E-World: Virtual Learning, Collaborative Environments, and Future Technologies

National Business Education Association Yearbook, No. 42

2004

Editor
Doris Christopher
California State University, Los Angeles
Los Angeles, California

Assistant Editor
Susan Jaderstrom
Santa Rosa Junior College
Petaluma, California

Published by

National Business Education Association
1914 Association Drive
Reston, VA 20191-1596
(703) 860-8300 • Fax: (703) 620-4483
www.nbea.org

E-World: Virtual Learning, Collaborative Environments, and Future Technologies

Copyright © 2004 by the National Business Education Association

National Business Education Association
1914 Association Drive
Reston, VA 20191-1596

ISBN 0-933964-61-7

TABLE OF CONTENTS

Preface vii

Chapter 1 1
Online Course Development for Business Education

Heidi R. Perreault
Southwest Missouri State University
Springfield, Missouri

Chapter 2 13
Student Values and Ethics in an E-Learning Environment

Patricia Theriot
Hinds Community College
Vicksburg, Mississippi

Chapter 3 26
Instructional Materials and the Internet

Nancy Groneman
Emporia State University
Emporia, Kansas

Chapter 4 42
Internet Use in Classroom Instruction

Theresa Yohon
Colorado State University
Fort Collins, Colorado

Chapter 5 67
Pedagogical and Technological Challenges of the Internet

Nancy D. Zeliff
Northwest Missouri State University
Maryville, Missouri

Chapter 6 89
Working Adults and Online Instruction

Rebecca J. Timmons
University of Arkansas, Fort Smith
Fort Smith, Arkansas

Chapter 7 .... **100**

E-Commerce Programs: What's Right for the Times?

Jo Ann Oravec
University of Wisconsin, Whitewater
Whitewater, Wisconsin

Chapter 8 .... **116**

E-Commerce Degrees: Are They Merely a Fad or Academically Sound Initiatives?

Richard Clodfelter
University of South Carolina
Columbia, South Carolina

Chapter 9 .... **127**

International Business Courses: Partnering with Overseas Students

Lila Waldman
Bloomsburg University
Bloomsburg, Pennsylvania

Chapter 10 .... **143**

Opportunity with a Capital E: The New E-Technologist

Sue Stidham
Pittsburg State University
Pittsburg, Kansas

Brenda Frieden
Pittsburg State University
Pittsburg, Kansas

Chapter 11 .... **160**

Collaborative Telelearning: Project Management

Tamra Davis
Tulsa Community College
Tulsa, Oklahoma

Chapter 12 .... **171**

Measuring the Teaching/Learning Process: Technology-Based Courses

Leslie Crair
McDonald Bradley, Inc.
Herndon, Virginia

Chapter 13 .... **180**

Distance Learning Success for the Business School: MERLOT's Facilitation Strategy

Joseph Otto
California State University, Los Angeles
Los Angeles, California

Gerard L. Hanley
California State University, Los Angeles
Los Angeles, California

Cathy Swift
Georgia Southern University
Statesboro, Georgia

Chapter 14 .... **195**
Distance Education Environment: Course Delivery in Cyberspace

Nanda Ganesan
California State University, Los Angeles
Los Angeles, California

Chapter 15 .... **209**
Essential Tips for Planning and Devlopment of Online Courses

Ok D. Park
University of Arkansas
Fayetteville, Arkansas

Frederick Nafukho
University of Arkansas
Fayetteville, Arkansas

Chapter 16 .... **223**
Educational Delivery: Intellectual Property Rights/Privacy Issues

Marsha Bayless
Stephen F. Austin State University
Nacogdoches, Texas

Betty S. Johnson
Stephen F. Austin State University
Nacogdoches, Texas

J. Keaton Grubbs
Stephen F. Austin State University
Nacogdoches, Texas

Table of Contents

PREFACE

NBEA's *2004 Yearbook* at its outset seemed to be a fairly modest undertaking. However, it soon became apparent that a wealth of information and techniques needed to be conveyed in an extremely concise and complete manner, without diluting substantive information. From this humble beginning, a substantial anthology of educational information has been developed for faculty at all stages of their teaching careers. As educators we are constantly involved in research, discussions, and quests for the most effective way in which to use technology as a learning tool to better serve our students. The *2004 Yearbook* undertook the process of delving into the questions of what constitutes an electronic educational environment, or E-world, and what present and future technological challenges teachers now face. The *Yearbook* can be used as both a resource tool and a methods book for secondary, postsecondary, undergraduate, and graduate business education students.

This *Yearbook* contains 16 chapters written by leading business educators who "teach what they practice and practice what they teach." The chapters are written by educators who are considered experts in their disciplines. These authors are recognized by their colleagues and students for their contributions to the field of academic technology.

The topics of the chapters are as follows:

Chapter 1: "Online Course Development for Business Education" contains an in-depth analysis of U.S. business educators' ideas and plans for designing, offering, and meeting the challenges of online courses at every level of instruction.

Chapter 2: "Student Values and Ethics in an E-Learning Environment" discusses e-learning in terms of student values and ethics.

Chapter 3: "Instructional Materials and the Internet" describes what an e-learning platform should include and provides practical "how to" guidelines for the delivery of an online course.

Chapter 4: "Internet Use in Classroom Instruction" presents various methods used to integrate the Internet into the classroom, and demonstrates how to use the Internet to enhance positive learning outcomes.

Chapter 5: "Pedagogical and Technological Challenges of the Internet" discusses various pedagogical challenges faced by teachers as they restructure their course content and classroom methods for online instruction.

Chapter 6: "Working Adults and Online Instruction" gives an in-depth view of the growth of e-learning in higher education among working adults, and the challenges it poses for academic institutions.

Chapter 7: "E-Commerce Programs: What's Right for the Times?" describes ways in which economic models of e-commerce programs have reshaped e-commerce instruction.

Chapter 8: "E-Commerce Degrees: Are They Merely a Fad or Academically Sound Initiatives?" explains how new e-commerce programs have impacted business and academia and analyzes the direction they will take in the future of business education.

Chapter 9: "International Business Courses: Partnering with Overseas Students" discusses the ways in which the Internet has changed the educational delivery mode of distance learning to international students.

Chapter 10: "Opportunity with a Capital E: The New E-technologist" discusses the emergence of business technologists—students who understand how to apply technology to solve business problems through the integration of classroom theory and hands-on, "real world" practice.

Chapter 11: "Collaborative Telelearning: Project Management" addresses the interesting computer-oriented and Web-based courses and activities that are taking place in the business education classrooms and curriculums throughout the nation.

Chapter 12: "Measuring the Teaching/Learning Process: Technology-Based Courses" explores the answers to such questions as, "How do you as an instructor evaluate your own and others' online material?" and "What kinds of assessments are available for students to evaluate instructors?"

Chapter 13: "Distance Learning Success for the Business School: MERLOT's Facilitation Strategy" examines the usefulness of the online research consortium, MERLOT (Multimedia Educational Resource for Learning and Online Teaching), and describes how it facilitates successful online business education.

Chapter 14: "Distance Education Environment: Course Delivery in Cyberspace" analyzes the technical issues related to online course delivery and examines one online learning model from the teachers' and students' perspectives.

Chapter 15: "Essential Tips for Planning and Development of Online Courses" chronicles the development of online courses and details the various instructional formats available for online delivery.

Chapter 16: "Educational Delivery: Intellectual Property Rights/Privacy Issues" discusses the ways in which copyright laws impact educational delivery, Web-based content material, and educators themselves.

The *2004 Yearbook* was written by dedicated business educators who expended an enormous amount of time and energy to undertake extensive research, writing, and rewriting of their chapters. I am most appreciative for their patience with each phase of the publication process.

I want to express my appreciation to all the chapter reviewers. Their dedication and expertise during the review process were evidenced by the extensive feedback given to authors. I am most grateful to Susan Jaderstrom, who served as a co-editor for the *2004 Yearbook*. Susan Jaderstrom's assistance came at a crucial time in the review process. I also want to extend my deepest gratitude to Susan O'Brien for her support in bringing this *Yearbook* to fruition. A special thanks is also extended to Ken Gorman and the NBEA Publications Committee for their help in providing me with the names of qualified, professional business education reviewers.

Finally, I want to extend a special thanks to Richard Valenzuela and Shanna Van Horn for their clerical help in handling the daily office tasks during the beginning phases of the *2004 Yearbook*.

Doris Christopher, Editor
California State University, Los Angeles
Los Angeles, California

ACKNOWLEDGEMENTS

The following business educators devoted their time, effort, and expertise to reviewing the *2004 NBEA Yearbook, E-World: Virtual Learning, Collaborative Environments and Future Technologies*:

Mary Ellen Adams

Marcia Anderson

Sherri Lee Arosteguy

Martha Balachandran

Carol Blaszczynski

Dianna Briggs

Gay Bryant

Jean Buckley

Judy Clark

John Clodfelter

John Clow

Donna Everett

Marie Flatley

Danny Frankl

Christine Givner

Ken Gorman

Dana Harader

Adam Huarng

Susan Jaderstrom

Marcia James

Carol Johnson

Marguerite Joyce

Lori Kievet

Judith Lambrecht

Peter Meggison

Bill Murphy

Mary E. Naftel

Sharon Lund O'Neil

Parviz Partow-Navid

Adam Reed

Sharon Reynolds

Nicole Rice

Kathleen Richards

Jim Scott

Jean Anna Sellers

Wanda Stitt-Gohdes

Allen Truell

Judee A. Timm

Kelly Wilkinson

Patricia Wilson

Martha C. Yopp

Holly Yu

Nancy Zeliff

Online Course Development for Business Education

Heidi R. Perreault
Southwest Missouri State University
Springfield, Missouri

Online courses are one segment of the educational market referred to as *distance learning*. Distance learning is the term used to describe any educational endeavor where the instructor and student are separated by physical distance. Advances in technology have contributed to the evolution of distance learning delivery formats, from correspondence to radio and television broadcasts to the Internet (Evolution of Distance Education, n.d.). The popularity and growth of courses offered over the Internet has been impressive. A 40% market growth for online courses is reported in a study conducted by Eduventures, a learning market research firm. The study also reported that online learning is the first distance learning format that comes close to engaging the student in a learning experience comparable to the traditional classroom experience (Gallagher, 2002). The ability to engage students, however, is not automatic with online courses. Careful course design and a command of the technology are required.

Business educators electing to design and/or deliver an online course face several challenges. Strategies and techniques that worked successfully for them in a traditional classroom may not be appropriate for an online class. They must modify their pedagogical approaches, learn new technologies, and incorporate additional time management and communication skills into their daily routines. It is not only educators who encounter challenges with the online course delivery format. Students enrolled in online courses also have to adjust to a different learning environment. Many students report feelings of isolation when participating in online courses, and others express frustration with the technology itself. This chapter provides an overview of the decisions required for designing a dynamic online course. A quality course design supports the student learning experience and provides opportunities for the student to communicate with other students and the instructor. The chapter also discusses the reasons for the growth in online learning opportunities and looks to the future of online course delivery.

DESIGNING ONLINE CLASSES

Glenn (2003) notes that designing an online course requires a very different approach to course development from that of a traditional course. Interactive components must be developed to introduce content, engage students, and provide assessment information. The course preparation time is considerable and the learning curve for the instructor is formidable, as both new technologies and new teaching methods must be mastered. Support is available for educators entering the virtual learning environment. Often school systems offer in-service programs and professional organizations provide information and publications.

Professional Organization Support

Professional education organizations, recognizing the interest in and growth of online courses, have expanded their membership services to include online learning issues. The organizations provide guidance by sponsoring research and by offering workshops and/ or publications. A model online business methods course was developed and implemented through a project sponsored by the National Business Education Association. The course is viewed as a means for helping to address the teacher shortage (National Business Education Association, 2001). Other professional organizations have assumed the role of a clearinghouse to provide members with information and contacts regarding online learning initiatives. The National Association for Business Teacher Education (NABTE), for example, provides a listing of 24 colleges and universities offering online courses for business teacher education. Newer organizations are being developed to support educators developing and delivering online courses. One such organization is the eLearning Guild (www.elearningguild.com). Its mission it to provide quality learning opportunities, networking services, resources, and publications related to online learning. Periodicals devoted to online learning are available. Four excellent resources include the WebNet Journal (www.aace.org/pubs/Webnet/default.htm), Syllabus (www.syllabus .com/mag.asp), THE Journal (www.thejournal.com), and Virtual University Gazette (www.geteducated.com/vugaz.htm).

Higher Education Programs

Postsecondary institutions offer both individual courses and complete educational programs online. Fifteen percent of higher education students in 2002 were expected to enroll in at least one online course as part of a degree program or continuing education plan (Pastore, 1999), and approximately 2% of higher education students were enrolled in programs being offered fully online (Gallagher, 2002).

Student demand and a flexibility advantage are two major reasons for the growth of higher education distance learning programs. The majority of students enrolled in courses at postsecondary institutions are employed adults living off campus. Working adults are the fastest growing demographic group in higher education. They appreciate the flexibility offered by online learning, so that they can better balance their work, family, and educational commitments (Gallagher, 2002).

Massey and Curry (1999) discovered that although many higher education institutions began offering online courses without having a specific strategy for their online learning initiatives, mission and policy statements soon were revised to reflect a commitment to online learning. Administrators devoted funds and efforts to establishing online learning programs so that their institutions would be competitive in reaching the adult student audience with specialized programs at both the undergraduate and graduate levels. Although postsecondary online learning programs are the fastest growing sector of the online learning industry, K-12 programs are expanding.

K-12 Education Programs

K-12 student participation in online learning has grown to an estimated 300,000 students taking at least one online course during the 2002-2003 academic year (Newman, 2003). Flexibility and access are the main reasons for offering online learning courses at the high school level. Students who are unable to attend traditional classes because of medical, disciplinary, or other reasons can complete a high school degree through online courses. Individual courses and complete programs are offered online to secondary students. Some programs are created to meet the needs of special populations, such as the self-paced curriculum available in the San Antonio area for at-risk students. The program provides the students with a second option for obtaining an education. The San Antonio program has successfully served students who are easily distracted by their peers in a traditional classroom setting, who are teen parents, or who are working to help support their families (Hurley, 2002).

Many K-12 school systems have joined with others to offer their students maximum access to online course offerings. The resulting consortiums can exist on a district or state level, and many include a partnership with a university. Some of the consortiums offer a limited curriculum focusing on English, math, and social studies. Others, however, offer an extensive listing of courses including business subjects. The Illinois Virtual High School offers several business classes, including Economics, Business Communications, Business and Personal Protocol, Consumer Education, International Business, and Personal Economics and Finance (Business and Economics, n.d.). Although many types of classes are available online, advanced placement courses are the most commonly offered online courses for the high school-level student (Clark, 2001).

Online courses often are developed to provide students at smaller schools with access to nontraditional or advanced courses not available at their schools. A higher proportion of high school students enrolled in online courses attend rural schools. Smaller school districts can expand their curriculums to include advanced placement courses and specialized electives by providing students access to online courses. The Virtual High School, a collaborative of national high schools, provides students access to nontraditional courses such as music appreciation and aeronautics. The courses could not be offered at local high schools because of low enrollment.

Newman (2003) recognizes that the rapid expansion of online course offerings has been due in large part to advances in technology and to organizations dedicated to supporting online instruction. The technology provides the platform that enables institutions to make quality online learning available to students. The course management systems, which are Web-based platforms, provide the framework for course delivery. The course designer inserts specific course content into the framework. Popular course management systems include WebCT, Blackboard, eCollege, and IntraLearn. Institutions without in-house expertise can provide quality online courses coupled with full student support services by contracting with online delivery organization such as Advanced Academy, Apex Learning, and Aventa Learning. These organizations provide consulting and technical expertise in the areas of faculty development, strategic planning, and systems integration.

Course Design Factors

While online courses expand the educational opportunities available to students at all academic levels, challenges exist for those who design and teach them. It takes considerable time, energy, training, and funding to provide students with quality online courses (Vail, 2002). One persistent problem is the higher dropout rate experienced with online courses. Reasons vary for not completing a course. For some students it is the frustration of too many technology-related challenges. For others, it is a lack of understanding that an online course requires as much, if not more, effort than a traditional course. Frankola's (2001) concern is that too often the reason why students do not complete a course is that it the course is not properly designed. Planning an online course begins with the same basic steps as does the preparation for a traditional course—set objectives, develop assessment tools, create activities, and locate resources. Decisions relating to the learning environment also need to be made. Those decisions include defining the audience, selecting the delivery format, and determining how to provide technology and support.

Define the audience. An important first decision is defining the expected audience (Vail, 2002). Whether the course is at the postsecondary or high school level, it should be tailored to meet the needs and expectations of a specific group. The course content and structure will be influenced by the students' academic history and maturity.

For distance learning courses at the postsecondary level, the students' prior college-level academic experience is an important design consideration. Students who just recently have begun or returned to a postsecondary education can be overwhelmed by an online learning course. The uncertainty of the new course delivery format, combined with the lack of experience, increases the stress associated with taking a course. It is not unusual for first-time distance learning students to become anxious and to begin to question if they are completing assignments correctly, if they are meeting expectations, and if they should or should not be contacting their instructor. Extra efforts on the part of the course designer to include clear instructions, sample responses for assignments, and opportunities to communicate with the instructor can help the student get a good start on the course. Designing multiple opportunities for communication and feedback at the start of the online learning course provides the support students new to Web-based learning need. One way to build in instructor interaction and feedback is to incorporate several small assignments at the start of the online course. As each assignment is submitted, the instructor interacts with the students, setting a pattern of open communication. The feedback lets the students know they are completing the assignments in the proper format or gives them the information they need to make changes by clarifying expectations and standards.

Courses designed for the experienced college student, such as advanced courses and graduate-level work, can have more flexible guidelines. The students have the confidence and experience to be able to set their own deadlines, determine when they need input, and select appropriate formats. Clear guidelines and interaction with the instructor are still important design factors.

At the high school level, the three groups most often served through online courses are advanced-placement students, homebound students, and at-risk students. Very different approaches to designing a course will be used, depending on the group being targeted. If the purpose is to offer advanced level courses and/or to supplement the current class offerings available to the student in the local high school curriculum, the audience will be students with a successful academic history. Communication and student interaction may be easier to design for high school students than for college-level students, because high school students often have a specific time set aside during the school day to complete the coursework. The students can share information online with other students involved in the program and/or with the instructor during that assigned class time. Challenging assignments, frequent sharing of information between the students, and multiple opportunities for exploring topics should be designed into the course. Flexibility on the assignments (students choose from a list of assignments or are encouraged to propose projects, for example) allows students to pursue areas of interest and promotes engagement in the topic.

If the purpose is to provide access to a course for students who are homebound or for individuals who have commitments keeping them from attending schools during normal hours, the course designer needs to consider that the students will be completing course work outside of a traditional, structured school setting. Directions and deadlines must be stated clearly. Small modules of instruction that can be completed in 20 minutes or less supports the student who is trying to complete his/her education while meeting other family or employment commitments. Having multiple opportunities for the student to interact with the instructor is important, so that the student doesn't feel isolated and so that guidance and encouragement can be provided if the student begins to fall behind or is confused by course concepts or requirements. The instructor interaction and feedback can be a combination of e-mail, online chat sessions, and/or phone calls.

Online courses designed for students who have been unsuccessful in the traditional classroom, or who are not allowed to attend regular classes due to disciplinary actions, need to have specific rules. For example, a student may need to complete work by a

certain day of the week and take quizzes on set days to provide proof of having completed the assignments. Interactions with instructors may be required on a daily basis, or
parents may be asked to verify the time spent working on the class.

Select the format. Along with defining the audience, decisions need to be made on
whether the delivery format will be asynchronous or synchronous. Asynchronous
delivery allows for the anytime, anyplace flexibility that many adults prefer. The student
has access to the course at any time and no set time is planned for students to be online.
The teacher can set guidelines such as providing due dates, so that the students are
required to complete sections of the course by a certain date. Synchronous delivery
requires the students to log onto the class at set times. It allows the flexibility for students
to be in different locations (such as at home) but maintains the traditional structure of a
set time for the course to meet. The synchronous delivery format is used to incorporate
more interaction between the students themselves and between the student and teacher
(Vail, 2002).

Plan for technology and student support. Technology and student services support
are important issues for schools to address. The "24-7" educational opportunity offered
through online learning requires considerable support. Both teachers and students may
be participating in the course outside of traditional school hours. How to provide
everyone with access to equipment and technical support needs to be considered. An
educator who has responsibility for an online course may need to have a home computer
upgraded or be provided with the equipment for the duration of the course. Students will
require access to equipment and technical support. Options include loaning the equipment to students and/or providing access to labs with generous evening and weekend
hours. Technical support should be available to students whenever they are online. If 24-
hour support is impractical for the school system, other means for support should be
provided. For example, a student may send an e-mail or call a toll free number to leave a
message regarding a technical problem. The school system guarantees that an answer will
be provided within 24 hours or less. Students will need ready access to course-related
information and to the resources required to complete course assignments. The server
hosting the course must be available whenever the student wants to access the course
material, and additional services such as online library access may be required. The
school system may need to install additional security measures or to provide more open
access to materials required by online students.

Access issues include more than access to technology and technical support. Students
taking online courses should have the same access to academic and instructional services
as do students taking traditional courses (Gallagher, 2002). Student academic services,
including advising and tutoring, are important factors for student success. These services
need to be made available to students in distance learning programs. The course designer
needs to work with the administration, academic services, technical support professionals, and librarians to assure that access to support services and to course-related
information are readily available to the online student.

ONLINE LEARNING CHALLENGES

Business educators moving from the classroom to an online delivery format will encounter many challenges. The teacher who relies heavily on visual and/or oral cues during a traditional lesson to determine student success may not be as successful with an online class delivery format (Valentine, 2002). The distance format requires a collaborative design where the teacher is a facilitator. Instead of providing the content and leading the learning process, the facilitator guides students by making materials available, developing engaging activities, encouraging sharing, and providing guidance and feedback. The instructor receives no visual cues to detect anxiety, boredom, or engagement. Lack of cues limits the instructor's ability to intervene at appropriate points to calm, clarify, challenge, or reward students (Valentine, 2002). In addition to visual cues, instructors traditionally rely on the interpersonal relationship formed between student and teacher to support learning. Developing a supportive and trusting learner relationship is one of the components of a successful learning environment. That relationship is difficult to achieve in an online learning environment. The foundation for a relationship is shared history. Since the instructor and student do not meet each other within the classroom as in a traditional setting, the shared history must be developed through communications and through the instructional content and delivery of the course (Stout, 2002).

Delivery and feedback methods are different for online courses (National Schools Board Foundation, 2002), yet most educators have not had formal training in teaching online. Sonwalkar (2001) notes that many instructors try to recreate a traditional class within an online environment. The approach often fails to develop the learner relationship and does not take advantage of the flexibility offered through online learning. To foster learning, online courses should provide students with choices and incorporate multiple learning modalities such as audio, graphics, video, and text (Glenn, 2003).

Professional Development

For a teacher moving from teaching a traditional to an online course, it is important to have opportunities to learn how to use new technologies and how to modify teaching methods. Professional development sessions can provide the new skills and a supportive environment where experienced teachers share their positive experiences and successful strategies for dealing with online delivery issues. The development opportunities can be workshops, meetings, one-on-one tutoring, or complete degree programs. Some universities such as the University of Maryland and Penn State offer certificate programs on developing and managing online programs. The teacher learns about online learning practices while participating in an online learning program.

Romkema (2003) encourages business educators to incorporate online learning into their traditional classes. A hybrid class is a traditional class that offers part of the curriculum through online learning. It is an excellent way for an educator to move gradually from traditional to online learning delivery (Stidham and Frieden, 2002). It also provides both educators and students an opportunity to experience online learning in a controlled, short-term setting.

Online Teaching Concerns

Those teaching in an online environment have noted their concerns. One common problem, say instructors, is that it is more time consuming to teach online than in a traditional format (Young, 2002). The online instructor spends considerable time updating Web pages, providing individualized feedback, and answering e-mail. Online educators soon learn the importance of timesaving strategies. Common strategies include how to grade and edit student assignments electronically, how to provide concise feedback through e-mail, and how to reduce the number of unnecessary e-mail messages. For example, one strategy to reduce e-mail is to place typical student questions with a related quality response on a frequently asked questions (FAQ) page. When an e-mail is received asking one of the questions, the instructor directs the student to the FAQ site. Another strategy is to post announcements at the same time on select days. Students are directed at the start of the online class to check the Web site on selected days after a set hour for new information, feedback, and directions. If a student does send an e-mail asking what he/she should do next, the instructor reminds the student to check the announcements on the set date/time for directions. Building information and consistency into the course design can reduce the number of repetitive e-mails. The valuable time saved can be used to provide one-on-one feedback and guidance.

Testing continues to be a concern for online learning course designers. Online objective and essay tests can be delivered, but special measures are required to know who is actually completing the test if the student is in a remote location. Requiring sign-in passwords and setting time restrictions provide some measures of control over the testing environment. Restricting access to the test to only those students who have the password and instituting time limitations reduces the ability of the student to cheat by consulting with other students or reviewing materials. Some online programs require students to take tests at centers where the test can be proctored. Many online instructors reduce their reliance on objective tests for feedback and evaluation. All tests are assumed to be open book. To determine student success, alternative assessment techniques are used. Projects, case studies, journals, and portfolios provide the student with multiple opportunities to demonstrate mastery of the material (National Business Education Association, 2001).

Student Concerns

Two problems that students often experience with online courses are feelings of isolation and anxiety. Without regular face-to-face contact, students feel that they are not noticed by the teacher. They may wonder if they are doing what is expected and whether anyone cares if they are on track. The distance learning instructor can reduce those feelings of isolation by building into the course multiple opportunities for sharing and communicating with others. Students can share information and ideas with other students through posting comments or by participating in a dialogue through the discussion feature provided with course management systems. Student to teacher interactions such as periodic meetings through computer conferences can be part of the course structure. Individual e-mail feedback on assignments, as well as group postings to the course site recognizing class efforts, are ways to let the students know that their work and input is being reviewed and acknowledged.

Anxiety levels increase when students are unsure of what they are expected to accomplish, where to find information, or how to submit materials. This discomfort can be reduced through the course management system's organizational framework. Course management systems provide a template for a consistent and organized format. The template includes features such as a course calendar, announcements, assignment page, e-mail option, and drop box. The instructor can insert due dates and expected timelines into the calendar and announcement page templates. All assignments can be listed in one location and presented in the order they should be completed by the student.

Related information sites, hints, guidelines, or examples showing acceptable formats are easily provided to students through active links. By selecting one of the links, a student can visit the Web site or document and then easily return to the original page within the course management system. Materials can be stored online and shared through attachments to e-mail or through course drop boxes, which allow students to send documents directly to the instructor or to other students. The course management system provides the technical framework, and the teacher provides the instructional details through posting due dates, updating announcement pages, providing examples, scheduling periodic e-mail communications, and incorporating online discussions or help sessions (Rosenblum, 2000).

THE FUTURE OF ONLINE EDUCATION

The experts agree that online learning will continue to grow. A study by the National School Boards Foundation (2002) study reported that K-12 school leaders believe that approximately 20% of their student body will complete at least a portion of their academic classwork through distance learning within the next three years. Enrollment in postsecondary distance learning is expected to be 2.23 million in 2004 (eLearning is burgeoning, 2001).

The increase in distance learning courses is both a response to student demand and a reaction to the technology that makes the delivery possible. Course management systems offer tools to allow the nonprogrammer to design and deliver a course online. Spending by institutions on distance learning technologies and services is expected to grow from $4.5 billion to $11 billion between 2001 and 2005 (eLearning is burgeoning, 2001). Both online students and those students in a traditional setting benefit from the upgrading of the infrastructure. Course management systems are used to some extent in 20% of all college-level courses (White, 2002). In traditional settings the course management system supports rather than delivers the instruction. Course assignments, schedules, and instructional materials are provided through the system. Students still come to class for the majority of the course lectures, activities, and assessments.

Higher education institutions are incorporating online learning into their mission statements. No longer an experiment, online classes are an integral part of the strategic plan for the institution (White, 2002). Educational institutions have business and government support for offering online education. In its report, *A Vision of E-Learning for America's Workforce*, the Commission on Technology and Adult Learning (2001) encourages business and government leaders to make online learning a "cornerstone of a national effort to develop a skilled workforce for American's digital society" (p. 27).

SUMMARY

Online learning, whether a full curriculum or an individual course, offers increased access and new educational opportunities for students at all levels. Online learning course offerings continue to expand at both the K-12 and postsecondary levels. One reason for the growth is student demand. The ability to access courses from virtually any location at any time has expanded the opportunity for obtaining an education (Gallagher, 2002). A second reason for the growth is the online learning support provided through technology. Course management systems provide the framework for designing and delivering online learning courses. To be effective, the courses need careful attention, so that the relationships required for student learning are integrated into the course design and delivery format. The course must be tailored to a specific audience and designed with maximum interaction.

Because the face-to-face communication is not available on a regular basis, the distance learning instructor needs to incorporate interaction in other ways, such as through e-mails, postings, and discussion boards. Frequent interactions with the instructor and with other class members can prevent feelings of isolation and anxiety. Scheduling specific opportunities to communicate with the instructor at the start of the course can prevent the student from falling behind or getting confused on expectations or deadlines. Student support services such as advisement, tutoring, technology, and library resources are important components of all academic programs including those offered online. Students taking courses online deserve the same level of support as that provided to students taking traditional courses.

Online learning is an important and growing educational market. Business educators at both the K-12 and postsecondary levels can expect online offerings to expand. Administrators plan to make online course offerings a viable option for students and expect online courses to provide a substantial portion of a student's educational experiences (National School Board Foundation, 2002). The reasons to offer the course are to increase opportunities for obtaining an education, to provide more access to select courses, and to meet student demand.

REFERENCES

Business and Economics. (nd). Retrieved March 18, 2003, from Illinois Virtual High School Web Site: http://www.ivhs.org/index.learn?action=academicinfo&subaction=

Clark, T. (2001). *Virtual schools: Trends and issues*. Retrieved November 22, 2002, from: http://www.dlrn.org/k12/virtualstudy.pdf.

Commission on Technology and Adult Learning. (2001). *A vision of e-learning for America's workforce.* Retrieved March 12, 2003, from http://www.astd.org/virtual_community/public_policy/jh_ver.pdf.

eLeaning is burgeoning. (2001, April 26). IDC eNewsletter. Retrieved February 28, 2003, from http://www.idc.com/getdoc.jhtml?containerId=ebt20010426.

Evolution of Distance Learning. (nd). Retrieved March 12, 2003, from University of Wisconsin, Collaborative Nursing Program Web Site: http://academic.son.wisc.edu/

Frankola, K. (2001). The e-learning taboo: High dropout rates in online courses, *Syllabus, 14(11),* 14-16.

Gallagher, S. (2002). *Distance learning at the tipping point.* Retrieved November 12, 2002, from: http://www.eduventures.com/research/industry_research_resources/distancelearning.cfm.

Glenn, J. (2003). E-learning e-volution: Your (digital) future awaits. *Business Education Forum, 57(4),* 8-15.

Hurley, R. (2002). Fine-tuning an online high school to benefit at-risk students. *T.H.E. Journal, 30(4),* 33-40.

Massey, C. and Curry, J. (1999). *Online postsecondary education: A competitive analysis.* Retrieved on August 23, 2003, from: http://gam-mlg.ic.gc.ca/en/docs/analysis/.

National Business Education Association. (2001, March). Assessing online learning. *Keying In,* 11. Reston, VA: Author.

National School Boards Foundation. (2002). *Are we there yet?* Retrieved on November 22, 2002, from http://www.nsbf.org/thereyet/index.htm.

Newman, A. (2003). Industry Focus. The Education Economy. *Vendors evolve product and service offerings to support the development of virtual learning.* Retrieved on August 20, 2003, from: http://www.eduventures.com.

Pastore, M. (1999, June 1). *Distance learning grows thanks to net.* Retrieved on February 28, 2003, from: http://cyberatlas.internet.com/markets/education/article/0,,5951_152731,00.html.

Romkema, P. (2003). The case for creating a hybrid international business course. *Business Education Forum, 57(4),* 43-44, 55.

Rosenblum, J. (2001). Design and development of online courses: Faculty working in collaboration. *Syllabus, 15(7),* 10-14.

Sonwalkar, N. (2001). Changing the interface of education with revolutionary learning technologies. *Syllabus, 15(4),* 10-13.

Stidham, S. and Frieden, B. (2002). 10 easy steps to online success. *Business Education Forum, 57(2),* 47-49.

Stout, V. (2002). Building relationships with learners at a distance. In A. Remp (Ed.), *Technology, methodology, and business education* (Yearbook No. 40, pp. 102-115). Reston, VA: National Business Education Association.

Vail, K. (2002, September). A new kind of school. *American School Board Journal.* Retrieved November 22, 2002, from http://www.asbj.com/specialreports/2002pdf/0902pdf/Sept02ASBJS1.pdf.

Valentine, D. (2002). Distance learning: Promises, problems, possibilities. *Online Journal of Distance Learning Administration, 5(3).* Retrieved November 22, 2002, from http://www.westga.edu/~distance/ojdla/fall53/valentine53.html.

White, E. (2002). *E-learning forecast*. Retrieved November 12, 2002, from: http://www.universitybusiness.com/story.asp?txtFilename=archives/Dec01Jan02/forecast.htm.

Young, J. (2002, May 31). The 24-hour professor. *The Chronicle of Higher Education, 48(38),* A31-A33.

Student Values and Ethics in an E-Learning Environment

Patricia Theriot

Hinds Community College

Vicksburg, Mississippi

The popularity and expected continued growth of distance learning methods, particularly online courses, appear evident. With this growth, however, comes the possibility of an increase in student cheating because of the ease and anonymity of Internet access and because of the proliferation of Web sites that actually encourage cheating. This chapter summarizes the research involving student cheating in traditional and online classes and discusses possible solutions for teachers to detect and deter student cheating in an online environment.

GROWTH OF ONLINE COURSES

While the merits of online courses are much discussed and debated, what cannot be denied is their increasing popularity and tremendous growth. Online courses are now available through most universities and community colleges throughout the country.

At the University of Colorado, during the period of the fall of 1996 until the spring of 1998, the number of students enrolled in online courses increased from 290 to 940, and the number of courses offered increased from 4 to 46 for that same period (Guernsey, 1998).

A report prepared by the National Center for Educational Statistics in 1999, as reported by Moore (2001), showed that over half of American higher educational institutions were offering online courses. Snow, Farris, & Levin (1999) reported that distance education was increasing at both two- and four-year postsecondary institutions in this country.

In Mississippi, the number of students enrolled in some form of distance learning at the state's eight universities from the fall of 2001 through the summer of 2002 was 27,684; the previous year's enrollment was only 9,742. Also, among the state's 15 two-year colleges the enrollment in Mississippi's Virtual Community College grew from 1,382 in the spring of 2002 to 12,594 in the fall of 2002 (Kanengiser, 2002).

In its brochure entitled *The University of Phoenix* (2002), the country's largest private online university offers 11 undergraduate and 12 graduate degree programs online and advertises that students can complete 100% of their education via the Internet, including administration and book buying. The number of students enrolled in these programs in 2002 was approximately 50,000, a 70% increase from the previous year (Hartigan Shea, 2002). Most of these students are working adults who must keep their full-time jobs while earning their degrees (Hartigan Shea, 2002).

REASONS FOR POPULARITY OF ONLINE COURSES

Interest in online courses is rapidly growing for many reasons. Online classes are attractive to students, teachers, and schools.

Benefits to students. The overwhelming reason given by most students enrolled in online courses is convenience (Guernsey, 1998). This is especially true in an asynchronous environment, where students can log on any time day or night, respond to e-mails from instructors, complete and submit assignments, or take electronic exams.

Many of the students enrolled in online courses have full- or part-time jobs while they are earning degrees, and these students simply do not have enough time to work and go to school without the advantage of online courses. Commuting students appreciate being able to save time, money, and gasoline while completing courses that are independent of time and place (Stidham and Frieden, 2002). Many students say that they would never be able to finish their degrees if they did not have the option of online courses (Guernsey, 1998).

Benefits to teachers. Online courses appear to be just as popular with instructors as they are with students. Moore (2001) reports on a survey of 40 college faculty members by NEA that found faculty were "generally enthusiastic about the idea of teaching distance education courses" (p. 1). Arthur McEntee, an instructor at the University of Maine at Machias, lives four hours from the university and can use his computer to teach from home ("Online Classes," 2002). To compensate for the lack of face-to-face personal contact between student and teacher, McEntee uses electronic bulletin boards, which allow his students to see, share, and comment on assignments.

While some skeptics claim that online instruction results in less personal contact with instructors, many instructors say that the opposite is true (Young, 2002). Before the Internet, in fact, the only time that students had a chance to talk with their teachers was either during class or during the instructor's office hours. In an online environment, however, students and their instructors can contact each other at any time of the day or night. To compensate for the lack of face-to-face contact, instructors often promise a quick response to student questions by e-mail (Young).

Benefits to schools. Online courses provide a cost-effective means for schools to reach more students. In online courses, students are typically responsible for their own equipment and supplies. Therefore, one teacher using one computer can teach a course to a "classroom" of online students without using a computer lab or additional equipment and supplies. According to Oliver (1999), the use of online technologies is "justified and premised by arguments and compelling evidence of their capacity to provide more cost-efficient programs to more students" (p. 241). Online teaching and learning "appear to offer many advantages over conventional formats including economics in cost, greater levels of access to students, more flexible teaching and learning approaches, and enhanced educational opportunities" (Oliver, p. 240). Virtual classrooms are not subject to the same space requirements as traditional classrooms and can, therefore, provide the same benefits as an in-class setting without incurring the costs (facilities, travel expenses, etc.) or inconveniences (Oakes, 2002).

Dr. Sylvia Charp, editor-in-chief of *T.H.E. Journal*, reports, "E-learning's future in education seems assured in both education and training" (Charp, 2002, p. 12).

STUDENT ETHICS REGARDING ONLINE INSTRUCTION

While the debate continues regarding the merits and quality of the online experience, distance learning will continue to grow. Those involved in this phenomenon need to focus on the issues that online delivery of instruction presents.

One prominent issue is whether online instruction increases the incidence of student cheating. How does an instructor ensure that his/her students are submitting their own work and not plagiarizing assignments? Since the work is submitted electronically, who is to say that a student is or is not completing his/her own assignments? How can cheating students be caught; and, if caught, what are the consequences?

Extent of cheating among students in general. Student cheating has and always will be a concern for teachers; and because of increased pressure on students to increase their GPAs, incidence of student cheating is on the rise in general.

In 1998, a survey of 3,123 students by *Who's Who Among American High School Students* discovered that 80% of the students admitted to cheating on an exam. This number is a 10% increase since the question was asked 15 years ago (Bushweller, 1999). In addition, 50% of the surveyed students did not believe that cheating was wrong; and 95% of the students said that they had never been caught. (Kleiner and Lord, 1999). Studies conducted by the Center for Academic Integrity at Duke University and others (as reported by Wilson, 1999) have shown that students do not think that cheating is a "big deal," and that professors are not doing much to discourage it.

The following quote from a college student, as reported in *U.S. News & World Report,* (Kleiner and Lord, 1999) typifies the attitudes expressed by students who cheat. This Duke University student had copied a friend's programming assignment and turned it in as his own. "There are times that you cheat because there aren't enough hours in the day. ...I understand how to do it; I just didn't have the time" (p. 3). McLeod (1997) reports that Bill Rukeyser, director of Learning in the Real World, an informational clearinghouse for educators, said that some students regard copying or buying material from the Web as just another form of research.

Unfortunately, the penalties for cheating are rarely very harsh. In most cases, students caught at cheating merely receive a poor grade for a particular assignment or course (Kleiner & Lord, 1999). At the University of Maryland, students caught cheating must attend a seven-week ethics seminar. Such minor consequences do little to deter students from cheating.

More serious consequences resulted, however, in Mississippi recently. Three University of Mississippi students had their degrees revoked when it was discovered that they received grades for online work that they did not do (Kanengiser, 2002). In 1998, a similar scandal involving Mississippi Valley State University made college officials realize the importance of assuring that the school's distance learning classes experienced the same integrity as traditional programs (Kanengiser, 2002).

Extent of cheating via the Internet. The Internet, while making it easy to locate and retrieve information, is also making it easier for students to cheat; and today's students are "a truly wired generation" (Schwartz, 2003). According to a study by the Pew Internet and American Life Project in Washington as reported by Schwartz, 86% of students have gone online compared with 59% of the general population. Students can search the Internet on virtually any topic and find a wealth of information. While this is an advantage in terms of research, the Internet has also resulted in the advent of several "paper mills" that allow students to download (either free or for a fee) entire documents, which students then print and turn in as their own.

Web sites such as Evil House of Cheat, which has as its slogan, "Download your workload" (McMurtry, 2001), and others such as 15000Papers.com and T.O.P. Thousands of Papers (www.termpapers-on-file.com), all owned by The Paper Store, offer a collection of papers to students. Other sites include Essay World (www.EssayWorld.com), Planet Papers (www.planetpapers.com), and Other People's Papers (www.oppapers.com).

McMurtry (2001) found 30 such sites, and if students don't know the particular Web address of one of these paper mills, they can type "free essays," and any Web search engine will provide a list of such sites. Some papers are free, others require a fee, and some sites offer custom essays costing from $18.95 to $35 per page. Brownstein (1999) reports finding as many as 70 Internet Web sites offering term papers for up to $200 each.

Kim McMurtry (2001), a college English teacher, reported that of the 61 students in an English composition class in spring of 1999, five plagiarists had downloaded papers from the Web and were caught. These students equal 8% of the class, and this percentage represents only the students who were caught.

Dr. Donald McCabe, a professor of organizational management at Rutgers University and founder of the Center for Academic Integrity at Duke University, appearing on the *Today* television show, December 27, 2002, reported that the most common reason students cheat is the GPA race. According to McCabe, the "ease and anonymity of the Internet can only increase the percentage of online cheaters" (as cited in Brownstein, 1999, p. 1).

On the same *Today* program (December 27, 2002), Omar Wasow, an Internet analyst, reported that over one-half to three-fourths of students who engage in online cheating do so by cutting and pasting, although many students buy entire papers (essays, theses, dissertations). Papers that are 8-10 pages long can cost from $50-$100 a paper. While most schools have (or should have) blocks to these sites on their school's file server, students can and do access the sites on their home computers.

Extent of cheating in distance education. Because of the lack of national data, measuring specifically the extent of online cheating is difficult. Carnevale (1999) reports that several colleges with extensive distance education programs (including Michigan State University, Ohio University, The University of Texas system, Park College, and Pueblo Community College) reported few, if any, cases where any disciplinary action was taken for online cheating. In fact, officials say that more cheating was reported in traditional classrooms (Carnevale, 1999). According to Zernicke (2002), cheating has become so common that experts say it often goes unreported and unpunished.

Determining if a student is cheating in a typical classroom situation can sometimes be difficult, but measuring the extent of online cheating can be even more difficult. Thus, online cheating will always be an issue for online instructors. However, according to Dee Stallings, director of academic programs at Vcampus, a company that helps colleges set up online courses, as quoted by Carnevale (1999), the "potential for cheating in distance-education courses is about equal to that in traditional courses" (p. 1). Mr. Stallings claims that teachers need to be made aware of how to detect and prevent cheating online. Several possible solutions for detecting or deterring cheating in an online environment were found in the literature.

POSSIBLE SOLUTIONS TO ONLINE CHEATING

Communication between student and teacher. Jeanne M. Wilson, president of the Duke Center for Academic Integrity, claims that the growth of online education makes it harder to be sure that the student turning in the work is actually the one who did the work (Carnevale, 1999); whereas Mr. Stallings contends that the opposite is true. According to Carnevale (1999), Mr. Stallings believes that online courses attract continuing education students who are usually more ethical than traditional 19-year-old graduates. Mr. Stallings further claims that because all communication between student and teacher is in writing, the "academic rigor is up," (p. 2) and an instructor can actually get to know a student better than in a typical classroom.

Darcy W. Hardy, director of the University of Texas' distance education component, Telecampus, agrees that the best way to catch cheaters is to know the students in the class (Carnevale, 1999). One way to get to know online students is through frequent e-mails. If a student consistently misspells or uses poor grammar in his/her e-mail message but turns in assignments that are grammatically and mechanically superior to the e-mail messages, that may be a clue that the assignments were done by someone other than the student. Ms. Hardy further suggests that a good way to get an idea of the quality of a student's writing is to require a 500-word essay at the beginning of the semester to give the instructor an idea of the student's writing style and abilities. It is important, however, that instructors give students enough time to complete such written assignments, and that a proposal or outline be required early in the semester to prevent the students from procrastinating. When students wait until the last minute to begin an assignment, they are more likely to resort to plagiarizing (McMurtry, 2001).

Instructors can use online chats and discussion boards in the same manner (Carnevale, 1999). Since the chats and discussions are recorded, the instructor can compare the quality of those with the quality of work turned in by the student. Other suggestions include making unexpected phone calls to a student to discuss a particular point or to ask a student how he/she found some piece of information (Carnevale).

According to Byrd and Lott (2003), online instructors cannot compare handwriting samples or font styles to detect dishonesty. However, online instructors who communicate frequently with their students can become more familiar with students' writing style, tone, and level of discussion than a teacher in a traditional classroom. In their survey of postsecondary computer teachers, 38% did not express concerns about validating whether the students turned in their own work, whereas 33% of those participating in the survey expressed concerns in this area (Byrd and Lott).

Proctored exams. Another possible solution to prevention of online cheating is to require students to take proctored exams. Luis Nazario, a composition professor at Pueblo Community College in Colorado, found three instances of cheating during six years of online teaching. The students were caught by comparing assigned work with other types of communication between him and the students, which included talking to his students at least three times each semester to discuss each student's progress. Mr. Nazario further stated that the best way to weed out those students is by requiring a proctored examination. These three students dropped out of the course when a proctored exam was required (Carnevale, 1999).

At the University of Southern Mississippi, Tim Hudson, provost of the school's Gulf Coast campuses and former dean of the College of International and Continuing Education, reports that all 11,988 of the USM students signed up on the Mississippi E-

Campus from the fall of 2001 to the summer of 2002 were required to take an in-person monitored test requiring changeable passwords and ID systems as a security measure (Kanengiser, 2002). Jason Pugh, director of distance education for the Mississippi Board for Community and Junior Colleges, likewise stated that students in the 569 distance learning classes in the Virtual Community College in the fall of 2002 were required to take either or both their midterm and final exams at a proctored test center (Kanengiser). Students must furnish a picture ID before taking tests at the proctor centers.

Teacher Web sites. In addition to proctored exams, several teacher Web sites are available to online instructors for use in detecting online cheating. Just as students can use the Internet and its many search engines to locate and possibly plagiarize papers, teachers have Web sites that they can access to help detect a plagiarized paper. Sites such as www.find-same.com, Plagiariam.org, or IntegriGuard allow teachers to enter key phrases from a student's paper, and these phrases are compared to their large database of papers, as well as to Internet databases and Web pages. The site will produce a report that highlights papers with those phrases in them. Usually, the instructor or the school will have to subscribe to these sites. Plagiariam.org charges an annual fee of $150, plus $1 per document, purchased in $50 blocks (McMurtry. 2001). HowOriginal.com is a free site that offers the same service. The world's most widely used resource for preventing Internet plagiarism is www.Turnitin.com, which also charges an annual fee that varies from school to school.

Some states have laws that prohibit the sale of papers through the Internet. In Massachusetts, a law banning the sale of term papers made it possible for Boston University to sue several Web sites that sold such papers to a school employee posing as a student. The site was charged with fraud, mail fraud, and racketeering (McLeod, 1997). The case was later thrown out by a federal judge, but the university planned to file charges again at the state level (Brownstein, 1999). Unfortunately, not all states have such laws in place. Thus, it becomes the teacher's responsibility to catch offenders and determine the consequences.

Hybrid courses. Another suggested solution is for schools to develop "hybrid" courses, versus strictly electronic ones in which instructors and students never meet. A hybrid course is described by Rabb (2000) as a "face-to-face course that is enhanced by distance learning applications" (p. 8). Hybrid courses incorporate online technology into the traditional classroom instruction. Rabb says that such a course provides for more student-teacher interaction and allows students more access to their instructors. Rabb further suggests that this type of blended learning environment may provide a better solution to meeting the diverse learning needs of today's students. For the many students, however, who by necessity must take their courses entirely online, hybrid courses would not be a solution.

Academic integrity policy. In most of the articles researched for this chapter, the most effective solution to reducing online cheating seemed to be developing and communicating to students a strong, clear policy of academic honesty. This policy should provide clear and severe penalties to anyone caught cheating.

Research shows that there is less cheating at colleges that exhibit strong honor codes (Zernike, 2002). Therefore, some schools are adopting codes for the first time. Others, like Duke, are rewriting and strongly enforcing their existing codes. At Duke, a new "community standard" for academic integrity will take effect in the fall of 2003. According to this standard, students will face punishment if they see cheating and do not report it (Zernike). Also, faculty are given more power to discipline first-time offenders.

The University of North Carolina, as a means of strengthening its honor code, is considering publishing a kind of "police blotter" of cheating incidents (without names) in the daily campus newspaper. The school is also considering adopting a grade of XF to indicate failure due to cheating (Zernike, 2002). Other schools, like the University of Maryland and Trinity College in Hartford, are requiring that their students sign an honor pledge or contract (Zernicke, 2002).

Omar Wilson, appearing on the *Today* show (December 27, 2002), reported that an investigation at the University of Virginia in 2001 uncovered 120 cheating incidents; and this investigation resulted in the dismissal of 48 students. Because of this scandal, a group of alumni at the University have since raised money to publicize the honor code and to promote it among the students (Zernicke, 2002).

While developing a new honor code or redesigning an existing code is important, such a code will only be effective if it is accepted by the students. Therefore, part of the success of these honor codes is dependent upon how well the institution promotes the code to its students. Various techniques can be used to communicate the importance of the honor codes.

Colgate University and Kansas State University both require an orientation session for their students as part of an academic integrity education campaign (Zernicke, 2002). McMurtry (2001) suggests that most colleges and universities do have academic integrity policies in place and that these policies need to be thoroughly explained to students. Students need to be made aware of the legal implications of plagiarism as well. Violation of copyright laws can result in stiff penalties, and some states actually have laws against the sale of certain kinds of papers (McMurtry). Students need to be aware of copyright infringement penalties and other laws regarding plagiarism.

Mark Jon Snyder, CIO with MSA Consulting Group in Baltimore, Maryland, developed for the state of Florida a set of 12 Internet Rules based on industry standards that he had created for his clients. He has presented these 12 rules in 21 states, and the school systems in all of these states are now using some form of these "rules" in their classrooms (personal communication, November 13, 2002). These 12 rules were subsequently condensed by a Georgia Assistant Attorney General because of redundancies (personal communication, July 28, 2003) and are presented in the following example of an Internet Use Policy:

XXXX Public Schools – Internet Use Policy:

- The computers, networks, hardware, software, peripherals, and configurations in this Internet classroom are the property of XXXX Public Schools. You will not alter, modify, damage, or degrade them in any manner.

- You will not install, upgrade, or modify any software operating system, application, or service.

- You will not view, print, distribute, display, send, or receive images, text, or graphics of obscene materials or material that violates laws relating to child pornography.

- You will not use an Internet workstation to view, print, send, or receive images, text, or graphics that contain hate speech, threatening, or harassing material.

- You will not engage in any activity that is deliberately offensive or creates an intimidating or hostile environment.

- You will not violate copyright or software licensing agreements. You will not download or exchange audio and video files including MP3 files and other similar files.

- You will not gain unauthorized access to any computing, information, or communications devices or resources.

- You will not copy, download, design, or create any software or component intended to damage, alter, or degrade software applications or network architectures.

- You will not use a workstation to conduct a business or participate in online buying or selling.

Any Violations of These Rules Will Result In Loss Of Internet Access, Disciplinary Action, AND Assessment of Monetary Damages. (attachment to personal communication, November, 2002).

These rules may be posted in the classroom. In some cases, the rules appear on the computer screens as part of the booting process so that students see them every time they log on to their networks. The rules describe specific restrictions to students on use of the Internet in the classroom and state very clearly the consequences students may expect for violation of any of these rules.

Schaefer (1998) reports that our young people are growing up in an environment that does not emphasize the importance of high moral and ethical values and that teaching values should continue to be a function of our schools. Robin Wilson (1999) reports that to stop students from cheating on exams and plagiarizing papers we must "tell them about honesty, trust, fairness, respect and responsibility" (p. 1).

SUMMARY

While there may be some disagreement among educators regarding the quality of online courses, what cannot be denied is their popularity and predicted continued growth. All forms of distance learning, and in particular online courses and curricula, will continue to experience rapid growth. Distance learning, and particularly online courses, makes education possible for a growing number of learners who cannot, for a number of reasons, pursue a degree in a traditional school setting. Online courses are popular with students because of their convenience and flexibility of scheduling. Faculty appreciates the flexibility of the scheduling as well, and schools appreciate the cost effectiveness that online courses provide.

What seems clear in the research discussed in this chapter is that because of increased competition for high GPA's, student cheating, whether in a traditional class setting or an online setting, will continue to rise. Most research seems to indicate that students are going to cheat both in class and in an online environment and that the online environment is not more conducive to plagiaristic acts than an in-class environment. The increased use of the Internet, however, in accessing and retrieving information is making it easier for students to cheat, especially in light of the preponderance of "paper mills" and "knowledge brokers" on the Web, which blatantly promote plagiarism. Online teachers must, therefore, develop new ways to detect such acts because of the lack of face-to-face contact with their students.

Some suggested techniques to detect and/or deter online cheaters include the following:

- Require students to take at least one in-person exam at a proctor center and require students to provide the proctor with a photo ID.

- Use a free or proprietary search engine (i.e., www.Turnitin.com) to detect similarities in student papers and other previously written papers and confront students with this information.

- Consider developing hybrid courses that combine both traditional in-class instruction with some online instruction.

Two of the most frequently suggested solutions to student online cheating (as appearing in much of the research used for this chapter) were the following:

a. Develop a relationship with students by communicating regularly with them via e-mail, chat rooms, and discussion boards. This frequent communication will give teachers some idea of the student's writing style, grammatical and mechanical skills, and communication skills. Occasional telephone calls to students throughout the semester may also deter cheating. Many students expect online courses to be completely devoid of any personal contact. This seeming lack of personal contact might tempt some students who would not cheat in a regular classroom to do so online. If they know that the instructor may, in fact, contact them via telephone to ask questions regarding particular assignments, they are less likely to cheat.

b. By far, most of the research indicates that developing and enforcing a strong, clear academic integrity policy and communicating this policy to students, together with strict enforceable penalties, is the most effective means of deterring online cheating. Students need to be made fully aware of the consequences that may result from plagiarizing.

Even with a strong academic integrity policy in place, institutions and teachers should incorporate moral and ethical education into their students' regular course work. The recent ethical scandals in corporate America, as well as in the political arena, provide poor examples and have thus contributed little toward strengthening the character of America's students. Likewise, the increased pressure for students to perform well and to maintain high GPAs, coupled with the ease and anonymity with which information can be accessed on the Internet, makes it easier for students to justify cheating. Incorporating values education into every curriculum, perhaps every course, may encourage the development of those qualities that would reject such unethical behavior.

REFERENCES

Brownstein, A. (1999, September 9). Beyond Cliff Notes: In college, online cheating is a grade-A problem. [Electronic version]. *Detroit Free Press*. Retrieved January 2, 2003, from http://www.freep.com/news/education/qfiller9.htm

Bushweller, K. (1999). Generation of cheaters. *The American School Board Journal*, April. Retrieved January 17, 2003, from www.asbj.com/199904/0499coverstory.html

Byrd, B. & Lott, K. (2003). Evaluation in online courses. *Business Education Forum*, 58(1), 48-50.

Carnevale, D. (1999). How to proctor from a distance. [Electronic version]. *The Chronicle of Higher Education, 46(12)*. Retrieved November 6, 2002, from http://chronicle.com/free/v46/i12/12a04701.htm

Charp, S. (2002). Administrative and instructional portals. *T.H.E. Journal, 30(2)*, 12-14.

Guernsey, L. (1998). Distance education for the not-so-distant. [Electronic version]. *The Chronicle of Higher Education, 44(29)*, A29. Retrieved from http://chronicle.com/data/articles.dir/art-44.dir/issue-29.dir/29a02901.htm

Hartigan Shea, R. (2002). E-learning today. [Electronic version]. *U.S. News & World Report, 133(16)*, 54-56. Retrieved November 5, 2002, from http://web10.epnet.com/citation.asp

Howland, J. L. & Moore, J. L. (2002). Student perceptions as distance learners in Internet-based courses. *Distance Education, 23(2)*, 183-194.

Kanengiser, A. (2002, October 21). Higher ed takes on high-tech cheating. [Electronic version]. *The Clarion-Ledger.* Retrieved November 6, 2002, from http://clarionledger.com/news/0210/21/m02.html

Kleiner, C. and Lord, M. (1999, November 22). The cheating game: Everyone's doing it, from grade school to graduate school. [Electronic version]. *U.S. News & World Report.* Retrieved January 17, 2003, from http://n13.newsbank.com/n1-search/we/Archives?p-action+doc&p_docid=0ED7DOA90441

McLeod, R. G. (1997, December 16). Classroom chronicles: Students Look to Internet for new ways to cheat. [Electronic version]. *San Francisco Chronicle.* Retrieved January 2, 2003, from http://www.sfgate.com/cgibin/article.cgi?file=/chronicle/archive/1997/12/16/MN16916.DTL

McMurtry, K. (2001). E-cheating: Combating a 21st century challenge. *T.H.E. Journal, November,* 37-41.

Moore, M. G. (2001). Surviving as a distance teacher. *The American Journal of Distance Education, 15(2),* 1-5.

National Business Education Association. (2002, November). Online classes and nontraditional students. *Keying In, 13(2),* 7. Reston, VA: Author

Oakes, K. & Rengarajan, R. (2002). E-learning. *T&D,* 56(9), 57-60. Retrieved November 5, 2002, from http://web10.epnet.com/citation.asp

Oliver, R. (1999). Exploring strategies for online teaching and learning. *Distance Education, 20(2),* 240-254.

Rabb, T. (2000). *Issues of education at community colleges: Essays by fellows in the mid-career fellowship program, 1999-2000,* (Doc. No 446 801, 170 pages). Princeton, NJ: Princeton University, Department of Education.

Schaeffer, E. F. (1998). Character crisis and the classroom. *Thrust for Educational Leadership, 28(2),* 14-17. Retrieved November 5, 2002, from http://web10.epnet.com/citation.asp

Schwartz, J. (2003, January 1). Professors vie with Web for class's attention. [Electronic version]. *The New York Times.* Retrieved January 2, 2003, from http://www.nytimes.com/2003/01/02/technology/02WIRE.html

Snow, K., Farris, E. & Levin, D. (1999). *Distance education at postsecondary education institutions: 1997-98.* Washington, D.C.: National Center for Education Statistics. (NCES No. 2000-013). U.S. Department of Education, Office of Education Research and Improvement.

Stallings, D. (2002). Measuring success in the virtual university. *Journal of Academic Librarianship, 28(1-2),* 47-53.

Stidham, S. & Frieden, B. (2002). 10 easy steps to online success. *Business Education Forum, 57(2),* 47-49.

University of Phoenix. (2002). *The University of Phoenix Online* [Brochure]. Phoenix, AZ.: Author.

Wilson, R. (1999). Colleges urged to better define academic integrity and to stress its importance. [Electronic version]. *Chronicle of Higher Education, 46(8),* A18-A20. Retrieved November 5, 2002, from http://web10.epnet.com/citation.asp

Young, J. R. (2002). The 24-hour professor. [Electronic version]. *The Chronicle of Higher Education, 48(38),* Retrieved November 6, 2002, from http://chronicle.com/free/v48/i38/38a03101.htm

Zernike, K. (2002, November 2). With cheating on the rise, more colleges are turning to honor codes. [Electronic version]. *The New York Times.* Retrieved November 17, 2002, from http://www.nytimes.com/2002/11/02/education/02HONO.html

Instructional Materials and the Internet

Nancy Groneman
Emporia State University
Emporia, Kansas

Using the Internet to provide instructional activities for students has created opportunities and challenges for students, teachers, and school administrators. Some of these Internet-based learning activities have changed instructional methodologies from teacher-centered to student-centered models. Student-centered learning activities help to make online instruction at least as effective as instruction in traditional classes and may make the instruction more effective. This chapter covers the factors involved in the development of effective Internet instruction.

BASIS FOR EFFECTIVE INTERNET INSTRUCTION

Some of the most effective teaching methodologies for Internet-based instruction are the ones suggested by Knowles (1984) as part of adult learning theory. Knowles' (1984) two major theories were that (1) adults learn more effectively through active training methods, and (2) adults learn through the application of knowledge based on their real-life experiences. Internet-based learning activities have applied those two theories effectively not only for adult instruction, but also for secondary school instruction.

The ultimate goal of Internet-based instruction is to have students achieve success in the course. Student success can be measured in several ways, including grades, completion rates, and feedback. In order to develop online instruction that allows students to achieve success, the factors need to be considered as follows:

- Nature of the course

- Overall benefit to students and schools

- Types, ages, and academic backgrounds of students

- Traits of teachers

- Availability of technical support and trainers

- Technology available to teachers and students

- Access to resource materials by students

- Type and number of learning activities

- Types of assessment tools needed

The ideas and resources described in this chapter should help teachers and administrators make wise choices, whether they are creating an entirely online course or supplementing a traditional course with Internet-based activities.

Internet-Based Course Selection Criteria

Course level. In the last few years, both educational institutions and businesses have offered Internet-based instruction. However, one should select very carefully the courses and course content to be taught over the Internet. Course objectives, learning activities, and grade levels of the courses are all related to whether students will be successful using Internet-based instruction.

Course objectives. The specific course objectives and related learning activities may determine whether instructional resources are available to teach a course effectively over the Internet. Course objectives related to the acquisition of business knowledge and skills are easier to achieve in Internet-based courses than ones that deal with the development of mathematical skills. A graduate level business education course may have an objective related to the analysis of business education issues. In such a course, students can analyze local issues or use Internet search engines or online databases such as InfoTrac or ERIC to identify the issues.

For most student populations, written communication competencies can be taught effectively and evaluated via the Internet, but oral communication and interpersonal (teamwork) skills may be difficult to teach and evaluate. Soft skills, sometimes called behavioral skills, should not be ignored (Fann and Lewis, 2001), no matter how difficult these skills are to teach. A study by Kaupins (2002) indicated that Web instruction using audios, videos, or keyboarded lectures were not effective training methods if the objective were to develop interpersonal skills.

Instructor evaluation of oral presentations given by groups of students in front of the rest of the class is a difficult activity to replicate in an entirely online course. Having students videotape their oral presentations provides a partial solution, but it does not give students experience speaking in front of an actual audience. As Fann and Lewis (2001) indicate, "It would not be practical (and perhaps even impossible) to observe a student's presentation before a group when a course is taught online." Offering an oral presentation course entirely over the Internet may not be a wise choice.

In addition to oral communication skills, interpersonal skill development may also be difficult to incorporate in Internet-based learning activities (Fann and Lewis, 2001). Team projects are often used in online instruction, but there is little evidence that student interaction via e-mails and chat rooms is equivalent to face-to-face interactions with students of other races, genders, and cultures.

Types and ages of students. Student success in Internet-based instruction is increased if students are mature, self-motivated, and currently employed in the field in which they are taking course work. Students of all ages may lack maturity and self-discipline, but the younger the students, the more likely that they will lack these attributes. In online classes, successful students are usually older and more academically experienced (Diaz, 2000). Exceptions are students who are currently in alternative schools or in at-risk programs (Hurley, 2002), students who have been home schooled, and American students who are at locations around the world and have taken traditional independent study courses in the past. As McEntee (Okula, 1999) indicates, some students "are not disciplined enough to complete work on their own schedule or do not possess other independent learning skills." Students of all ages may need to be given deadlines for completion of assignments.

Before selecting a course to be offered online, at a minimum, teachers and administrators should gather and analyze the following types of data on the target group of students: (1) age, (2) grade level of education completed, (3) maturity, (4) previous experience with independent study classes, and (5) work experience related to the online course.

Instructor Issues

Several issues related to instructor training and support can affect the quality of online learning materials and effectiveness of Internet-based courses. A top-down administrator-directed approach to online course development will probably not be effective. Teachers are the best judges of whether a course or a portion of a course can be effectively delivered via the Internet. However, after offering one or two courses over the Internet, teachers may discover teaching methods that will allow them to offer more courses online.

Effective online instructor traits. Online instructors should be able to organize learning materials in a logical order, write clear directions, evaluate assignments in a reasonable time frame, set deadlines for assignments, be flexible, and be willing to change assignments based on student feedback. In fact, formative feedback should be gathered from students midway through a course in order to determine whether the students are overwhelmed with work, understand the assignments, and have received enough background information to complete the assignments. If the feedback from formative evaluations is negative, instructors should be flexible enough to revise the assignments or activities immediately.

Training, Support, and Teacher Incentives

Faculty training, faculty incentives, and technical support are essential for the success of Internet-based instruction. Training needs to cover both the online technologies and the student-centered teaching methodologies. Technical support personnel are needed to train the instructor and to keep online classes up and running. Additionally, faculty should be provided incentives or rewards for the creation of online courses since course development time is much greater than for traditional courses.

Teacher training. In order to create effective learning activities, teachers need to be aware of the capabilities of the technology and be trained to use it. Trainers should show teachers examples of other online courses, so that teachers can visualize an actual online course. Technical training should be given on Web page creation, the use of online course authoring software, e-mail, and scanners. Tutorial books and software can be helpful as an introduction, but some teachers prefer to be trained in a hands-on classroom situation. Spaced practice is better than massed practice with one-hour training sessions being preferable over three- or four-hour sessions. Teachers also need time to use new technologies between training sessions. Teachers should apply this instruction very soon to one of their own courses by creating course components.

Hricko (2002) suggests that teacher training be designed to have the teacher become a student in someone else's online course and use it as a model both for course structure and for teaching methods. When teachers take online classes themselves, they see the course from a student's perspective. As a student, one can see how time consuming it is to review 50 or more Web sites to find only two or three sites that actually provide the needed information. In addition, many commercial Web sites promote their own products and contain biased or inaccurate information. From those experiences, teachers may learn to provide URLs for a few Web sites specifically related to an assignment, thereby focusing the instruction and saving students' time and effort.

Student-centered teaching methods. Another main aspect of teacher training deals with instructional methodologies needed to create a student-centered course. Instructional designs that utilize student-centered learning approaches support problem-solving, application, and other higher order thinking skills (Land & Hannafin, 1997).

Curriculum directors and teachers. Curriculum directors/developers may need to work with teachers to help them make the transition from teacher-centered courses to student-centered courses, since curriculum specialists have expertise in creating student-centered learning activities (Perreault, et al., 2002). Effective student-centered teachers should coach, provide guidance, observe, and offer hints, reminders, and regular feedback (Hazari, 1999). Student-centered teaching methods include using team projects, gathering information directly from business representatives in the local community, locating and reading information on Web sites, and using discussion forums/boards to share and answer questions.

Peer training. Besides developer-directed training, peer training and support can also be effective. Through faculty sharing sessions or via e-mails, online teachers can share techniques for creating online learning materials with other teachers. Some higher education institutions encourage peer training by organizing a mentoring or coaching relationship among online teachers (Perreault, et al., 2002).

Technical support staff. No matter how outstanding the learning activities, the course will not be successful if the students cannot access the course content. Technical support staff are needed to help students access course materials, enter student names and e-mail addresses in directories, help teachers develop online materials, troubleshoot technical problems, select online technology, and provide help desk support and electronic troubleshooting.

Technological Choices

Before choosing a specific computer user interface for an online course, two questions should be answered: (1) What computer user interface will make learning easy for students? (2) What computer user interface will allow instructors to create all course components in the least amount of time with the least amount of training? Some instructors place all the learning activities and assignments on a school's Web site, while others create their course materials using an online course authoring software program such as WebCT or Blackboard. Developers of online courses may incur a large financial outlay for the technology.

Course authoring software. Online course authoring or delivery programs make it easy for an instructor to create a course and provide a consistent user interface. The ease of use of online course software makes course development time shorter than if all materials were created in HTML programming language. Online authoring/delivery programs include WebCT, Blackboard, LearningSpace5, E-College, TopClass LCMS, and Anlon. Generally, these programs have a prepared skeleton course structure with menus and buttons. Most of the software programs allow a student to do the following:

- View course syllabi, announcements, assignments, and lectures

- Take online tests

- Link to external Web resources

- E-mail the instructor and other students

- Read the instructor's resume and view a photograph

- Post items to a bulletin board

- Access a chat room/virtual meeting room

- View grades for individual assignments

Before selecting course-authoring software, teachers should consider the following factors: software cost, reliability, features, and ease of use. Some Internet-based courses use multiple course authoring features; others do not. Some courses require students to read a textbook and complete assignments printed in the textbook or online, while others use no textbooks or online lectures. Online computer applications courses often use a tutorial textbook and no online lectures. Assignments identified by page number may be provided under an "Assignments" button for students to read. Once assignments are completed, students send them to the instructor. If using course authoring software, student assignments can be turned in by placing files in a "digital drop box." Students may also send assignments by attaching files to an e-mail sent to the instructor.

Administrative technology requirements. Both administrative and instructional needs may determine the type of technology used and the features needed. School administrators and instructors are concerned that online courses cover the same material and involve the same amount of time as traditional classes. Some high schools that offer online classes have to verify the amount of time individual that students have spent on an online class. These schools must track student login sessions reliably to allow verification of student "seat time" or the school will not receive state funding (Hurley, 2002).

Availability of technology. Instructional activities created and used for Internet-based instruction depend on the availability of certain types of technologies for both students and instructors. Normally, the minimum technology needed by students is a computer with Internet access and e-mail capabilities.

Before creating learning activities that use audio, video, or plug-in software programs, the target student population needs to be identified, as does the students' technology and their technological literacy level. Although instructors may have multimedia technology, if all students do not have speakers and sound cards on their computers to receive those messages, this technology should not be used. The file size of online lectures and the transfer speed over the Internet are two of the most common limiting factors when using multimedia in online courses (McManus, 2003). By using low-level technologies to deliver a course, the prospective student population that can access the course will increase, but the variety of learning activities will decrease.

For Internet-based instruction, technology does drive the learning activities. Technology is available that allows all types of multimedia to be used. Instruction can even involve two-way, audio-video satellite transmissions, but only if students and instructors have personal computers with high-speed processors, large memory capacities, laser technology, and voice recognition systems (Morrison, 1996).

Video and audio presentations require large amounts of bandwidth not available through ordinary dial-up Internet service providers in many parts of the U.S. (Gehris, 2001). The target market of students can decrease dramatically if students need Internet2, high-speed digital access, broadband Internet access, or special computer hardware or software. Although video lectures may add little educational value to some classes, in others they could be very useful. However, it may take students 30 minutes to download a 5-minute video clip using dial-up Internet service. An alternative is to store videotaped lectures on CDs and send them to students through the mail.

Students' technological expertise. Students who lack basic computer and Internet skills may struggle with online learning activities. The success rates of business students in online classes may be higher than for other students because business students have used computers extensively. However, to relieve student anxieties, teachers can send an e-mail to students prior to the start of the course telling students step-by-step how to (1) access the course URL, (2) enter the user ID and password, (3) select the course by name, and (4) locate the course syllabus and assignments. This initial mailing increases the opportunity for students to have a positive learning experience.

Access to Student Resource Materials

Not all resource materials in online classes are provided online. Teachers may want to reinforce or supplement textbook material. Those supplementary materials can be created using HTML, a Web editor software program, or a word processing program, which is then uploaded to the course Web site. Students in traditional courses know how to obtain textbooks for courses, but instructors must tell students how to obtain textbooks for online classes. Some schools use an online textbook service, and students purchase textbooks either online or call a toll-free telephone number. In other cases, students are told to contact any bookstore locally or online to order the textbook.

Online databases and journals. Students may need access to online databases such as InfoTrac, ERIC, Periodical Abstracts, and ProQuest. When online databases are not available, students may have to locate alternative resources through local community libraries. Online journals such as *Information Technology, Learning, and Performance* (http://www.osra.org) and *BusinessWeek* (http://www.businessweek.com) can be useful instructional resources too. For example, in a business curriculum class, a specific research-based article on the most used computer skills in business can be a useful resource.

Student software needs. Resource materials need to be accessed easily by students. Reading materials can be sent to students by mail or can be scanned and made available on Web pages, often as PDF files. Other resource materials may include PowerPoint presentations. When using PDF or PowerPoint files, instructors must inform students prior to the start of the course that they will need to download Adobe Acrobat to view PDF files or to have PowerPoint software/viewer files installed on their computers. The instructors should also make available specific step-by-step instructions on how to download such files.

Course Objectives, Learning Activities, Assessment, and Relationships

As in traditional classes, online course objectives, learning activities, and assessments should be closely related and instructors must make an effort to establish relationships with their online students.

Course objectives and normative evaluation. During the first half of an online course, the instructor should obtain normative feedback from students on three things: (1) the length of time it takes to complete assignments, (2) the clarity of instructions, and (3) the usefulness of online lectures, printed materials, and other resources. Based on normative evaluations and the quality of students' work during the first part of the course, the teacher can create or revise assignments and deadlines for the second half of the course.

Number and type of learning activities. Using a wide array of learning activities in an online course can hold students' interest; otherwise, working at home alone on very similar kinds of assignments can become boring. (Assignments, however, should maintain some consistency in terms of format to provide students a sense of security.) If students are in the workforce, assignments should make use of those work experiences. Having assignments that make use of community resources such as Chambers of Commerce, businesses in a local community, and local libraries can also be very beneficial to students.

In online classes, teachers need to select enough assignments to meet the course objectives, even though these assignments may not exactly be the number of assignments given in face-to-face classes. To make up for time spent on teacher demonstrations in face-to-face computer classes, distance education teachers may give more assignments to their online students. Too many assignments become a problem, however, when the teacher receives hundreds of assignments from students over a weekend. If the grading burden is overwhelming, the teacher cannot provide student feedback in a timely fashion.

Assessment. Assessment methods should be closely related to both course objectives and learning activities. In classes such as computer networking classes, both assignments and formal objective examinations are evaluated. In other classes, especially graduate level classes, evaluation of daily/weekly projects may indicate whether students have achieved the objectives and no objective exams are given.

Building relationships. To develop relationships with their students, instructors can use the following methods:

- Post the instructor's and the students' resumes.

- Post a photo of the instructor and of each student on the Web site.

- Give quality feedback on assignments in one- or two-paragraph e-mails.

- Require paired/team assignments.

Another way to build class relationships is to have a getting-acquainted assignment as the first one. This assignment may involve having students and the teacher write one to three paragraphs about themselves in an open forum/discussion board (Gehris, 2001). The assignment deadline may be within a day or two after the course begins to show the instructor that all students have been able to log on to the course. If open forums or discussion boards are not available for this activity, one can use group e-mails.

Online Course Design

Creation of online assignments/lectures. The teacher creates many online instructional materials. Online lectures may be necessary to explain in simple, easy-to-understand language the concepts presented in a textbook, to give examples, and to outline the most important points in a textbook. Teachers do not need to know how to use HTML programming language to create online lectures. They can create Web pages using Web editor software such as Dreamweaver or FrontPage, or word processing programs. Web editor programs are relatively easy for instructors to use. Additionally, some online course authoring software programs contain text boxes to fill in, eliminating the need to create files using HTML, Web editor software, or a word processing program. The technical aspect of Web page development should not deter teachers from the creation of online courses.

Once they create online lectures, teachers can easily upload word processing or Web page files into a prepared skeleton course, an advantage of using course authoring programs. The main student benefit of using course authoring programs is that students become familiar with a consistent course structure, lessoning their anxieties while taking a course, and making it easier for them in future online courses.

Textbooks. Online learning activities may include the use of a textbook. Some teachers may think the creation of an online course means creating the equivalent of all of the information that is in a textbook, while most supplement the textbook with online lectures and other learning activities that they create themselves.

Course segments. Generally, an online course should be divided into small segments (assignments) rather than having all assignments presented together. Each assignment should have a deadline attached to it regardless of the age of the student population. In a semester-long course, usually a couple of assignments per week is more realistic than daily assignments. A single term paper or project is not usually considered online instruction; if used, students should turn in a partial term paper or project several times during the semester to get ongoing instructor feedback.

Design principles for online lectures. A common teaching method involves the use of an online lecture or a combination reading assignment in a textbook followed by an online lecture. By using eye-catching, easy-to-read online lectures, students will focus on the important points. To create attractive online lectures, the following design principles are recommended:

- Use a large font size to make the text easy to read.

- Use colored text for headings or bulleted items for emphasis.

- Use bulleted lists frequently.

- Use short paragraphs of text or outlines.

- Use short Web pages that branch or link to other Web pages.

- Use graphic images when they add to the content.

- Use no more than one or two graphic images per Web page.

- Copy multimedia presentations to CD-ROM disks.

- Select multimedia that all students can access.

- Embed complete URLs to have active links to other Web sites.

- Provide clear and concise instructions.

- Create short paragraphs that link to other Web pages.

Instructors may believe that links to World Wide Web sites will be read by all students, but that is probably a false assumption for three reasons: First, links must include complete URLs or they will not be active links. Second, links that worked yesterday may not work today because the linked Web sites may be under reconstruction. Third, unless students are required to complete an assignment directly related to the linked material, they may not read it. For these reasons, nearly every online lecture page needs to encourage student feedback, possibly in the form of hidden questions within the lectures or quiz questions covering them. These types of student activities encourage thoughtful reading (Arsham, 2002).

Graphic images. Graphic images should be used to enhance an online lecture but should not distract from it. If not related to the subject matter, graphic images can be distracting. Animated GIF files are not recommended because of the distraction factor. Many graphic image files in the gif or jpg formats are available free of charge on World Wide Web sites; however, few are related to business courses. Taking pictures yourself with a digital camera may take less time than searching the Internet for images.

Locating appropriate graphic images that are not copyrighted or registered can be difficult. Although images and text in magazines can be scanned and added to a Web page, instructors should follow copyright laws. Using an image with a registration mark

® without getting approval from the organization that has registered the image is trademark infringement. However, the use of copyrighted (versus trademarked) works for instructional purposes is considered "fair use" as indicated in the Copyright Act (17 U.S.C. 107). To be legal, teachers may want to only scan images in publications that are not copyrighted such as some computer catalogs.

In general, the use of one or two graphic images per Web page is all that is recommended, because too many high resolution images in a single file can cause a Web page to download very slowly. A practical method to determine the speed at which Web pages will load is to load each Web page on several computer models having various amounts of RAM memory and using various Internet communication speeds.

Discussion forums. One of the most valuable experiences students have in face-to-face classes is networking with other students, which is especially true for adult students. Discussion forums or paired/team assignments can facilitate networking. In a graduate level "issues and trends class," each student could post an issue on a discussion board and then be required to help two or three other students solve their issue by posting a reaction to the initial postings.

Teamwork activities. Online classes can effectively incorporate teamwork (Fann and Lewis, 2001). Students may communicate with team members by e-mail, phone, faxes, chatrooms, or virtual meeting rooms. Videoconferences may be a very effective technology to develop teamwork skills but may not be available in remote geographic locations. As in face-to-face classes, the instructor may never know who has done the most work or whether some students did any work unless students fill out a peer evaluation form and rate the team members. This form may have students rate the amount of time and effort other team members have spent on the project, each student's punctuality in terms of meeting deadlines, and a ranking of the effort and quality of each student's work. Teamwork assignments can break up the monotony of sitting at home and doing the class assignments alone, but it would be unusual to have all assignments be team assignments. However, team assignments can be a problem when online students work at their own pace. When one student is ready to begin the team assignment, other students may not have the background knowledge needed for it. This problem is another reason to set deadlines for the completion of assignments.

Online teachers may want to have at least one paired or teamwork assignment and one discussion board or discussion forum activity in each course to build a "learning community." In fact, one rubric designed for the evaluation of online courses indicates that an exemplary online course will provide multiple opportunities for students to interact and communicate with the instructor and other students (Rubric for Online Instruction, 2003).

An instructor can "meet," share ideas, and delegate work to a team of students using an online chat room or virtual meeting room. The logistics of organizing these sessions at a compatible time with five or six teams of students is a primary constraint. Teachers may wish to keep students on a rigid assignment schedule so that all students are ready for a chat room discussion on a given day.

Hands-on computer instruction. Computer hands-on instruction is one of the most popular teaching methods used in online computer software classes such as word processing, spreadsheet, database, or desktop publishing classes. The primary teaching resources used in computer applications courses include a tutorial textbook for introductory assignments and a project-oriented textbook for advanced assignments or classes. Teachers usually test students in computer classes by giving them an application problem or project, having them create an appropriate document, and having them turn the file(s) in by an e-mail attachment or an electronic drop box. However, some schools have students meet at the school on a given day to take the major exams. This prevents the problem of teacher uncertainty about whether students are completing the tests themselves.

Student questions. The freedom students have to ask questions in online classes should be considered another teaching methodology. Students' questions should be encouraged by the instructor in order to clarify material in textbooks, online lectures, or other resource materials. Students are much freer in online classes to ask the instructor questions without feeling "dumb" in front of a group of students and may ask more questions than in a traditional class. Usually questions are sent by e-mail, but instructors should also be available to answer questions over the telephone during specified office hours. By holding online office hours, students can e-mail the instructor and receive an answer back almost instantaneously.

Assignment deadlines. Having deadlines for student assignments is an important aspect of an online class. The younger the student, the more important are assignment deadlines. Even adults want and need to have deadlines to stay motivated. Without deadlines, some students will complete all the assignments for a course during the last week of the course or not at all. If students are not completing the assignments accurately, the instructor does not have time at the end of the course to provide feedback to students and prevent other assignments from being done incorrectly.

On the surface, open entry/open exit course offerings that allow students to start and finish courses whenever they desire seem appropriate for online courses. However, a main reason for not making online classes open entry/open exit courses is the high student dropout rates ranging from 25% – 44% in such online classes (Kiser, 1999; Gehris, 2002; Hurley, 2002). Students need definite deadlines to complete assignments, or they are more likely to drop out of the course.

Assignments. As described previously, teachers of online classes can select from a wide array of learning activities, including,

- Textbook reading assignments and questions

- Online lectures created by the instructor

- Reading articles in online journals

- Web sites as learning resources

- Online database searches for journal and newspaper articles

- PowerPoint types of presentations that may correlate with a textbook

- Multimedia presentations

- Paired or team assignments

- Discussion forums

- Hands-on computer assignments

- Interviews with business people in the local community

Certainly, most online teachers do not have the time to utilize all of those types of activities, nor will all course content be enhanced by these activities. The idea is to select among them to the extent that they complement the course of study.

Elements of Assessment

Student assessment methods should be linked as closely to learning activities in online classes as they are in face-to-face classes. In many classes, project-based activities allow students to achieve course outcomes without using objective (multiple choice, true-false, or short answer) examinations. Graduate students may be required to create an ideal business curriculum for the school in which they teach. In a computer applications class at the undergraduate or secondary school level, application exams may require students to create a document and send it to the instructor. The course objectives and the level of cognitive skill students need to demonstrate will determine whether to use objective tests or project-based assessments, or both.

Feedback. Instructor feedback to students becomes an integral part of the learning activities and the assessment system. Feedback can be in the form of one or two paragraph reviews sent to each student by e-mail or handwritten notes on printed assignments that are scanned and sent immediately to a student's e-mail address. Many scanners have an e-mail button making this task easy to accomplish. Writing one or two paragraph evaluations for 15-20 students in a class takes a lot of instructor time but should be valued as an instructional activity in and of itself. If more than twenty students are in a class, the quality and quantity of student feedback will diminish. Students expect quick feedback, but instructors cannot work 24 hours a day or 7 days a week; consequently, students' expectations are not always realistic. Some teachers send a brief note to each student indicating that an assignment has been received, even if the teacher does not have time to grade it immediately.

Feedback provided to students is often longer and of a higher quality in online courses than in traditional courses. In traditional courses, some teachers only give a letter grade or total points on a 15-page term paper. In online courses, teachers can send e-mails to students with their scores, as well as make specific comments about correct or incorrect answers. By placing the assignment description and the points or letter grade in a subject line of an e-mail, students can easily see them. If using online course authoring software, an online grade book can be used to enter student scores; students can view their scores but not other students' scores. Some online instructors use a combination of e-mails and online grade book to provide feedback only to students who do not receive perfect scores on the assignments.

Online testing and posting grades. Online objective tests can be just as useful in online classes as they are in traditional classes. In fact, for classes such as business law, accounting, or marketing, objective exams may be a necessity. Many online course authoring programs such as Blackboard and WebCT provide built-in quiz and examination features with automatic grading of students' responses to questions, but the exams must be considered open book unless taken under supervision. Some programs have more powerful testing tools than Blackboard or WebCT, and some are designed just to administer tests and assessments. Mallard (http://www.cen.uiuc.edu/Mallard/) and Question Mark Perception for Web (http://www.questionmark.com/uk/perception/index.htm) are two examples of online testing programs. Online testing features allow an instructor to set a specific time and day to administer the test and to set the length of time allowed for students to take it. Students learn their scores immediately and see which questions they have missed when using online tests.

Cheating. Cheating on learning activities and exams probably occurs as often in traditional classes as it does in online classes, but it is an issue of great concern to most online instructors. Teachers often ask, "How can I tell if a student has completed an assignment or test himself/herself?" Many course authoring software programs provide built-in test generators that allow the instructor to designate starting and ending times for exams. However, these online tests provide no effective way to determine whether students are looking at the textbook or notes, soliciting help from another student, or having someone else take the test (Gehris, 2001). Some instructors design online tests as open book exams, telling students that they may use textbooks and notes. Usually, the tests are used to make sure that students have read the resource materials, and they may be considered by the instructor as an en-route learning activity that leads to some other form of assessment. The amount of weight given to those open book tests is often less than that given to other assignments or forms of assessment.

Besides cheating on tests, students can cheat on all types of learning activities, including projects and case problems. Development of a "learning community" within an online class means that students who have problems with assignments quickly "learn" to e-mail other students for help. Asking other students for help also occurs in on-campus, face-to-face courses and is considered part of the learning process. Feedback to some students should occur after the assignment deadline to prevent giving correct answers to students who in turn give them to other students.

Weighting of assignments and tests. The weighting of assignments and tests can become an art form in online classes. In terms of points or percent of the total grade, enough weight needs to be given to individual assignments to motivate students to complete them. Since cheating is possible in some online classes, more weight may be given to assignments on which students cannot cheat easily. Having self-assessment quizzes and tests can alleviate some of the burden of grading, but frequently students skip those self-assessment tools and immediately go to the assignments that actually count toward their final grade.

Monitoring exams. One solution to the problem of cheating is to have someone monitor the tests. Finding a monitor can be accomplished in a variety of ways. One way is to have students meet at a local school where a local teacher monitors the exams and sends completed exams to the course instructor. A second method is to have students identify by name, position, address, e-mail address, and telephone number someone who can monitor the tests. The exam is sent through the postal service or by e-mail to that individual. A third way to handle tests is to have all students come to the school offering the online course for face-to-face classroom testing. This works only if all of the online students live within a short distance of the school, but it could be used for online courses offered by a high school during summer months when regular school is not in session.

Assessment of student achievement in online classes can be as varied as in traditional classes. Assessment in an online class involves more than grading papers and tests; it involves selecting the correct weight to give to assignments, selecting a reasonable number of online tests, and providing written feedback to students via faxes or e-mails.

SUMMARY
Many factors need to be considered to deliver effective online learning activities, including the age and academic level of students, the technology available, training requirements, students' technological expertise, course objectives, resource material availability, and the assessment methods needed. Course objectives, learning activities, and assessment methods need to be intrinsically joined together when developing online courses.

REFERENCES
Arsham, H. (2002) *Interactive education: impact of internet on learning & teaching.* Retrieved November, 2002, from University of Baltimore, 1995-2002 Web site: http: ubmail.ubalt.edu/~harsham/interactive.htm.

Diaz, D. (2000). *Comparison of student characteristics, and evaluation of student success, in an online health education course.* Unpublished doctoral dissertation, Nova Southwestern University, Fort Lauderdale, Florida. Retrieved January 12, 2003, from http://www.ltseries.com/LTS/pdf_docs/dissertn.pdf

Fann, N. & Lewis, S. (2001). Is online education the solution? *Business Education Forum,* 55(4), 46-48.

Gehris, D. (2001). Exploring Web-based business instruction. *Business Education Forum,* 56(1), 44-46.

Hazari, S. (2002). Evaluation and selection of Web course management tools. Retrieved January 19, 2003, from http://sunil.umd.edu/lectures/effteach/sld018.html

Hricko, M. (2002). Developing an interactive web-based classroom. *USDLA Journal.* Retrieved December 18, 2002, from http://www.usdla.org.html/journal/NOV02_Issue/article05.html.

Hurley, R. (2002). Fine-tuning an online high school to benefit at-risk students. *T.H.E. Journal,* 30(4), 33-40.

Kaupins, G. (2002). Trainer opinions of selected computer-based training methods. *Journal of Education for Business,* 77(6), 319-323.

Kiser, K. (1999). Ten things we know so far about on-line learning. *Training.* November, 66-74.

Knowles, M.S. (1984). *The adult learner: A neglected species.* (3rd ed.) Houston: Gulf Publishing.

Land, S. & Hannafin, M. (1997). Patterns of understanding with open-ended learning environments: A qualitative study. *Educational Technology Research and Development,* 45(2), 47-73.

Mass Communication and Campaign Strategy. Retrieved July 30, 2003, from http://apps.internet2.edu/.

McManus, T. (1995, August) *Special considerations for designing Internet instruction: Size and speed.* Retrieved July 29, 2003 from http://www.svsu.edu/~mcmanus/papers/special.html#Delivery_Methods__Advantages__and_Limitations

Morrison, J. (2002) Distance learning: Extending business education beyond electronic walls. *Journal of Education for Business,* 71(4). 189-190.

Okula, S. (1999). Going the distance: A new avenue for learning. *Business Education Forum,* (53(3). 7-10.

Perreault, H., et al. (2002) Overcoming barriers to successful delivery of distance-learning courses. *Journal of Education for Business,* 77(6). 313-318.

Rubric for Online Instruction. Retrieved July 30, 2003 from California State University, Chico Web site: http://www.csuchico.edu/tlp/webct/rubric/rubric_final.pdf.

Internet Use in Classroom Instruction

Theresa Yohon
Colorado State University
Fort Collins, Colorado

Internet use in education has increased since the introduction of the World Wide Web in 1991. Today the Internet offers an interactive means of connecting teachers and students with educational resources, colleagues, and professional development. In this chapter, how the Internet is used in education, the Internet's effect on teaching and learning, educational changes to be addressed in Internet-based learning activities, and training for effective Internet use are discussed.

The Internet employs technology that has been around for over thirty years. The Internet, which is literally a system of equipment and software that connects computers and networks around the world, allows for communication and information sharing across a variety of different types of computer systems. U.S. military installations first used the Internet for communication, and then college and university researchers started using this network to share data (Lewin, 2001). In 1991, researchers at the European Organization for Nuclear Research conceived the idea for the World Wide Web (WWW), an online environment in which documents are linked to other documents or files by comments or hyperlinks embedded in the documents themselves. Since then the Internet has moved from a text-based file system to include audio, video, interactive Java and Flash-based programs. New technologies such as cable modems, T1 lines, DSL (Digital Subscriber Line), and satellite connections allow the Internet user to access these larger file-sized mediums.

The advent of the World Wide Web and a more graphical-based browser interface sparked interest in the Internet for broader educational use. The Internet offers an environment for professional development, extended learning options, and increased connections with fellow teachers. Teacher benefits from Internet use include having an expanded classroom and making the educational process more authentic and exciting for their students (Barron and Ivers, 1998). Many teachers also have Web pages or Web sites on the Internet for one or more of the following reasons: (1) as a source of information for parents, (2) for public relations, (3) for student information, and (4) as a publication site for student work (De Cicco, Farmer, & Hargrave, 2001). For students, the Internet provides an archive of endless information, collaboration opportunities, interactive activities, and a presentation format for self expression. Students find that the Internet makes learning more relevant and authentic, opens new ways to learn, and allows them to be more analytical and curious (Barron and Ivers, 1998).

Today it is not a question of whether or not to use the Internet in education, but it is a matter of finding effective methods of Internet integration into the teaching and learning environments. In general, Internet use in the classroom is too new to have been studied in depth (Garner & Gillingham, 1996; Schofield & Davidson, 2002); however, smaller studies have indicated that teachers using the Internet exhibit more pedagogical changes to collaborative and problem-solving classroom environments than do teachers who make less use of the Internet (Becker, 1999). To the extent that the changes in educational practice will lead to improved learning for students, Internet use in the classroom looks encouraging. Though little compelling evidence shows that the Internet raises the academic success of students, particularly for high school students (Schofield & Davidson, 2002), schools continue to look for ways to integrate the Internet into the classroom because of other benefits gained through Internet use in the classroom such as increased collaboration and challenging and real-life tasks (Jones, Valdez, Nowakowski, & Rasmussen, 1995).

HOW THE INTERNET IS USED IN EDUCATION

Internet access does not guarantee Internet use. Furthermore, Internet activities planned for students may not be a part of a thoughtful instructional plan. According to Keating, Wiles and Piazza (2002), the Internet has been used effectively for the following purposes: (1) to add rich and up-to-date resources for information and lesson planning, (2) to support research, (3) to increase communication among teachers, students and parents, (4) to increase collaboration between students, content experts, and other teachers, (5) to individualize student experiences by creating Web -based curriculum projects, activities, and virtual field trips that provide opportunities for critical and creative thinking skills through student support activities, and (6) to provide additional coursework avenues via online learning.

Teacher and Student Resources

Teacher resources. Curriculum planning materials, classroom materials, textbooks, and even courseware and testing systems are available online. The most common use of the Internet for teachers is information gathering for lesson preparation (Becker, 1999). Many organizations have created online teacher resources, such as the following:

- Education World (http://www.education-world.com)

- TeachNet.com (http://www.teachnet.com/lesson)

- Global School House (http://www.globalschoolhouse.com/)

- Gateway of Educational Materials (http://thegateway.org)

- Knowledge Network Explorer (http://www.filamentality.com)

- Kathy Schrock's Guide for Educators (http://school.discovery.com/schrockguide/index.html

- Internet Innovations (http://www.biopoint.com/)

- Marco Polo (http://marcopolo.worldcom.com/)

- Educational Resource and Information Clearinghouse (ERIC) (http://www.askeric.org/)

- Wall Street Journal (Classroom Edition) (http://www.wsjclassroomedition.com/index.html)

- Discovery Channel (http://school.discovery.com/)

Teacher resources also include productivity templates that help teachers develop lesson plans, Web-based project pages, worksheets, or Web pages. My Project Pages at (http://www.myprojectpages.com/) provide directions for developing online curriculum pages, project pages, and MiniQuests, which are problem-based learning activities that utilize online resources to solve the problem. At High Plains Regional Technology in Education Consortium (http://wizard.hprtec.org/), teachers can build a worksheet, lesson plan, or class page. Other productivity tools include Rubistar (http://rubistar.4teachers.org/), an online rubric maker; Zoomerang (http://www.zoomerang.com) for online surveys; BackFlip (http://www.backflip.com) for online bookmarks to Web sites; and Quiz Star (http://quiz.4teachers.org/index.php3) and Quiz Center (http://www.school.discovery.com/quizcenter/quizcenter.html), both online quiz generators.

Professional journals and teacher magazines are also available on the Internet. Classroom Connect (http://www.classroom.com/) is a monthly magazine that offers Internet lesson plans and articles about online learning. The Awesome Library (http://www.awesomelibrary.org/) contains over 22,000 reviewed resources, including over 70 magazines.

Student resources. Student resources can also be found at many of the teacher resource Web sites. However, additional Web sites for reference material are available for students. The High School Hub (http://www.highschoolhub.org/hub/hub.cfm) is a noncommercial learning portal to high quality, free online educational resources for high school students. It features interactive learning games, puzzles, and quizzes. Other reference Web sites include Reference Desk (http://www.refdesk.com), Britannica Internet Guide (http://www.britannica.com), The U.S. Library of Congress (http://www.loc.gov), Internet Public Library (http://www.ipl.org), Library Spot (http://www.libraryspot.com), Information Please (http://www.infoplease.com), and eLibrary (http://www.encyclo-pedia.com/). Up-to-date business information can also be found on the Internet, such as information on companies at Standard and Poor (http://www.standardpoor.com), on entrepreneurship at YoungBiz (http://www.youngbiz.com), and current business news at Business Week (http://www.businessweek.com/).

Internet student resources allow students to participate in experiments or activities that they normally would not be able to access. Complete digital objects that students can freely interact and manipulate are accessible online. For example, in a biology class, students can manipulate, dissect, rotate, and watch a three-dimensional, digital video of a human heart. Business and financial math models are available for students to compare leasing versus buying of equipment and to understand the time value of money. Even though availability of these online media has increased, students (as well as teachers) may be unable to access them because of their file size. Some Internet connections at schools and at homes are not fast enough to allow for a file download or for the video or interactive activity to be "streamed" onto a computer for playback.

Research

Teenagers have replaced the library with the Internet as the primary tool for doing research for significant projects. Almost all online teens (94%) use the Internet to do research for school (*Teenage Life Online*, 2001). The Internet provides access to a range of online periodicals and up-to-date news sources. Current statistics and economic and business data are available and searchable.

Unfortunately, most students don't have the search skills to effectively use the Internet for research. School librarians report that teachers send students to the library with instructions to "use the Internet," without realizing that the students need specific search skills in order to find needed information (Schofield & Davidson, 2002). Wallace, Kupperman, Krajcik, and Soloway (2000) found that sixth-grade students were not successful at finding useful information on the Internet or using the information they did find in a thoughtful manner.

Communication and Collaborative Spaces

Not only is the Internet a source of information, but the Internet also supports collaborative working practices. Students who would otherwise work in isolation or only with their classmates can now work with students around the world. Teachers can collaborate on projects with other educators and interact with colleagues via online professional development activities (Weller, 2002). The most common collaborative tools used on the Internet are e-mail, listserv, instant messaging, chat, and video conferencing. E-mail and listservs are asynchronous collaborative tools, while instant messaging, chat, and video conferencing are synchronous.

E-mail. E-mail is the most frequently used collaborative tool by teachers and students. Not only can messages be delivered electronically, but other documents such as papers, presentations, and spreadsheets can be attached to the e-mail and sent with it. Instructionally, e-mail supports Electronic Pen Pals (such as KidLink at http://www.kidlink.org or ePals at http://www.epals.com/), online tutoring and mentoring (Net Mentors at http://www.netmentors.org/Home.asp or National Mentoring Partnership at http://www.mentoring.org/index.adp), conversations with experts (Ask an Expert at http://www.askanexpert.com/), collaborative story building, and student gallery development (Barron & Ivers, 1998).

Listservs. Discussion groups, or listservs, extend the e-mail concept beyond the individual (Picciano, 2002). Rather than sending mail to individuals, mail is posted and resent to listserv members to read and to respond as they wish. To become part of a listserv, the student or teacher must subscribe to the listserv. If a listserv doesn't provide the information that is needed, a person unsubscribes to the listserv.

Listservs can be one-way information distribution lists, which means one can receive messages from the list, but cannot post a message on the list. Many of the listservs for teachers at Global School House Web site (http://www.gsn.org/lists/index.html) are constructed in this way. If the listserv is a discussion list, listserv members can post messages to the list, which means questions and responses to questions may be posted. These types of listservs are very similar to Web-based bulletin boards. Listservs are set-up by the local school district or through a third-party on the Internet. NetPals at http://netpals.lsoft.com/licenseapp.html provides free listserv software to school districts.

Instant messaging (chat), video conferencing, and shared workspaces. Over the past few years, instant messaging or "chatting" has become increasingly popular. Educationally, instant messaging allows for real time idea exchange, interactive mentoring (including online office hours), and connections to remote guest speakers (Barron & Ivers, 1998). On the Internet, text-based "chat rooms" are available on a variety of topics.

To use an instant messaging system, some type of Internet Relay Chat (IRC) software is installed on a computer's hard drive (Picciano, 2002). After installation, the teacher or student registers a log-in with a central computer server, along with anyone else's user name with whom they wish to communicate. To start a messaging or chat session, the IRC software program is activated, which notifies the central server of the person's online presence, which in turns allows the co-communicators to see that the person is online and available to chat (Mambretti, 1999). The most popular instant messaging systems today are supported by major computer portals such as MSN.com (messaging software is MSN Messenger) or Yahoo.com (messaging software is Yahoo! Messenger).

To use this Internet tool, teachers need to identify chat rooms that are safe for students. Additionally, teachers should plan to record the chat conversations to ensure the appropriate use of language and content (Valauskas & Ertel, 1996). Online messaging or chat rooms that support educational objectives are Nicenet Internet Classroom Assistant (http://www.nicenet.org/) and Global School House (http://www.globalschoolhouse.com/cu/index.html).

Video conferencing is similar to chat or instant messaging, in that it allows for real time conversations via the Internet. However with video conferencing, a Web-enabled camera and microphone is used to communicate. Video conferencing software is also needed; the most common products are NetMeeting (free at http://www.microsoft.com/windows/netmeeting/) and CU See Me (http://www.cuworld.com/). Schools use video conferencing to connect with experts, other students, view live press conferences and newscasts, and to share project work. In many cases, the need for a computer with at least 128 to 256 RAM and a high-speed Internet connection prohibit most K-12 schools from using this online capability. Ideally, an ISDN or T1 line is needed to support audio and video over the Internet.

Shared workspaces are virtual (or online) spaces where documents, pictures, PowerPoint presentations, and drawings can be shared among people who are logged in. Often shared workspaces are provided through groupware, or software that supports the online collaboration. In most cases, software costs and the need for a high-speed Internet connection prohibit schools from using this online environment. Additional information about groupware can be found at http://www.usabilityfirst.com/groupware.

Student Support Activities
The Internet provides multiple student supports, such as online field trips, projects, tours, simulations, and interactive games. The Internet allows for virtual field trips to locations previously impossible. Teachers can also design their own field trips by using available Internet resources, putting their own pictures and videos online, or going to Web sites maintained by governmental agencies, universities, or commercial companies. The following Web sites are a subset of the online locations where virtual field trips available.

- Global SchoolNet Foundation (http://www.gsn.org/project/fieldtrips)

- TramLine (http://www.field-guides.com)

- Virtual Field Trip (http://www.uen.org/utahlink/tours)

- Biz/Ed Virtual Field Trips (http://bized.ac.uk/virtual/home.htm)

- Plant Tours (http://bradley.bradley.edu/%7Erf/plantour.htm)

- Virtual Tour of the Federal Reserve Money Museum (http://www.rich.frb.org/research/econed/museum)

Various Internet project designs and templates have been developed for teacher use. Web Quests are inquiry-based activities in which most or all of the information needed by the learner is online. The authoritative Web site on Web Quests can be found at San Diego State University at http://Web quest.sdsu.edu. Web Quests that have already been developed can be found at Internet Expeditions (http://eduscapes.com/sessions/travel/index.html) and EdHelper (http://www.edhelper.com/cat311.htm). Specific business Web Quests can be found at: http://imet.csus.edu/imet1/peaty/Web quest/, http://www.nevada.edu/~ldr/, and http://Web quest.sdsu.edu/matrix/9-12-Bus.htm. A tutorial on Web Quests is provided at http://www.teachersfirst.com/summer/Web quest/quest-a.shtml. ThinkQuests are similar to Web Quests, however through the ThinkQuest Internet Challenge (http://www.thinkquest.org/library/JR_index.html), students have the opportunity to compete in the development of Web -based activities.

Some Web sites provide a variety of Web-based student support activities. The Blue Web 'n Library (http://www.kn.pacbell.com/wired/blueWeb n) lists Web-based tutorials, projects, and activities. Marco Polo (http://marcopolo.worldcom.com/) is an educational portal that provides search capabilities across seven educational Web sites: ArtsEdge, EconEdLink, EDSitement (humanities), Illuminations (math), Read«Write«Think, Science NetLinks, and Xpeditions. These Web sites were specifically chosen because their online activities are interactive and support critical thinking and problem solving. Lesson plans, interactive models, video cases, and business statistics can be found through Marco Polo's search engine.

With faster modems and better file compression, students can view video footage of business-related reports, interviews with corporate managers and small business owners, and participate in interactive simulations. For example, students start an e-business at the online simulation located at http://www.bizworldgame.com/thegame/, make money in a virtual stock market game http://www.smgww.org., or balance the federal budget at http://www.budgetsim.org/nbs/. Students can test their knowledge of economics and sport trivia at a Federal Reserve supported Web site at (http://www.bos.frb.org/peanuts/leadpgs/intro.htm).

A student support activity does not need to be online. An electronic sheet or "e-sheet" of Web-based resources will focus students on quality links to data and articles on a particular theme. The benefit of an e-sheet is that each student can look at his or her own copy of the material online (versus needing to share one copy of a book from the library). The hyperlink environment provides options to read additional related material, and the student has more control over his or her learning (Lewin, 2001). A detailed list of ten to fifteen Web sites could be divided among students, so that students are not all visiting the same Web sites.

Other online environments are MOOs and MUDs. Multi-user object-oriented environments (MOO) and Multi-user domains (MUD) are forms of text-based virtual reality that users can access and interact with over the Internet. Both MOOs and MUDs are software programs that accept multiple users across a network and provide each user access to a shared database. Participants have the appearance of being in an artificially constructed place (a "room") that also contains other people who are connected at the same time (De Cicco, Farmer, et al., 2001). They emphasize social interaction and the ability of users to create their own virtual objects, allowing students to create and explore their own "virtual communities." The educational value of these environments is the ability to collaborate in real time; to explore virtual rooms where students can tour famous cities; to take part in lab experiments or meet fictional characters; and to have students create their own buildings, games, or worlds.

Coursework through E-Learning

Schools that support e-learning, or electronic learning, either have a locally developed online course system or have purchased a course management "shell" in which course tools (i.e. e-mail, chat rooms, quiz makers, etc.) and content spaces are available and can run through a computer's browser. The most common features of a course management system (CMS) are, (1) password security, (2) ability to deliver and manage course material, (3) ability to deliver and manage classes and groups, (4) pupil tracking and assessment capability, (5) communication capabilities, and (6) the ability to change the look and function of the system (De Cicco, Farmer, et al., 2001). Most all CSM packages provide a course template that makes developing a Web-based course no more difficult that completing a survey (Picciano, 2002). Often CMS-based course sites are used to extend an on-campus class, provide additional resources, and increase opportunities for communication through e-mail, discussion boards, and chat. The two most common course management systems are Web CT and Blackboard.

The advantages to e-learning are numerous. Educational materials can be altered or amended quickly and easily. New materials or information can be added. To accommodate different student learning styles, students can choose their own path through the material and can work through the material at their own pace. Course management tracks students' use of the material and their progress through the material (De Cicco, Farmer, et al., 2001). An obvious advantage for students is the ability to take a course anytime, anyplace. To effectively use e-learning, teachers and students need regular access to a computer and the Internet and a basic level of technology skill. Additionally, teachers require support in terms of time (for course development and delivery) and adequate compensation for the increased student connection.

Critics of e-learning state that it will not fully replace face-to-face delivery (De Cicco, Farmer, et al., 2001). Some online instructors find it difficult to develop a genuine dialogue between students who don't know each other (Engler, 2000). A recent National Center for Educational Statistics (NCES) study of distance education in postsecondary institutions found the program development costs (77%) and lack of instructor interest

(63%) were major inhibitors to starting or increasing distance education course offerings (Waits, Lewis, & Greene, 2003).

Still, examples of successful e-learning can be found at most colleges and universities. For high school level courses, the Virtual High School (http://www.govhs.org/Web site.nsf) and Class.com (http://www.class.com) provide examples of online coursework across various content fields. Online courses increase the availability of coursework to high schools and postsecondary students. Additionally, business teachers can upgrade their technology skills through online workshops and courses. For example, the Public Broadcasting System (PBS) through TeacherLine (http://teacherline.pbs.org/teacherline/) offers inexpensive courses on technology integration in various content areas. Microsoft© offers free online tutorials (http://www.microsoft.com/education/ ?ID=Tutorials) on how to use their products in the classroom. To search for a tutorial in a specific instructional area on the Internet (i.e., e-commerce, accounting, etc.), use the keywords "online tutorial" and instructional area name.

The Internet is used in various ways in education by providing a rich supply of teacher and student resources. Two major educational Internet uses are for research and collaboration through e-mail, listservs, and chat. Opportunity for coursework is extended through the Internet for the student as well as for the teacher.

THE INTERNET'S EFFECTS ON TEACHING AND LEARNING

Research suggests that some applications of home and school computers, e-mail, and multimedia projects lead to success in advanced courses, as well as gains in critical thinking, complex problem solving, understanding the scientific method, and synthesizing different points of view. One of the most highly rated reasons for using the Internet is that the Internet expands the student's classroom and provides a natural setting for inquiry skills (Barron & Ivers, 1998). However, most research doesn't separate the Internet's effect on teaching from technology integration's effect in general. The following section summarizes the available research on the Internet's effects on the classroom environment, the teacher's role in the classroom, on instruction, and on student learning and which classroom factors most strongly predict a high level of Internet use by teachers and students.

Classroom Environment

Internet use may influence the configurations of classrooms. According to Ravitz, Wong, and Becker (1999), the highest level of student use in the classroom environment, whether it involved student research or posting student work on the Internet, was reported by teachers who had high-speed direct access to the Internet in their own classrooms, with at least four computers available in that classroom. However, in spite of the communication potential with students and experts around the world, only 7% of the teachers had their students use the Internet to communicate with other students or to post their work (Becker, 1999). Besides access to computers, another major reason for low Internet usage among teachers is their frustration due to a mismatch between the technical capabilities of the computers being used and the capabilities needed to access the Internet (Schofield & Davidson, 2002).

Overall, using computers may influence student self-esteem and positive teacher behavior. Archer (1998) found that where teachers used computers for more sophisticated activities than drill-and-practice, school officials were more likely to report higher teacher and student attendance, less tardiness, and better morale. One reason for this is that computers provide instant, nonjudgmental feedback, a characteristic beneficial for building self-esteem and morale,.

Teacher's Role in the Classroom

Part of the teacher's role in utilizing the Internet is to have a deep understanding of its capabilities (Schofield & Davidson, 2002). So it is not surprising that computer expertise was the second most important predictor of frequent Internet by teachers and their students (Ravitz, Wong, & Becker, 1999). Teachers with substantial computer skills in such areas as file handling and using presentation and multimedia authoring software were twice as likely to use the Internet in the classroom (Ravitz, Wong, & Becker, 1999).

With the inclusion of the Internet in the classroom, teachers need more time to update materials and their knowledge of the Internet. Because of the fluidity of the Internet, online resources change, disappear, or move (Schofield & Davidson, 2002). With little discretionary time for exploring resources during the school year, teachers have little opportunity to track these changes. To increase available time to integrate Internet activities, teachers turn to other teachers. Not surprisingly, connections to other teachers and to professional development opportunities also indicate potential high levels of Internet use in the classroom (Ravitz, Wong, & Becker, 1999). Additionally, teachers who report a high level of informal contacts with other teachers at their schools were also more likely to use the Internet than teachers with fewer of these informal contacts (Ravitz, Wong, & Becker, 1999). In the use of new educational tools, community discussions of their challenges and successes support continued use of the tools.

Through the use of the Internet, the teachers' role becomes more facilitative in nature. Teachers using the Internet identify themselves as guides, mentors, and facilitators, whose roles are to motivate students and engage them in discussion and reflection (Moller, 1998). As students become more self-directed via Internet integration, teachers (as well as students) need to change the way they think about the teaching/learning process. The teacher needs to become comfortable not being in front of the classroom and needs to learn to spend instructional time as a guide versus a lecturer (French, Hale, Johnson, & Farr, 1999).

Teachers and students work together differently when Internet-based activities are used. Students indicated that teachers controlled and directed student work to a much lesser degree when students worked online than at other times (Schofield & Davidson, 2002). Teachers reported that they circulated when students were working on an Internet activity and provided help only when students requested it. Teachers felt that if the Internet could provide students with certain information that they had previously provided, they felt less obligated to provide it themselves. This placed the burden for education more directly on their students. Other teachers reported improved relationships with students, because they did not have to exert the same sorts of control strategies that they felt compelled to use in the regular classroom. Because students enjoy using the Internet, students were more interested and less disruptive (Schofield & Davidson, 2002).

Instruction

In the integration of the Internet in an urban school setting, Schofield and Davidson (2002) found that 46% of teachers required students to complete research via the Internet; 40% required Internet resources to interact with others; and 18% had students publish their information onto the World Wide Web. Teachers who believed strongly that good teaching involved facilitating independent student work, rather than emphasizing direct instruction and skills practice, along with the emphasis on complex thinking, were more likely to have their students use the Internet than were those who put limited value on such approaches to teaching (Ravitz, Wong, & Becker, 1999). Additionally, teachers who used more constructivist methods were two-and-one-half times more likely than traditional teachers to use the Internet for teaching (Ravitz, Wong, & Becker, 1999).

Student Learning

The Internet's impact is variable, often positive, and strongest on dimensions other than academic achievement. Internet use differs from school to school and the learning goals for using the Internet vary. The driving forces for Internet integration are to increase teachers' and students' use of up-to-date and extensive materials and provide new opportunities to learn in the context of meaningful experiences in a real world framework (Schofield & Davidson, 2002). Internet usage often increased students' motivation and acquisition of technical skills, and improved their ability to work cooperatively (Archer, 1998).

Most Internet projects' primary objectives do not include improvements in academic achievement. The fact that the Internet is a flexible tool that can be used for a variety of reasons makes precise assessment of its impact more problematic. However, evaluators from West Virginia found that the more access to technology students had, and the more their teachers believed that technology could help, and the better trained they were to use the technology, the higher students scored on the Stanford 9 (McNabb, Hawkes, & Rouk, 1999). Internet access also brings the possibility of creating active, empowering roles for students (Peck, Cuban, & Kirkpatrick, 2000) such as student assistant, collaborator, tutor, and technical assistant, using the tools (i.e. e-mail, chat, etc.) that facilitate their new roles.

The Internet's effect on education is difficult to separate from overall technology use in the classroom. However, Internet use seems to positively influence student self-esteem and positive teacher behavior. As more active learners, students develop an ability to use a broader range of materials and learn in more contextual environments.

EDUCATIONAL CHANGES DUE TO INTERNET-BASED LEARNING

The inclusion of the Internet in teaching and learning raises issues about what changes in pedagogy, the classroom, and school should be expected and supported. Also with increased avenues for resources and collaboration, the additional issues of copyright protection, privacy of student information, security and protection of students, and equal access to the Internet need to be addressed.

Pedagogical Changes

The Internet isn't the answer for every educational activity. Nor should the Internet be used in the classroom without a clear instructional goal. Questions to ask before deciding to use the Internet are the following (Barron & Ivers, 1998):

- Can I teach the goals or concepts of the lesson just as effectively or more effectively through the use of the Internet?

- Is the Internet the most effective way to obtain information?

- Am I taking advantage of the benefits of the Internet, i.e., developing connections with people, accessing multiple resources, and gathering timely information?

- Will the activity increase the student's ability to conduct information searches and retrieve relevant resources?

- Will the student's technology skills increase through the use of the Internet?

The key is to develop the "right kind" of Internet assignment. Internet-based assignments teach students "how to teach themselves," a critical workplace skill in an uncertain future labor market (Salpeter, 2003). David Jakes and his partners at Internet Innovations, Inc. (http://www.biopoint.com) suggest starting an Internet project with an essential question, i.e., a question such that students have to solve a relevant problem by collecting, synthesizing, processing, assembling, and expressing information (Salpeter, 2003). For example, in an entrepreneurship course, an essential question is, "What type of business would be successful in a particular community?" For this project students can use U.S. census data at http://www.census.gov/ to determine what type of business may be successful in a locality, and then check at Superpages (http://www.super pages.com/) as to what businesses in that category (i.e. florist, accountant, etc.) are already in that community. A comparison of businesses would be made using Web site information from each company. Based on this comparison, students decide whether to start the new business in that community, emphasizing the competitive advantages of the proposed business.

With the Internet, teachers can seamlessly link Internet resources, interactive activities, and text. These Internet tools, along with collaborative tools such as e-mail, support constructivism—a practice in which students construct their own knowledge, based on their experience and relationship with concepts (Weller, 2002). For example, through various career development Web sites and e-mail interviews with business owners, students can construct their own knowledge regarding career trends. By e-mailing other business students in different parts of the United States, students can compare the factors that influence the economic health of a particular location. In addition, teachers can develop a Web page of online financial calculation resources that students can access to complete various finance projects.

Because of increased access to resources, students have the opportunity to find resources that best suit their learning styles. Therefore, students need more extensive skills in searching the Internet and analytically evaluating the resources found. With the Internet, control is increasingly being relinquished to the learner; students are no longer passive recipients of knowledge (Weller, 2002), and the focus of education shifts from the teacher to the learner. This shift of control should be supported by professional development in collaborative and authentic instructional strategies for the teacher. Suggested pedagogical strategies for in-service training include collaborative learning, problem-based learning, inquiry-based learning, and situated learning.

Collaborative learning. Collaborative learning is an instructional approach in which students of varying abilities and interests work together in small groups to solve a problem, complete a project, or achieve a common goal (Bransford, 2000). Teachers use the Internet to increase student opportunities for collaborative learning in virtual classrooms via chat rooms, e-mail or video conferencing. In many collaborative learning activities, students have individually assigned tasks that they can accomplish using Internet resources. Information exchanges and database creation with students around the world allow students to become both the creators and consumers of the information that they exchange (Harris, 1998). Peer feedback activities are done electronically with experts and other students. Chats are held among students to solve a particular problem.

In business education, collaborative learning via the Internet could take place, for example, by student groups across a state completing a research survey in their individual communities, then e-mailing all responses to a central location for data analysis. Each student group then draws conclusions based on the data and posts those conclusions on a project Web page. In another collaborative activity, students presented with a business case problem then contact various experts and fellow students via e-mail or chat to receive help in solving the problem.

Problem-based learning. Internet use increases problem-based learning. Students can discuss issues, find information required, and present solutions to real problems. One way to do this is through a parallel problem-solving activity, in which students in several locations solve a problem and then share their problem-solving methods, using collaborative methods. For example, the problem of deteriorating downtown business areas could be discussed among business students from different communities. Problem-based learning also takes place via virtual simulations such as the online Stock Market game (found at Denver Post's education Web site— http://www.postnews-education.com/curriculum.asp) and virtual worlds such as those found at http://

www.bized.ac.uk/virtual/. For more information on problem-based learning through projects, go to http://4teachers.org/projectbased/.

Inquiry-based learning. Inquiry-based teaching is also a teaching strategy more often used by teachers who use the Internet. The process begins when students notice something that surprises them or stimulates a question, i.e., something that may not make sense in relationship to the learner's previous experience or current understanding. Rather than focusing on information, inquiry-based teaching focuses on questions that motivate learning (Feldman, 2000). The student then takes action through continued observing, raising questions, making predictions, testing hypotheses, and creating theories and conceptual models. In business education, whether in a finance, marketing, business law, or international business course, students will have questions that are "researchable." The Internet, through its search engines, provides a rich environment for information.

Situated learning. Situated learning occurs when students work on authentic and realistic tasks that reflect the real world. By embedding subject matter in the ongoing experiences of the learners and by creating opportunities for learners to live subject matter in the context of real-world challenges, knowledge is acquired and learning transfers from the classroom to the world of work. According to Stein (1998), "situated learning places the learner in the center of an instructional process consisting of *content*— the facts and processes of the task; *context*—the situations, values, beliefs, and environmental cues by which the learner gains and masters content; *community*—the group with which the learner will create and negotiate meaning of the situation; and *participation*— the process by which learners working together and with experts in a social organization solve problems related to everyday life circumstances" (¶ 5). Situated learning options are enhanced through Internet use. Situated learning includes Internet-based case problems, such as those found at (http://www.econedlink.org/). In another example, the online video case about the economics of professional sports at http://www.econedlink.org/lessons/index.cfm?lesson=NN146, puts students in a real-life situation looking at value of work and money. Online communication via the Internet allows students to participate in discussions with actual practitioners, either business people in the local or surrounding communities or expert, such as Ask an Expert (http://www.askanexpert.com/), where students can ask questions of international marketers, family financial expert, or business etiquette consultants. Collaborative avenues allow students to share internship experiences with their teacher or other students, or to maintain contact with a business mentor.

Classroom Changes

Obviously Internet usage has the potential in enhance curriculum through more interdisciplinary activities and authentic learning experiences and can support new curriculum models and major changes in pedagogical practice. However Internet use also adds another layer of classroom management and organization strategies due to the increase in technology tools in use. Barron and Ivers (1998) provide the following considerations in the implementation of Internet strategies:

1. Practice first. Work with the computers and Internet resources that you plan to use.

2. Focus on curriculum. Focus on standards to be accomplished and teaching methodologies to be utilized to enhance standards mastery.

3. Preview Internet resources on all computers that will be used to view them, or be sure that computers to be used have the same configuration of hardware and software (i.e., Web browsing software, plug-ins, etc.).

4. Make alternative instructional plans when the school's network is down or is unavailable, or is running slowly.

5. Provide instruction in basic computer and Internet skills. Though students today are more computer literate than in the past, and in some cases, more comfortable with computers than their teachers, students do not ordinarily have the skills to effectively search the Internet for information or critically evaluate resources that are retrieved.

6. Conduct some activities off-line. In most schools, teachers will not have access to computers every day at any time. Combining off-line activities (such as planning before Internet-based research, reviewing information from other sources first, writing an outline for an e-mail to a pen pal, etc.) with online activities allows for flexibility of computer lab time.

7. Monitor student work online.

With the Internet, the classroom can now exist in "cyberspace." The Internet has the potential to open learning opportunities to a wider audience by allowing students greater flexibility regarding where, when, and how they will learn. Important questions need to be answered, however, prior to using e-learning in a school:

- Do the students have the potential to be good online learners?

- Do the students and teachers have adequate technology skills?

- Is there enough time for course development and increased connections to students?

- Is there enough time for constant updating of hyperlinks to Web resources?

Online classrooms are not successful learning environments for all students. Students who do best in online courses are focused, self-directed, independent, motivated, and comfortable in expressing themselves (Engler, 2000). Online courses often require a far greater time and effort commitment from students than a face-to-face course. Although research shows there is little significant improvement in student learning through the use of online technologies, the reason for continued growth is the perceived benefits of just-in-time learning and time and location flexibility for the student in class attendance (Weller, 2002).

School Changes

To support Internet integration, a solid technology plan should be developed to support the technical infrastructure to fulfill both the school's educational mission and essential school services (enrollment, records, etc.). Increased security is needed to protect electronic data and the privacy of school and student records. Monies need to be allotted each year to maintain and update computer networks and Internet connections. Computer support personnel are also needed to sustain the increase in technology use. Professional development activities for teachers need to be supported with continued technical assistance available to teachers as well as administrative staff. Technology access for parents also needs to be considered.

Copyright

Copyright laws are based on the premise that people should have the right to compensation for their creative works because compensation encourages more creative works. A creative work is automatically protected by copyright from the moment of creation. The "fair use doctrine" provides a limited basis by which people can use a copyrighted work without getting permission from the creator.

One reason for the fair use doctrine was the immediate need for the use of the material by teachers and the difficulty of contacting the copyright owner for permission. However, the ease with which one can communicate directly with the owner of a work on the Internet may begin to restrict the use of the fair use doctrine. Training on copyright law needs to be included for all teachers and students using computers and the Internet.

In general, if a Web site is clearly copyrighted, contact the owners to request permission to use items from it. If the site has no copyright statement, reference the Web site via its URL and organization or owner's name. Some Web sites allow materials to be used freely for educational use. In other cases, the organization may ask for credit for providing the material or request a link to their Web site be included on the Web page. On the other hand, if the educational materials produced will be sold, the copyright to the material must be owned or permission to use it must be obtained.

For additional information on copyright law, go to the following Web sites:

- Fair Use of Copyrighted Materials (http://www.utsystem.edu/OGC/Intellectual Property/copypol2.htm)

- Copyright Basics by the U.S. Copyright Office (http://www.loc.gov/copyright/circs/circ1.html)

- Fair Use Guidelines For Educational Multimedia: Background and Summary (http://www.libraries.psu.edu/mtss/fairuse/dalziel.html)

- The Copyright Web site (http://www.benedict.com/)

The Technology, Education, and Copyright Harmonization Act (TEACH) expanded the range of copyright-protected works that may be used for distance learning and, in some cases, allows educators to digitize and use materials not already available in digital form. More details on this legislation can be found at http://www.ala.org/washoff/teach.html.

Privacy and Security

Students must be responsible Internet users. All schools need to write an Acceptable Use Policy (AUP) for the Internet. An AUP states the Do's and Dont's of Internet usage on school property and requires signatures of agreement from students and their parents/guardians. An AUP should include how the Internet is connected to teaching and learning expected in the classroom, student responsibilities while online, and consequences that will result from policy violations (Provenzo, Brett, & McCloskey, 1999). Most AUPs address issues such as student e-mail ethics, plagiarism and inappropriate Web surfing (Poftak, 2002). Many schools also include inappropriate use of laptops, handheld computers, cell phones and calculators, particularly in the accessing of a wireless network. An example of an AUP can be found at http://connectedteacher.classroom.com/tips/aup.asp

Obviously, the Internet has materials that teachers and parents do not want their students to see. In 2001, the National Center for Educational Statistics found that about 74% of public schools were using some type of software to filter the Web's over two billion pages. Filtering software such as Cyber Patrol, Cyber Sitter, and Net Nanny prohibits access to Web sites based on keywords and/or a list of off-limit Web sites. Teachers also can randomly check the History, i.e., the list of the sites visited, from the Web browser to review the student's trail of Web sites visited. Most vendors also extend filtering capabilities to filter or block instant messaging (MSN Messenger), chat rooms, and e-mail (such as Hotmail and Yahoo). Because of increased student use of Hotmail and Yahoo accounts in order to e-mail themselves project and homework files, some schools allow students to access their e-mail at designated times or grant special permission to log-on to their e-mail accounts (Poftak, 2002).

In using the Internet, students and teachers may decide to post pictures or documents of students online. To protect student identities, permission from the student and parents for any pictures or documents must be gathered prior to posting online (De Cicco, Farmer, et al., 2001). In captioning pictures or documents, do not use the student's complete name or any additional information that might identify the student. It is also important to monitor students' Web pages, particularly to ensure that they do not reveal their full names and/or personal information. (De Cicco, Farmer, et al., 2001) Rules for online safety are found at http://www.safekids.com/.

Equity

In spite of government efforts to equalize Internet access through financial subsidies of up to 90% of the access cost for schools in the poorest districts, patterns of inequality persist (Schofield & Davidson, 2002). A survey of one thousand public schools found that classrooms in well-off schools were nearly twice as likely to have Internet access (74% to 39%) as those in poor schools (Mendels, 1999). Additionally, teachers in well-off schools reported receiving more technical and instructional support to help them use technology effectively (Ronnkvist, Dexter, & Anderson, 2000). Students also need continuous training and access to Internet tools to gain the benefits before Internet integration takes place.

Internet access does not guarantee effective Internet use. According to Schofield and Davidson (2002), although educators at high and low Internet use schools devised a variety of uses for the Internet in the classroom, teachers at high-use schools tended to develop more Internet-based projects and implement intensive projects that had a recurring and substantial impact on the students' school experiences. These projects were integrated into the curriculum rather than appended to it. Schofield and Davidson identified eight factors that must be in place to support effective Internet integration: (1) team cohesion, (2) project ownership, (3) collaborative structures, (4) active librarian involvement, (5) strong teacher leadership, (6) ease of integration, (7) discretionary professional time and (8) technical reliability.

Economically disadvantaged students. According to the U.S. Commerce Department's July 1999 report, *Falling through the Net: Defining the Digital Divide*, only about 20% of households with incomes below $30,000 own computers, as opposed to 80% of those with incomes over $75,000. Community-based organizations such as YMCA/YWCAs, libraries, Girls and Boys Clubs, etc. are mounting efforts to develop after-school technology centers and programs. Schools also need to make computer labs available to students after school hours.

Ethnic groups also have different experiences with computers and Internet access. For example, only 23% of Hispanic households have Internet access, compared to 46.1% of Whites and 56% of Asian Americans (Trend Watch, 2001). How the Internet is used is also different among ethnic groups. According to Archer (1998), 31% of white students used computers mostly for simulations and applications, in other words, for more critical-thinking activities. This is contrasted with just 14% of black students using computers for simulated activities. At the same time, more than half of America's black students use computers mostly for drill and practice, compared to only 30% of white students. Even though some strides have been made in Internet access at schools, the digital divide still exists in how technology and the Internet are being used to enhance learning.

Disabled students. Through the use of assistive technology, the Internet is available to students with limited sight, manipulative skills, and reading difficulties. Text recognition software reads a Web site; monitor resolution and text size can be changed; and adaptive keyboards and pointing devices allow Internet access for challenged students. Web site development guidelines also have been developed for accessibility. Some key design components for accessible Web sites are to use a consistent temple with no tables or frames, keep the navigation system in the same place on all pages, and add alternative text to all graphics. The World Wide Web Consortium (W3C) has developed these guidelines and can be found at http://www.w3.org/TR/ATAG20/.

The Internet influences pedagogy, the classroom, and the school environment. Additionally, special copyright issues and student privacy and security issues need to be addressed. Even though the Internet provides educational opportunities, some students, particularly economically disadvantaged and disabled students, need special support to access the benefits of the Internet.

TRAINING FOR EFFECTIVE INTERNET USE
Teacher Training
According to a report released by the CEO Forum (1999), a national group of business leaders, "Schools are spending less than $6 per student on the computer training of teachers, contrasted with more than $88 per student on computers, computer programs, and network connections" (p. 8).

Because of the fairly recent development of the Internet for educational use, many teachers need upgraded technology and pedagogical skills to effectively integrate the Internet into the classroom. What training individual teachers need depends on their use of the Internet. Internet skills and knowledge can be tiered into three areas: *basic skills, collaboration skills,* and *development skills.* The basic skills level details the beginning skills and knowledge needed for basic Internet understanding, activity development, and integration into the classroom. The collaboration level of skills requires teachers to be more sophisticated in Internet searching, use of collaboration tools (e-mail, chat, and video conferencing), and use of teacher-based Web sites in the classroom. The development skill level requires teachers to be able to develop Web sites and other Internet-based tools and develop a simple online course.

Depending on the teacher's technology comfort level, online tutorials may provide the needed skill and practice needed. For other teachers, hands-on activities are best. Internet workshops composed of two to three afternoon sessions can cover a basic Internet based tool (i.e. quiz maker, Web Quest, e-mail project, basic course Web site, etc.) and allow time for development and sharing among colleagues. More complex Internet skills, such as Web site or online course development, would require more time.

Student Training
To be Internet literate, students not only need to be technically familiar with computers and how to use the available Internet tools, but they also need to be "manipulators of information to the extent that they can find it, think about what they have found, sort through various points of view, and then form their own opinions" (Valauskas & Ertel,

Table 1. Internet Training Topics for Teachers		
Level One (Basic)	**Level Two (Collaboration)**	**Level Three (Development)**
Technical Skills	Technical Skills	Technical Skills
Search techniques using one search tool	Conduct searches using Boolean logic	Develop basic Web site
Plan lessons for technology integration	Use collaborative tools	Upload and download files for a Web site
Bookmark Internet Web sites	Use teacher-based Web sites to support interactive environment for students	Use course management software
Download and install plug-ins	Create e-mail distribution lists	Develop multimedia files (such as audio and video files, digital pictures, etc.)
Use keyboarding skills		
Create and read e-mail messages		
Manage files		
Knowledge	Knowledge	Knowledge
Internet Terms (such as URL, File formats)	Understanding various collaborative tools (such as e-mail, chat, video conferencing, instant messaging, etc.)	Understanding Web design issues, including accessibility
File formats and how to download and/or use each format		Understanding and using online best teaching practices
Copyright regulations		
Privacy and security issues		
Web site evaluation (for accuracy and quality)		
Internet etiquette (Net-etiquette)		
Pedagogical changes		

1996, p.198). Students need training in two areas: conducting Internet research and evaluating Internet resources.

Conducting research. One of the most frustrating features of the Internet is the difficulty of finding information. Think about what it would be like to search the world's largest library without a complete list of book titles, keywords or subjects, and no organizational strategy. In general, Internet resources exist in this type of environment.

To find information on the Internet, over 75% of Web users use search engines (Sullivan, 2000). Though search engines abound on the Internet (i.e. Google, Northern Lights, Alta Vista, Metacrawler, etc.), no search tool has an index or search "menu" to the entire contents of the Internet. In a 1999 report (Albert, Jeong, & Barabasi, 1999), Northern Lights, the number-one rated search engine at the time, only indexed 16% of the entire Web. Additionally, each Internet search tool uses a slightly different search technique and builds its index (or table of contents) in a different way. Even in a search engine with a large database of Web sites, the student may not find the results of the search to be particularly useful or relevant.

In training the student to use the Internet for information to aid in problem solving, efficient searching techniques need be taught (De Cicco, Farmer, et al., 2001). Barron & Ivers (1998) suggest that these steps be followed:

1. Know specifically what you are searching for, i.e., what specific questions need to be answered. For example, searching for answers to the question "What is the stock market?" yields hundreds of thousands of results or "hits."

2. List the keywords or subject headings that clearly identify the information that is being sought. Use distinctive words to pinpoint information. For example, use the term "depression" with stock market to find information about the stock market during the depression era.

3. Try out the keywords you have identified and revise the keywords that are used based on the results. Use Boolean operators to combine or eliminate phrases of portions of the subject matter that are not important.

4. Gather resources using the refined keyword list. Quickly access the value of the information before downloading and capturing files.

5. Sift and sort through data and information. Organize information into categories.

6. Synthesize information. Use the information gathered to answer the question(s).

7. Evaluate whether the question(s) was adequately answered.

A variety of Internet search tools exist. Subject directories such as Yahoo are complied by humans and organized into subject areas. To be part of the directory, a Web site must be submitted and then it is assigned to an appropriate category. Search engines such as Excite, HotBot, and Alta Vista use a software program to look for keywords embedded in a Web site and rank the Web site in terms of where the term appears on the Web site or how the keywords are placed in proximity to each other. Metasearch engines such as MetaCrawler, Google, and DogPile search across a variety of search engines.

Which search engine is used for research depends on the information to be gathered. If one knows the general category in which the information will be found (e.g., career information), a subject-based search tool like Yahoo works well. If a specific term is being searched (such as inflation, shopping cart software, torts, etc.), search tools such as Alta Vista or Google allow a search by keywords. Also, since each search engine or tool has its own way of using Boolean-like operators (for example, using "and" or "+" to combine keywords), it is a good idea to review the search engine's Search Tips or Advanced Search. To more fully search the Internet, more than one search engine is required.

To learn about the advantages and disadvantages of different search engines, go to Gregg Notess' Web site at http://www.notess.com/search/reviews/. For other types of search sites (e.g. multimedia search engines, search sites for kids, etc.), check out Search Engine Watch at http://searchenginewatch.com.

Evaluating Internet resources. Since anyone can place information on the Internet, students need to develop skills to critically assess the quality of information provided at a Web site. According to a UCLA report cited by Poftak (2002), 51% of Internet users ages 12-17 believe that all or most of the information found on the Internet was reliable and accurate.

In general, information from Web sites with an education (.edu), government (.gov), or organizational (.org) extension is more credible as a source of information. French et al. (1999, p. 82-83) suggest four quality indicators for Web sites:

- Authority: Does the Web site have a clear "owner"? Is contact information about the Web site's owner or sponsor easy to find? Are links to the sponsor's purpose included on the Web site? What other Web sites link to this Web site?

- Accuracy: Can the sources of information provided be verified by another source? Are sources documented with footnotes or hyperlinks to other Web pages? Is it clear who holds responsibility for the information?

- Timeliness: Do the documents or Web pages have the date that the document was last revised?

- Bias: From what viewpoint was the content written, i.e, personal, factual, etc.? What are the author's credentials?

Good tools exist online to help teachers and students evaluate the information available on Web sites. Evaluation instruments can be found at discoveryschool.com: http://school.discovery.com/schrockguide/eval.html. Libraries also provide tips and instructions on how to evaluate Web resources such as,

- http://www2.widener.edu/Wolfgram-Memorial-Library/Web evaluation/Web eval.htm,

- http://www.lib.berkeley.edu/TeachingLib/Guides/Internet/Evaluate.html, and

- http://www2.vuw.ac.nz/staff/alastair_smith/evaln/.

To effectively use the Internet, teachers and students need specialized training. Teachers need professional development not only to learn how to use the technology, but how to effectively integrate the Internet into relevant, critical thinking activities. Students, though often more comfortable in the Internet environment than their teachers, need to learn how to effectively conduct research on the Internet and evaluate Internet resources.

SUMMARY
The Internet is one of the most dynamic digital technologies ever introduced. Since the development of the World Wide Web environment on the Internet, tens of millions of people have used Internet services. The Internet is suffering growing pains because of its increased commercialization, which slows down Internet connection time due to online "traffic."

New technologies being perfected such as wireless communications, handheld computers, and cell phones will increase Internet use and are potential educational enhancements. These telecommunication tools and more sophisticated computers have unique capabilities for enhancing learning through "distributed learning" in which classrooms, workplaces, homes, and community settings are linked for education activities. This continuing development of Internet technology and infrastructure is being accomplished by a number of collaborative projects. The most recent efforts involve the Next Generation Internet (NGI) and Internet2 projects.

Pedagogical change is slow, while technology change proceeds at a speed-of-light pace. Teachers who have successfully made shifts in their teaching to incorporate Internet enhancements report the shifts to this new teaching environment may take three to five years to complete (Feldman, 2000). For successful Internet integration into quality teaching and learning, teachers will need long-term professional development in Internet content, pedagogy, and technology.

REFERENCES
Albert, R., Jeong, H., & Barabasi, A. L. (1999). Internet: Diameter of the World Wide Web. [Electronic version]. *Nature, 401*(6749), 130-131. Retrieved February 1, 2003, from http://www.nature.com
Archer, J. (1998). The link to higher scores. *Education Week on the Web*. Retrieved February 1, 2003, from http://www.edweek.org/sreports/tc98/ets/etc-n.htm
Barron, A. E. and Ivers, K. S. (1998). *The Internet and instruction*. Englewood, CO: Libraries Unlimited, Inc.

Becker, H. J. (1999, April). *Changing teachers' pedagogical practices through the use of the World Wide Web*. Paper presented at the annual meeting of the American Educational Research Association, Montreal, Canada.

Bransford J. (2000). *How people learn: Brain mind experience and school.* Washington D.C.: National Academy Press.

CEO Forum on education and training. (1999, February 22). *Professional development: A link to better learning.* Retrieved February 1, 2003, from http://www.ceoforum.org/reports.cfm?RID=2

De Cicco, E., Farmer, M., & Hargrave, J. (2001). *Using the Internet in secondary schools.* London, UK: Kogan Page Limited.

Engler, N. (2000). Distance learning in the digital age. In D. T. Gordon (Ed)., *The digital classroom* (pp. 51-59). Cambridge, MA: The Harvard Education Letter.

Feldman, A. (2000). Distance learning in the digital age. In D. T. Gordon (Ed)., *The digital classroom* (pp. 90-102). Cambridge, MA: The Harvard Education Letter.

French, D., Hale, C., Johnson, C., & Farr, G. (1999). *Internet based learning: An introduction and framework for higher education and business.* Sterling, VA: Stylus Publishing, Inc.

Garner, R. & Gillingham, M. (1996). *Internet communication in six classrooms: Conversations across time, space, and culture.* Hillsdale, NJ: Erlbaum.

Harris, J. (1998). *Design tools for the Internet-supported classroom.* Alexandria, VA: Association for Supervision and Curriculum Development.

Jones, B.F., Valdez, G., Nowakowski, J., & Rasmussen, C. (1995). *Plugging in: Choosing and using educational technology: New times demand new ways of learning.* Retrieved February 1, 2003, from North Central Regional Educational Laboratory Web site: http://www.ncrel.org/sdrs/edtalk/newtimes.htm

Keating, M., Wiles, J., & Piazza, M. W. (2002). *LearningWebs: Curriculum journeys on the Internet.* Upper Saddle River, NJ: Merrill Prentice Hall.

Lewin, L. (2001). *Using the Internet to strengthen curriculum.* Alexandria, VA: Association for Supervision and Curriculum Development.

Mambretti, C. (1999). *Internet technology for schools.* Jefferson, NC: McFarland & Company, Inc.

McNabb, M., Hawkes, M., & Rouk, U. (1999). Critical issues in evaluating the effectiveness of technology. In *The Secretary's conference on educational technology-1999.* Retrieved February 1, 2003, from http://www.ed.gov/Technology/TechConf/1999/confsum.html

Mendels, P. (1999, September 8). Survey finds teachers unprepared for computer use. *New York Times.* Retrieved February 1, 2003, from http://www.nytimes.com/library/tech/99/09/cyber/education/08education.html

Moller, L. (1998). *Designing communities of learners for asynchronous distance education.* Paper presented at the annual conference of the American Educational Research Association, San Francisco, CA.

Peck, C., Cuban, L., & Kirkpatrick, H. (2000). *Techno-promoter dreams, student realities.* Unpublished manuscript, Stanford University, Department of Education.

Picciano, A. G. (2002). *Educational leadership and planning for technology*. Upper Saddle River, NJ: Pearson Education, Inc.

Poftak, A. (2002). Net-wise teens: Safety, ethics, and innovation. *Technology & Learning, 23*(1), 36-49.

Provenzo, E. F., Brett, A., & McCloskey, G.N. (1999). *Computers, curriculum, and cultural change: An introduction for teachers*. Mahwah, NJ: Lawrence Erlbaum Associates, Inc.

Ravitz, J. L., Wong, Y., & Becker, H. J. (1999). *Teaching, learning and computing: 1998*. Retrieved February 1, 2003, from University of California, Irvine, and University of Minnesota, Center for Research Information Technology and Organizations Web site: http://www.crito.uci.edu/tlc/findings/special_report

Ronnkvist, A. M., Dexter, S. L., & Anderson, R. E. (2000). *Technology support: Its depth, breadth, and impact in American schools*. Retrieved February 3, 2003, from University of California, Irvine, and University of Minnesota, Center for Research Information Technology and Organizations Web site: http://www.crito.uci.edu/TLC/findings/Internet-Use/startpage.html

Salpeter, J. (2003). Web literacy and critical thinking: A teacher's tool kit. *Technology & Learning, 23*(4), 22-34.

Schofield, J. W. & Davidson, A. L. (2002). *Bringing the Internet to school*. San Francisco, CA: Jossey-Bass.

Stein, D. (1998). *Situated learning in adult education*. (ERIC Digest #195). Retrieved August 22, 2003, from http://ericacve.org/docs/situated195.htm.

Sullivan, D. (2000). Survey reveals search habits. *The Search Engine Report*. Retrieved February 16, 2003, from http://www.searchenginewatch.com/sereport/article.php/2162681

Teenage Life Online: The rise of the instant-message generation and the Internet's impact on friendships and family relationships. (2001). Retrieved February 1, 2003, from Pew Research Center Web site: http://www.pewinternet.org/reports/reports.asp?Report=36&Section=ReportLevel2&Field=Level2ID&ID=221

Trend Watch. (2001, May). *TechLEARNING, 21*(10), ¶ 4. Retrieved February 1, 2003, from http://www.techlearning.com/db_area/archives/TL/200105/trendwatch.html

Valauskas, E. J. & Erthel, M. (1996). *The Internet for teachers and school library media specialists*. New York: Neal-Schuman Publishers, Inc.

Wallace, R., Kupperman, J., Krajcik, J., & Soloway, E. (2000). Students online in a sixth-grade classroom. *Journal of the Learning Sciences, 9*(1), 75-104.

Weller, M. (2002). *Delivering learning on the Net*. London, UK: Kogan Page Limited.

Waits, T., Lewis, L., & Greene, B. (2003). *Distance education at degree-granting postsecondary institutions: 2000-2001* (NCES Publication No. 2003-017). Washington, DC: U. S. Department of Education.

Pedagogical and Technological Challenges of the Internet

Nancy D. Zeliff
Northwest Missouri State University
Maryville, Missouri

Today's learners face a world in which they will assume new roles as consumers, citizens, and workers. Technology defines these roles very differently today than just 20 years earlier. Technology brings the conflict of war into our living rooms; laser surgical methods allow patients quick recovery times; online learning brings education and training to the learner in a 24/7 environment; and online shopping alters the way consumers choose products and services.

Today's learners in business education programs at middle, secondary, and postsecondary institutions are citizens of the net generation, identified by Tapscott (1998) as those born between 1977 and 1997. This group of learners has the characteristics of independence, innovativeness, immediacy, and emotional and intellectual openness.

"N-Geners" accept diversity, are curious, and tend to be assertive and self-reliant. Although the perception may be that N-Geners may have a smaller attention span, in fact, these learners can adapt their attention to what is required, allocate their attention to the task at hand, and multitask (Tapscott, 1998). Not only do members of the net generation now outnumber the baby boomers, they have been exposed to digital technology from birth. While television was the primary communication media for baby boomers, computers, CDs, and the Internet are the communication primers for the net generation. Television requires only passive involvement. Digital technology requires interaction, allowing learners to control their level of involvement and direction. Interaction demands in learners the abilities of higher-order thinking and evaluation. Technology allows learners to center on the learning experience rather than the delivery method or person (Tapscott, 1998).

Business educators utilize the Internet in classroom instruction in varied ways. Mrs. Black's middle school computer applications class researches vacation sites around the world such as Hawaii, Florida, France, and Sweden. Students then develop their dream vacation plans in a PowerPoint presentation that is presented to the entire class. Mr. Hanson's high school economics class monitors stock prices of selected companies via the Internet. Students chart the daily prices of the stock as part of their investment portfolio. Ms. Shandy's high school management class downloads programs from the Internet to handheld computers to make management decisions in the business simulation under-way. Dr. Johnson's collegiate business communications students research job vacancies via the Internet and then complete a resume and letter of application for their jobs. Students also complete Web-based virtual job interviews to help them prepare for actual interviews.

What are the pedagogical and technological challenges of using the Internet that face Mrs. Black, Mr. Hanson, Ms. Shandy, and Dr. Johnson? This chapter will explore the challenges business educators face in using the Internet in business education programs in middle, secondary, and postsecondary programs. Means by which these challenges can be reduced and eliminated will be highlighted.

Pedagogical Challenges

Business educators who utilize the Internet in classroom instruction are faced with pedagogical challenges. These challenges include Internet access, assistive technology for learners with special needs, appropriate content and activities, educational copyright issues, assurance that technology improves student achievement, technical support and professional development, and classroom management in the technology classroom.

Internet Access

The U.S. Department of Commerce study (2002) on how Americans use the Internet reinforces statistics and shows gains made from findings in an earlier study called the Digital Divide. More than half (54%) of the U.S. population is online with 2 million new Internet users per month. Computer users number 174 million or 66%. Of these, the largest group of users of computers and the Internet are children and teenagers. Family households with children under the age of 18 are more likely to have Internet access (62%) than family households with no children (53%). It is evident that computer and Internet use at school helps narrow the gap that exists between high and low income families who use computers at home or have home access to the Internet. Of all school-aged children (ages 5-17), 90% use computers and 59% use the Internet at home, school, or other places. Teens in particular are among the population that uses the Internet the most, with 75% of 14-17 year olds and 65% of 10-13 year olds using the Internet (U.S. Department of Commerce).

Internet use is most affected by school attendance among 18-24 year olds, those of traditional college age. Of individuals in that age group, 98% use the Internet if they are in school or college; only 51.5% of those in that age group who do not attend school or college use the Internet. It is evident that school access helps decrease the digital divide by providing computer and Internet access to learners at all levels. This is especially important when household income is considered. Only 33% of students in the lowest income level of households have computers in the home compared to 92% of homes at the highest income level (U.S. Department of Commerce, 2002).

Accessibility to broadband and high speed Internet is often related to the geographic region and the infrastructure of telecommunication in those areas. Rural area use of the Internet has grown by 24%. The percentage of rural area residents who have Internet access is now 53%, almost the national average of 54% (U.S. Department of Commerce, 2002). Yet, particularly in rural areas, dial-up services remain the primary mode of service. As more powerful and affordable Internet systems are made available, high speed Internet access will be available in rural areas.

How does the largest population to access the Internet use the Internet? While adults use it to check weather, sports, news, or health information, children and young adults use it for school assignments and entertainment. The Internet is used for schoolwork among 50% of students over the age of 10. Schoolwork is the predominant use of the Internet by users of 18-24 years of age. Twenty percent of elementary school-aged students use it for schoolwork. E-mail use is a close second to schoolwork. The percentage of the U.S. population that uses e-mail on the Internet is 45%. Sixty-five percent of young adults (18-24 years old) and 63% of teenagers (13-17 years old) use e-mail as a primary communication tool. It is evident by these statistics that the Internet is a daily routine among the majority of school and college learners for schoolwork, communication, and entertainment (U.S. Department of Commerce, 2002).

How accessible is the Internet to educational institutions, and more importantly, how accessible is high speed Internet access? An intensive study completed between 1995-2000 in varied states uncovered several factors that affect the use of technology for teaching and learning. The most common barriers to the integration of technology into educational settings include inadequate networking infrastructure and inadequate Internet connectivity or access to broadband connections (SIER-TEC, 2001).

An additional study by the Web-based Education Commission (2000), which included testimonies and interviews from teachers, administrators, government officials, higher education faculty, researchers, students, and parents, arrived at the same outcome—affordable and available Internet access is imperative. Workplace and educational institutions have more ready access to broadband Internet service. However, residential use of high speed broadband service that is affordable and available is still a problem—even though it has increased substantially (US Department of Commerce, 2002). Broadband allows larger transmission of electronic data by wire or wireless methods. More interactive multimedia learning opportunities are available with broadband service, which provides a more interactive and richer online experience for the user. Online learning environments used in distance education require these broadband systems (Web-based, 2000).

Two initiatives are underway to bring affordable and available broadband systems to educational institutions. Internet2 is a consortium of nearly 200 U.S. universities working with industries to "develop and deploy advanced network applications and technologies for research and higher education." The second initiative is the Next Generation Internet (NGI). NGI agencies work with Internet2 members to bring this high-performance network to states and K-12 educational districts (Web-based, 2000, p.23).

Just as past technologies have proven, high speed Internet access will increase in power and decrease in cost, bringing more interactive and meaningful learning opportunities. E-rate funds granted to states for distribution to educational institutions allow the delivery of discounted Internet and communication services to schools and public entities, an additional source of increasing high speed Internet access (Web-based, 2000).

Another factor affecting the accessibility of the Internet is the availability of computers and computer networks. Internet access and service is not the only requirement for Internet use in educational environments. Up-to-date computer hardware and network systems are crucial. Funding for computers and technology are a critical component of all educational budgets. Grants and donations can supplement education budgets for computer hardware. K-12 public, private, and home schools and nonprofit educational agencies are eligible for donations through the Computers for Learning (2003) program sponsored by the U.S. General Services Administration. Excess federal computer equipment is transferred to schools and educational organizations in need.

Assistive Technology for Learners with Special Needs

Learners with special needs and disabilities having access to the Internet are a second pedagogical challenge. Even with high speed Internet access and up-to-date computers, learners with special needs may have limited mobility or use of hands for traditional computer input devices; they may be blind or have visual impairments that prohibit them from seeing what is on the computer monitor; or they may be deaf and do not benefit from the multimedia sounds and voice synthesized output of the Internet. People with physical disabilities are less likely to use computers or the Internet (U.S. Department of Commerce, 2002). Nearly 60% of those with a disability have never used a computer, compared with 25% without a disability. Those with visual impairments or manual dexterity problems use the Internet and computers less than those with hearing or mobility disabilities (Web-based, 2000). Among learners, 11% of K-12 students and 7% of beginning postsecondary students have disabilities.

The Americans with Disabilities Act requires that educational institutions that receive federal funds must offer equitable technology access to all students (Web-based, 2000). The World Wide Web Consortium (W3C) has prepared guidelines for Web accessibility. These guidelines list problems experienced by those with disabilities and solutions to make Web content available to the disabled (Maddux, 2001). W3C identifies the following physical disabilities that need to be addressed through assistive technologies:

1. Visual impairments, including blindness, low vision, and color blindness

2. Cognitive impairments, including Downs Syndrome and Alzheimer's disease

3. Seizure disorders

4. Hearing impairments

5. Mobility impairments

6. Reading and learning disabilities

7. Nonfluent speaking or inadequate understanding of the language of the document (WebAIM, 2002-2003).

These hardware/software limitations are addressed as well:

1. Text-only screen, small screen, or slower connection to the Internet

2. Different browser (Maddux, 2001)

Solutions proposed by WC3 to the above problems can include "text descriptions on all nontext elements in a page" (Maddux, p. 4, 2001). Braille displays, speech synthesizers, or large print displays will take these text descriptions and apply them to graphics and pictures. Color is another consideration that is not transferable into oral, Braille, or print output. Text-based strategies should be used as an alternative to color, and background and foreground colors of low contrast should not be used. HTML coding should also be used to control the structure of the page rather than trying to control the actual physical layout. All images should contain an ALT tag to describe the image. Navigational strategies of a Web page also need to be modified. Movement by links needs to be descriptive and the use of "Click Here" should be avoided (Maddux).

Section 508 (1998 Amendment to Section 508 of the Rehabilitation Act) requires that electronic and information technology of all federal agencies must be accessible to people with disabilities. Like ADA and WC3, equal access to electronic and Internet information for those with disabilities is required by federal agencies regarding their Web pages and electronic information (Section 508, 2002). To ensure that Web pages meet the WC3 standards, a support tool called Bobby has been created by the Center for Applied Special Technology (CAST). Bobby is a Web-based "tool that analyzes Web pages for their accessibility to people with disabilities" (Web-based, p. 30, 2000). Bobby is free, and when a Web page meets the standards outlined by CAST, the site displays a "Bobby Approved" icon (Web-based, 2000).

All learners have benefitted from the efforts to open up accessibility to electronic and Internet information to those with disabilities. Research with multiple intelligences and learning styles proves that when multiple senses are utilized and users take varied paths to learning,, they are more engaged in the learning process and achievement increases.

Appropriate Internet Content and Activities

The third pedagogical challenge is creating appropriate content and activities that utilize the Internet. To meet this challenge, teaching strategies and classroom activities must undergo a change. Active learning and the integration of technology, rather than isolated "kill and drill" or learning games on computers, leads to higher student achievement (SIER-TEC, 2001). Because of the interactive potential of the Internet, how people learn when using the Internet requires research. As with traditional delivery methods and media, academic standards need to be met. Therefore, quality Internet activities and content is just as important as high-quality textbooks and materials (Web-based, 2000).

Standards. The foundation of what all students should "know, do, and be like" are educational standards. Learned societies and professional organizations develop national standards, such as those developed by the National Business Education Association (NBEA, 2001). These standards illustrate the foundations of business and information processing/technology classes in the body of business education knowledge.

The International Society for Technology Education (ISTE) has developed standards for students, teachers, and administrators. These standards are a framework that "define the fundamental concepts, knowledge, skills, and attitudes" (NETS, 2003) for computers and technology. The NETS for students can serve as a basis for developing technology-based activities for students. They include specific performance indicators for students at the following grade levels: K-2, 3-5, 6-8, and 9-12. The six foundational areas include,

1. Basic operations and concepts

2. Social, ethical, and human issues

3. Technology productivity tools

4. Technology communication tools

5. Technology research tools

6. Technology problem-solving and decision-making tools (NETS)

State educational agencies and local school districts use these national standards to develop standards used at those organizational levels. With standards as the basis for all classroom activities and learning, the selection of teaching strategies and the nature of Internet projects and activities are the next curriculum development elements business educators will select.

Teaching strategies. The study conducted by the SIEC-TEC (2001) indicated that teaching strategies used today need to embrace technology. Technology integration and use of the Internet in business courses allows teachers to diminish the use of teacher-centered teaching strategies and to employ more student-centered learning strategies. Lao (p. 2, 2000) states that one "positive implication of technology integration is that it allows the teachers and the learners to be involved in the learning process." Once the teacher has received training in a technology, he/she needs to be given opportunities to put into practice what was learned. Time for practice and technology access are critical to the teacher as well (Lao). The teacher is no longer the "sage on the stage" or *the* only knowledgeable one in the classroom. Students and teachers both become facilitators in courses where technology integration is rich. This is a paradigm shift for teachers—one some are not ready to make.

Becker and Ravitz's (1999) study on the influence of computer and Internet use on teachers' pedagogical practices revealed similar findings. Frequent use of the Internet and computers are related to

1. Teachers allowing themselves to be taught by students

2. Orchestrating multiple simultaneous activities occurring during class time

3. Assigning long and complex projects for students to undertake

4. Giving students greater choice in their tasks and the materials and resources they can use to complete them (Becker & Ravitz, p. 14)

The researchers found these events to occur more commonly in high school social studies, science, and "most often in business and other occupation-related fields" (Becker & Ravitz, p.14).

Becker and Ravitz (1999) also discuss the movement toward more teaching practices matching those of the constructivist theories of learning. Constructivism involves designing activities around teacher and student interest rather than a mandated curriculum; having students work in collaborative group projects where skills are taught in context; granting attention to student understanding of complex ideas rather than just facts and definitions; and the teacher engaging in learning with the students rather than appearing as the all-knowledgeable sage. Computers can help teachers employ constructivist teaching methods. The Internet and computers provide a "rich array of easily accessible and relevant information" (Becker & Ravitz, p. 2) for students to explore and then analyze.

Internet activities. Technology alone does not make the educational experience effective. Internet-based projects and activities that are appropriate and sound are critical to successful integration of the Internet in student learning activities. Business educators, such as Mrs. Black, Mr. Hanson, Ms. Shandy, and Dr. Johnson utilize the Internet as sources of authentic information and resources, bringing real-world activities into their classroom instruction.

Internet-related information available for K-12 and postsecondary business courses is available from several public sector providers that include "federal agencies, museums and science centers, professional organizations, teachers, and students" (Web-based, 2000 pp. 70-71). "Many private-sector providers have changed their focus from producing content to aggregating instructional information" (Web-based, p. 70) through a portal or content-based information source. Both public and private sources provide information, as well as prepared lessons that utilize the Internet.

Traditional teaching strategies have included the use of computers, field trips, and mentoring. With resources now available with the Internet via the World Wide Web and e-mail, activities such as telecomputing, telefield trips, and telementoring are available. Harris (2001) describes telecomputing activities to include "key pals," by which students communicate with other students at remote sites; electronic appearances through live chats or asynchronous correspondence; and telefield trips that allow students to share findings from local field trips with students at a remote site. Harris encourages teachers to develop their own activities rather than take "canned" lesson plans from the numerous Internet sites that host prepared lesson plans and activities for varied grade levels and content areas.

There are numerous templates for Internet-based activities. Two of the more well-known and more commonly utilized are WebQuest and Filamentality. WebQuest is an "inquiry-based activity in which some or all of the information that learners interact with comes from resources on the Internet" (Dodge, 1997). The attributes of WebQuest include an introduction, a task, a set of information sources, a description of the process, some guidance to organizing the information, and a conclusion. More commonly, WebQuests are completed in groups, include motivational elements, and can be interdisciplinary (Dodge). Once a WebQuest is prepared, it is hosted on any Internet server for access to the learner. Web development skills and the capability to host the activity on a server are requisites for the developers of this type of Internet activity.

A Filamentality (2001) is a template-building and hosting service for Internet activities, perhaps more usable to a developer who has less Web development experience or no server available to where Web pages and Internet activities can be hosted. Hosted by Pacific Bell, five templates are available. These include a Hotlist, Multimedia Scrapbook, Treasure Hunt, Subject Sampler, or a Webquest.

For the adventuresome or more computer-savvy teacher, one can create an Internet-project from scratch. Kelly (1999) outlines four levels of projects, from simple to complex, that can be developed by individual teachers. A Level One activity uses a Web page to augment a lesson or topic. Level Two uses the Internet as a "static information collection tool," (Kelly, p. 4) such as a scavenger hunt or Filamentality Subject Sampler. This takes students to specific Internet sites the teacher has identified. Using the Internet as a "dynamic information tool" (Kelly, p. 5) is the Third level project. Given specific questions to research related to a given topic, students search the Internet for answers, utilizing search engines and evaluating Web sites for appropriate content and sources. Level Four uses the Internet to "collect, manipulate, and publish information" (Kelly, p. 6) in a Web site, research paper, class presentation, or other distribution method.

Ms. Shandy's high school management students use a Level One activity as they download programs for their handheld computers. Dr. Johnson's collegiate business communications students use a Level Two activity to collect information from online job vacancy sites for which they will develop resumes and application letters. Mrs. Black's middle school computer applications students work with a Level Three activity by utilizing search engines and researching states or countries from which they plan their dream vacation. A Level Four activity completed by Mr. Hanson's economics students allows them to collect and manipulate current stock market quotes gathered from the Internet.

Evaluating Internet sites. Kelly's (1999) Third Level Internet activity uses Internet sites to gather information in response to questions. Learners must be able to effectively evaluate the content of Internet information found. Browne, Freeman, and Williamson (2000) discuss the importance of preparing students to critically view information from the Internet. Students need to continually look for "evidence, arguments, or information on the Internet until they have looked at several sites" (Browne, Freeman & Williamson, p. 5).

One model for evaluating Web sites is the ADAPT model (Owens Library, 2003). The model includes the evaluation of the following Web page elements:

A – Authority

D – Design

A – Accuracy

P – Purpose

T – Target

Evaluating the authority of a Web page means reading the author's or sponsoring organization's credentials. The domain of the Web page usually reveals the type of organization that sponsored it, whether it is commercial, organizational, or governmental page. The final element to evaluate regarding authority is the contact information of the author or sponsoring information. An e-mail address is not sufficient. A mailing address, name, and phone number would attribute more credibility to the page (Owens Library, 2003).

"Consistent appearance and ease of navigation"(Owens Library, 2003) are both essential when evaluating the design of a Web page. Look for consistency in color scheme, fonts, and navigation bar. Links to previous or main pages also contribute to good design. Easy-to-read backgrounds and typography and a search engine for the site would also be sound elements for good design. Accuracy is equally as important as authority. Information presented needs to be bias free, links and works cited need to be verified, and an appropriate date of creation or update will contribute to accurate information on a Web site. The reader of a Web page needs to identify the ultimate purpose of the page. Is the purpose to persuade, educate, or entertain the reader? The target audience is commonly revealed through the Web page's purpose (Owens Library). This model is sound in helping both learners and teachers effectively evaluate the content of Internet information.

Filtering and security measures. Additional measures to protect learners and users of the Internet are needed. The Children's Online Privacy Protection Act (COPPA) has been in effect since April 2000 and requires parental permission to collect information on Internet users younger than age 13 (FAQ, 2003). COPPA does not cover the second largest group of Internet users—teens—who can be a very vulnerable online population. Public libraries and schools must have filtering software in place to qualify for e-rate funding. However, filtering does not ensure that all inappropriate sites are blocked or that even appropriate sites are made available (Web-based, 2000). Agencies receiving federal funds must have filtering measures in place in order to continue to receive e-rate breaks for Internet access and telecommunication services.

In addition to filtering methods, other measures can be used in attempts to keep objectionable and inappropriate sites and information from young learners. Monitoring systems provide a record of site visits. Rating systems, like those for motion pictures, gives the power of choice to schools, agencies, or parents. Portals offer to Internet users preselected sites related to an area of interest or topic. Acceptable use policies are in place at schools and colleges. The policies outline what computer usage is acceptable and allowed regarding resources, networks, e-mail, and the Internet. Consequences of misuse or abuse are also mentioned. Users are asked to sign the policy, and parents may be asked to sign or at least review the policy in the case of younger learners. Educating learners on the glut of appropriate and inappropriate information on the Internet is also essential (Web-based, 2000).

Protecting an educational institution's computer hardware and software is an integral part of the challenge of appropriate Internet activities. Anti-virus software needs to be in place to guard against viruses that can be downloaded from the Internet intentionally or unintentionally. Frequent updates to this anti-virus software also need to be set. Educating computer users on the possibility of viruses and virus hoaxes is also critical.

Educational Copyright Issues

The issue of legally using copyrighted material for education is a persistent challenge of Internet utilization. The study undertaken by the Web-based Commission on the power of the Internet (2000) stated that changes in copyright regulations were needed. This included a directive from Congress to the U.S. Copyright Office of the Library of Congress to "study the impact that copyright laws might have on online education" (Web-based, p. 95). Educational institutions, as well as Congress, contend that online students need to access educational materials in a 24/7 remote environment.

In December 2002, the Technology, Education, and Copyright Harmonization (TEACH) Act was passed. It provides exemptions to "allow for the digital transmission of copyrighted materials, including on Web sites, so they may be 'viewed' by enrolled students" (Russell, 2002, p.1). Accredited, nonprofit K-12 and postsecondary schools are able to use this exemption. TEACH allows teachers "to copy an analog work to a digital format for use without prior permission of the copyright holder when a digital version of the work is not available" (Russell, p. 2). TEACH is a huge step forward in alleviating the restrictions imposed by the former copyright challenges to online courses and many Internet-based projects.

Assurance Technology Improves Student Achievement

Another challenge is determining whether technology and the Internet have a value-added effect on student achievement. Schacter (1999) reports on over 700 empirical research studies to determine if students with access to computers, technology, and the Internet show positive student gains in achievement. Varied studies in Schacter's research (by researchers Kulik, Sivn-Kachala, Baker-Gearhart-Herman, Mann, Wenglinsky, and Scardamalia-Bereiter) reveal the following in relation to student achievement when using technology:

Positive findings:

1. Students who used computer-based instruction scored at the 64th percentile on achievement tests, compared to students in control conditions without computers (50th percentile).

2. When students receive computer-assisted instruction, it takes less time to learn more.

3. Students enjoy their computer-oriented courses more and have more positive attitudes towards those classes.

4. Increased achievement in K-12 and postsecondary education was achieved by regular and special needs learners.

5. Student self-concept improved when computers were used.

77

Chapter 5

6.   Teaching strategies changed toward more cooperative work groups and less teacher-centered teaching strategies.

7.   Girls and boys did not differ in achievement, access, or use of computers.

8.   Use of technology was more cost effective in improving student achievement than class size reduction, increase in instructional time, and cross-age tutoring programs.

9.   Students whose teachers received professional development on computers showed gains in math scores.

10. Computer use encourages reflection, independent thinking, and multiple perspectives among learners (Schacter, 1999).

Negative findings:

1.   Positive effects were not present in all areas studied.

2.   Drill-and-practice use of computers led to lower student achievement on standardized tests.

3.   Playing learning games on computers only led to a slight increase in student achievement.

4.   Computer use is less effective or ineffective when learning objectives are not clear and use of the technology is not focused or planned (Schacter, 1999).

Technical Support and Professional Development

Another challenge of utilizing the Internet in classroom instruction is the need for technical support and professional development. Technology integration is not an overnight process, and with some projects, can take years to accomplish. Technology integration can be achieved with visionary educational leadership, the activation of a technology committee, the formulation of a formal technology plan, and the implementation of a teacher training and professional development program (SIEC-TEC, 2001).

Training and professional development for administrators and faculty are important. Success is best reached when varied training models are used and when teachers become coaches and mentors among their peers. Technical support is also needed, with best results from at least one full-time technical support person per building. This individual would not only support the infrastructure and maintain equipment and the network, but also facilitate training and professional development. In many situations, this position is a part-time responsibility of a classroom teacher (SIER-TEC, 2001).

The National Education Technology Standards for Teachers (NETS-S) and the National Education Standards for Administrators (NETS-A) outline the "concepts, knowledge, skills, and attitudes for applying technology in educational settings" (NETS, 2003). The NETS for teachers target what preservice teachers should meet so they can be effective integrators of technology. The six standards areas include,

1. Technology operations and concepts

2. Planning and designing learning environments and experiences

3. Teaching, learning, and the curriculum

4. Assessment and evaluation

5. Productivity and professional practice

6. Social, ethical, legal, and human issues (NETS, 2003)

Only about 50% of all U.S. teachers use technology in their teaching (Starr, 2003 February). Almost two-thirds of U.S. teachers feel they are not prepared to use technology. Even some young teachers hold the same perceptions. Although they may have the basic technology skills, they do not feel prepared to integrate technology in their teaching (Web-based, 2000).

How effective is the professional development given teachers? In 1998-99, 78% of public school teachers received technology professional development. But that training was only 1-5 hours for 39% of teachers and just 6-10 hours for 19%. Training in business organizations is tailored and focused and held during the workday on tools found in the workplace. Training in educational organizations is often held after school or during summer vacations and not with the same tools teacher have access to after the training. Teachers usually are not rewarded with stipends or convenient times for training (Web-based, 2000).

However, the larger problem associated with K-12 teachers is the feeling of isolation (Web-based, 2000). Can the Internet change this? Yes! Listservs or electronic discussion groups can provide a question/answer or help forum for teachers. Missouri business educators have had access to the Missouri Business Education Discussion List for several years. Over 500 business educators subscribe to this valuable communication tool, whereby isolation among business teachers is diminished by the hundreds of colleagues who are able and willing to share their knowledge and information with those who have questions or inquiries (Missouri, 2003).

Schools with successful technology integration encourage use of technology in all aspects and among all staff members. All staff members, including custodians and cafeteria staff, have e-mail addresses. Daily bulletins are sent via e-mail; no paper bulletins are printed. Students and teachers both have folders on the network server, making uploading and downloading of files possible. Class attendance and grades are posted to an electronic program. Educational technology specialists employed by districts also aid in the integration of technology. Such personnel manage the network and maintain computers. Professional development for teachers and staff, enabling them to better use technology, is often a responsibility of these technology specialists (Starr, 2003, February).

Starr (2003, March) reports on effective professional development models. Multifaceted training includes introductory training at the beginning of the year, training during the school year over several days, and training at the end of the school year over several days that includes a skills inventory checklist to assist in planning for training in the next school year. Extrinsic rewards can be offered to encourage teachers to participate in voluntary training. Stipends are awarded in some districts when staff members take technology workshops. Project-based learning not only includes training with equipment and software, but also concludes with an integrated project that the teacher must use in his/her teaching (Starr).

Guidelines for effective professional development are offered by Starr (2003, March). These guidelines include soliciting support from administrative leadership, encouraging administrators to attend, including teachers in the planning of training to be offered, rewarding teachers for participating in training by granting stipends or compensatory time, giving teachers choices among training, offering training at convenient times and days, and using technology training and integration in teacher observations and evaluations (Starr).

Classroom Management in the Technology Classroom

The final challenge to utilizing the Internet is keeping technology-rich courses motivational and enjoyable to all students enrolled. However, computer classes are unlike regular classrooms. Students are involved in exploration, collaboration, and movement, all leading to possible classroom management situations that need control and attention (Jackson, 2002). Computer activities often require "frequent directions and explanations, as well as individual support and supervision, which slows down instructional time" (Jackson, 2002, p.1). Student seating and arrangement of computers in the room can vary and contribute or diminish classroom management problems.

Starr (2002, February) provides the following guidelines to manage the technology learning activities. Teachers need to be prepared for technology and Internet activities by going through the activity in its entirety before presenting it to students. A backup activity should be planned in case technology is not available. Students should turn off monitors when directions are given. Technology managers can assist the teacher in varied classes by helping students with the assigned technology or software. These technology managers can be paid paraprofessionals or students who earn either course credit or community service hours. Classroom managers (students from within the class) can take attendance, turn computers on/off, and perform other housekeeping tasks for the teacher before and after each technology class. A list of rules and procedures for using technology should be posted. Business educators should wear comfortable shoes and be prepared to walk the classroom, as teachers in technology classes are on their feet helping students and often troubleshooting equipment (Starr). These pedagogical challenges of the Internet, although not all present in every educational setting, are real and pose threats to true technology integration and use of the Internet.

Technological Challenges

Business educators who utilize the Internet in classroom instruction are faced with technological challenges as well as pedagogical challenges. These include the widening of the digital divide among learners, ensuring that students use proper keyboarding techniques, having concern for repetitive stress injuries in students, teaching technology to already computer- and Internet-savvy students, preparing students to be ethical users of the Internet and technology, and keeping current with the growing online education environment.

Widening of the Digital Divide

The first technological challenge of utilizing the Internet in classroom instruction is the digital divide, which identifies inequities and differences in access and the use of computers and the Internet due to demographic variables. According to a U.S. Department of Commerce (2002) study, over 54% of the U.S. population is online and 66% of the U.S. population uses computers. Disparities of computer and Internet use prevail among special populations.

Children and teens are the largest sector of the population to use the Internet. Households with children under the age of 18 are more likely to have Internet access than households without children. Teens (ages 14-17) and college-aged students (ages 18-24) are the heaviest Internet users. Household income and geographic location also affect Internet use and access. Only 33% of homes in the lowest income bracket have Internet access, while over 90% of homes in the highest income bracket have access to the Internet. The 53% of rural areas having Internet access is almost equal to the percentage of the population who use the Internet (U.S. Department of Commerce, 2002). Yet, the digital divide is widening, leaving the "have-nots" without reliable and high speed Internet access, while the "haves" continue to increase use and access.

School- and college-age learners prefer the new paradigm of teaching strategies. Historically, teaching strategies included "broadcasting, with the teacher using top-down, authoritative, teacher-centered methods" (Tapscott, 1998, p. 129). Rather, these learners of the net generation prefer multimedia-rich, interactive and student-centered strategies (Tapscott, 1998). Today's business educators must realize that most students in their classrooms are of the net generation and more interactive, technology-rich teaching strategies and classroom activities will be needed to better serve the learners.

Levin and Arafeh (2002), in a study of how college students use the Internet, identify the major uses of the Internet among postsecondary students. Of the college students surveyed, 85% owned their own computers and 66% used at least two e-mail addresses. In weekly Internet use, 74% used the Internet four or more hours a week, and 19% use the Internet 12 hours or more per week. Both statistics reveal more hours on the Internet than spent studying. College students used the Internet predominantly to engage in e-mail with professors in academic settings and with others in social settings. For research, 73% of students used the Internet more than library resources. Only 6% took online classes, but 68% subscribed to academic-based mailing lists (Levin & Arafeh).

Ensuring Learners Use Correct Keyboarding Techniques

The second technological challenge is the concern that all computer and Internet learners use sound keyboarding techniques and touch keyboarding skills. Keyboarding instruction, once an important part of the secondary business curriculum, is now found in the upper elementary and middle school curricula. Secondary school students are the heaviest users of the Internet, with 75% of all 14-17 year olds using the Internet. The middle school business education curriculum (commonly ages 11-14) includes keyboarding instruction and computer applications. With 65% of 10-13 year olds using the Internet (U.S. Department of Commerce, 2002), it is expected that most students will have keyboarding experience, although it may not include touch keyboarding and proper keyboard techniques. A major challenge to middle school keyboarding teachers is to motivate students to use correct keyboarding techniques and touch keyboarding skills. Having used a computer for years and not keying correctly, students find it difficult to break poor habits; and business teachers find it difficult to motivate students to key with correct techniques and methods.

Concern for Increase in Repetitive Stress Injuries

Because of early computer use, and not always with correct keyboarding techniques, Barksdale (2001) warns of increased repetitive stress injuries (RSIs) among young keyboarding users. No longer are RSIs only occurring in older office workers. The combination of athletics, the playing of musical instruments, and the prevalent use of the computer keyboard and mouse from a young age contribute to RSIs in children of pre-adolescent age. Stressing sound keyboarding techniques; having ergonomically sound furniture, devices, and workstations; and using alternative input devices such as speech recognition software are possible answers to reducing keyboarding injuries to middle school and secondary business education students.

Teaching Computer- and Internet-Savvy Students

Another technological challenge to utilizing the Internet is that now a "digital disconnect" also exists, a major challenge to teachers who integrate computers and the Internet. The digital disconnect is the "widening gap between Internet-savvy students and their schools" (Levin & Arafeh, 2002, Part 3, p.1). Business educators who utilize computers and the Internet are faced with the challenge of "what to do with computer- and Internet-savvy students" who finish early or become unmotivated in class. Students with technology expertise, extensive computer experiences, and competence with the Internet feel they are at times not challenged appropriately in technology-oriented classes. Some teachers motivate these students by asking them to complete challenging enrichment or authentic activities. Advanced students can also share their expertise by serving as technology managers or assistants in classes. Other business educators choose to limit the computer- and Internet savvy students by "keeping all students together" or allowing those who finish early to "surf" or play games on the Internet. The latter is a common and easy response by business educators, although an incorrect one, and one that is frustrating to the highly computer literate students (Levin & Arafeh).

Van Horn (2003) reports that about 30-40% of teenagers are in the category of being Internet savvy. In his work with focus groups from 36 different schools and 200 voluntarily submitted online essays, the following uses of the Internet were discussed with Internet-savvy students: (a) the Internet is a source of primary and secondary materials for school assignments and serves as supplemental information when outdated textbooks are used; (b) students also use the Internet as a virtual tutor or study group; (c) students access sites for additional information on topics discussed in class; and (d) students converse with others to compare notes or seek help. With the abundance of colleges and universities with Web-based information and admission procedures, Internet-savvy students have less reliance on information from parents and guidance counselors on colleges and careers. Finally, the Internet serves as a virtual organizer. Students e-mail themselves electronic files that contain unfinished assignments, so they can complete the assignment from any Internet connection (Van Horn, 2003).

These Internet-savvy students reported two barriers to Internet use at school. A six-period school day left no free period for students to use the Internet. Therefore, Internet use was predominantly occurring at home. A second barrier to student Internet use at school was the use of filtering software with school networks (Van Horn, 2003)

Levin and Arafeh (2002) also revealed barriers that Internet-savvy students experience. The first barrier is that schools need to increase the quality of access to the Internet in schools and not restrict use on those already present. Secondly, more technical support and professional development is needed for teachers, so that they can develop effective Internet-based activities. Digitized worksheets are not what these Internet-savvy students want. They seek rich, interactive activities where they can use critical thinking. A third suggestion by the Internet-savvy students is that schools need to ensure that *all* students have keyboarding, Internet, and computer literacy skills. Even students who are frequently online do not always have the appropriate skills. These same students are frustrated with the inappropriate and unsound sites available on the Internet. Even to these Internet-savvy students, seeking the correct information via the Internet can be difficult. Finally, the Internet-savvy students are keenly aware of the digital divide and want school administrators and policymakers to take these inequities seriously. They see the disadvantages that face students who do not have ready access to the Internet outside of the school environment (Levin & Arafeh, 2002).

Preparing Students to be Ethical Users

Ethical issues create technological challenges. Rader (2002) reports three ethical challenges that face business education teachers when using the Internet in class activities. These three challenges are "appropriate use, privacy, and security and copyright/intellectual rights" (Rader, 2002, p. 73). These three topics have already been discussed in this chapter as pedagogical challenges and are now reinforced as important ethical topics that students need to be knowledgeable about and to which they need to appropriately respond.

Rader (2002) offers instructional strategies to help students become ethically sound computer and Internet users:

1. Establish an acceptable use policy.

2. Communicate ethical codes.

3. Model ethical behaviors and articulate values.

4. Encourage classroom discussion on ethical issues.

5. Reinforce ethical conduct and enforce codes of conduct.

6. Monitor students' behaviors.

7. Secure computer systems and software.

8. Discourage Internet surfing.

9. Monitor e-mail systems and Web sites.

10. Reinforce all school policies for technology (Rader, pp. 75-77).

Growing Online Education Environment

There is no doubt that there are hundreds of thousands, if not millions, of lesson plans and educational activities available on the Internet. But using Internet-based activities is not fully harvesting the power of the Internet. As universities and colleges have progressed into online courses, programs, and degrees, K-12 educational institutions are also moving to that delivery system. Advanced Placement (AP) courses and elective courses are offered online to high school students through consortiums and third-party online entities, and several states are developing virtual high schools. The accreditation and regulations states impose on K-12 schools serve as challenges to bringing more online offerings to K-12 students (Web-based, 2000).

Postsecondary institutions offer online courses, programs, and degrees with more frequency than K-12 institutions. More technical and financial resources, different targets of student populations, and meeting the expectations of the Net-generation students are reasons postsecondary institutions offer more online offerings. Challenges to offering online courses, programs, and degrees include faculty resistance, lack of technical support and training for faculty, time involved in online development, and lack of professional and financial rewards for faculty to be involved with online offerings (Web-based, 2000).

Conclusion

The challenges of integrating technology and the Internet can create real barriers for business educators. Pedagogical challenges affect how business educators teach. These pedagogical challenges include Internet access, assistive technology for learners with special needs, appropriate content and activities, educational copyright issues, assurance that technology improves student achievement, technical support and professional development, and classroom management in the technology classroom.

Governmental and legislative efforts have created grants and funding for educational and community-based institutions to make computers and the Internet available to populations who may have had restricted access. As technology increases in power and decreases in cost of access and distribution, broadband and high speed Internet access will become prevalent in more geographic areas. Regulations also mandate accessibility to the information from the Internet. All federal and state governmental agencies with Web-based information and sites must employ assistive technologies that allow those with disabilities to access the information and equipment.

As business educators utilize the Internet in classroom instruction, Web-based activities need to be developed that increase student achievement. Today's students of the net generation want to work with technology and other interactive learning strategies. As Internet resources are used, business educators need to evaluate and select appropriate Web-based information and lead learners themselves to evaluate information gathered from the Internet as well. Although public institutions and agencies must have filters and security measures in place to guard against inappropriate Internet sites, students must be wise users and evaluators themselves.

Technical support and professional development from educational institutions for business educators is essential. In most settings, business educators train peers, administrators, and community members in technological advancements and Internet applications. However, in order for the business educators to implement the Internet, they must be given the financial support, time, and opportunities to learn themselves. This training should also include classroom management strategies to help business educators successfully manage learners and technology.

Technological challenges affect what is taught. These technological challenges include the widening of the digital divide among learners, ensuring students use proper keyboarding techniques, having concern for repetitive stress injuries, teaching technology to already computer- and Internet-savvy students, preparing students to be ethical users of the Internet and technology, and the growing online education environment.

The gap between the "haves" and the "have-nots" is increasing in some areas, although minority populations have increased their overall use of the computer and the Internet. Governmental and legislative efforts need to continue to help technology and telecommunication companies bring high speed Internet to more geographic regions and special populations. Business teacher education programs and state education agencies need to work together to implement elementary and middle school keyboarding methods courses in teacher education programs other than those in business education.

When computer users learn proper keyboarding techniques and touch keyboarding skills when first using the computer, repetitive stress injuries and bad habits diminish. The use of alternative input devices such as speech recognition and handwriting recognition will also help alleviate RSIs.

Business educators must "raise the bar" and continually modify the content and knowledge base of the technology-based curriculum. Each year, business technology-rich courses need to be modified to match the skill level of the learners. Assignments and software may have to be offered at advanced levels to match the skill levels and knowledge of the learners. Utilizing the computer- and Internet-savvy student as a classroom manager and assistant is a better way to motivate that student than allowing the student to "surf the Net and play games." And within each course that utilizes technology, students must be encouraged and led to be ethical users of technology and the Internet. It is not enough to have students sign an acceptable use policy. The actions of students must be monitored with technology and human means. Business educators and educational institutions need to model ethical practices as well.

As more educational opportunities are offered online for learners of all ages, business educators need to develop meaningful learning opportunities online. Most teaching strategies and assessment measures need to be modified for use in online instruction. Educational institutions need to offer technical assistance and training opportunities to prepare business educators to develop, teach, and manage online educational environments.

Regardless of these challenges, today's learners are of the net generation and prove to be highly computer- and Internet-savvy. These learners expect multimedia and interactive-rich classroom activities. Business educators can and must meet these challenges and bring the power of the Internet to all their students.

REFERENCES

Barksdale, K. (2001). Using speech recognition to prevent middle school keyboard injuries. Retrieved March 31, 2003. http://speakingsolutions.com/news/middleschoolrsi.html.

Becker, H. J., & Ravitz, J. (1999, Summer). The influence of computer and Internet use on teachers' pedagogical practices and perceptions. *Journal of Research on Computing in Education, 31*, 356-385. Retrieved March 29, 2003, from the Academic Search Elite database.

Browne, M. N., Freeman, K. E., & Williamson, C. L. (2000, September). The importance of critical thinking for student use of the Internet. *College Student Journal, 34*, 391-399. Retrieved March 29, 2003, from the Academic Search Elite database.

Computers for Learning. (2003). Retrieved March 29, 2003. http://www.computers. fed. gov/Public/home.asp.

Dodge, B. (1997, May). *Some thoughts about WebQuests.* Retrieved March 29, 2003 from the San Diego State University Web site: http://edweb.sdsu.edu/courses/edtec596/about_webquests.html.

Federal Trade Commission. (2003, March). *Frequently Asked Questions about the Children's Online Privacy Protection Rule* (2003, March). Retrieved March 29, 2003. http://www.ftc.gov/privacy/coppafaqs.htm.

Filamentality. (2001). Retrieved March 30, 2003. http://www.keithstanger.com / filamentality.html.

Harris, J. (2001). TeleComputing-based Activity Structures. Retrieved March 29, 2003 from http://www.esc20.net/etprojects/training/structures.html.

Jackson, L. (2002). Teaching in a tech-ing classroom. Retrieved March 29, 2003. http:// www.education-world.com/a_tech/techtorial/techtorial007.shtml.

Kelly, D. (1999, Summer). Creating your first Internet project. Retrieved March 29, 2003. http://connectedteacher.classroom.com/newsletter/firstproj.asp.

Lao, T. (2000, August). A position paper on technology integration in the classroom. Retrieved October 28, 2002. http://pt3.nmsu.edu/educ621/teresa4.html

Levin, D. & Arafeh, S. (2002, August). The digital disconnect: The widening gap between Internet-savvy students and their schools. Retrieved March 29, 2003. http:// www.pewinternet.org/reports/toc.asp?Report=67.

Maddux, C. D. (2001, Fall). Solving accessibility and other problems in school and classroom web sites. *Rural Special Education Quarterly, 20,* 11-18. Retrieved March 29, 2003, from the Academic Search Elite database.

Missouri Business Education Discussion List. Retrieved March 31, 2003. http:// www.dese. state.mo.us/divvoced/biz_business_ed_discussion_list.htm.

National Business Education Association. (2001). *National standards for business education.* Reston, VA: Author.

National Education Technology Standards (2003). Retrieved March 30, 2003. http:// cnets.iste.org/.

Owens Library. Northwest Missouri State University. Retrieved March 30, 2003. http:// www.nwmissouri.edu/library/courses/usingcomputers/evalonline.htm.

Rader, M. H. (2002, Spring/Summer). Strategies for teaching Internet ethics. *Delta Pi Epsilon Journal, Vol XLIV,* pp 743-78.

Russell, C. (2002, December). New copyright exemptions for distance educators: The technology, education, and copyright harmonization (TEACH) Act. Retrieved March 29, 2003. http://www.ericit.org/digests/EDO-IR-2002-10.shtml.

Section 508 (2002, January). Retrieved March 29, 2003. http://www.section508.gov/

Schacter, J. (1999, February). Impact of education technology on student achievement: What the most current research has to say. Retrieved March 29, 2003. http://www.mff.org/ pubs/ME161.pdf.

SIER-TEC (2001). Factors influencing the effective use of technology for teaching learning: Lessons learned. Retrieved March 29, 2003. http://www.seirtec.org/ publications/lessons.pdf.

Starr, L. (2002, February). Managing technology: Tips from the experts. Retrieved March 29, 2003. http://www.educationworld.com/a_tech/tech116.shtml.

Starr, L. (2003, February). Encouraging teacher technology use. Retrieved March 29, 2003. http://www.educationworld.com/a_tech/tech159.shtml.

Starr, L. (2003, March). Technology training programs that work. Retrieved March 29, 2003. http://www.educationworld.com/a_tech/tech165.shtml

Tapscott, D. (1998). *Growing up digital: The rise of the net generation.* New York: McGraw Hill.

U.S . Department of Commerce (2002, February). A nation online: How Americans are expanding their use of the Internet. Retrieved on March 29, 2003 from http://www.ntia.doc.gov/ntiahome/dn/index.html

Van Horn, R. (2003, January). Internet-savvy students. *Phi Delta Kappan 84*, p 3430344. Retrieved March 29, 2003, from the Academic Search Elite database.

Web Accessibility in Mind (WebAIM). (2002-2003). Retrieved March 29, 2003. http://www.section508.gov/.

Web-based Education Commission. (2000, December). The power of the Internet for learning: Moving from promise to practice. Retrieved March 29, 2003. http://www.ed.gov/ offices/AC/WBEC/FinalReport/Preface.pdf.

Working Adults and Online Instruction

Rebecca J. Timmons
University of Arkansas, Fort Smith
Fort Smith, Arkansas

"To educate is to teach a student that he/she can learn without a teacher."
                                                                    –Anonymous

Just as businesses have expanded their markets to offer their products and services to foreign as well as American consumers, education has expanded beyond the classroom walls to offer educational opportunities across geographic boundaries. During the 20th century, the educational ideology evolved that, for people to become educated, they had to be able to educate themselves. Educators refer to this as "lifelong learning." Online learning reinforces this tenet. In order to meet the needs of different generations of working adults, education has adapted its delivery method to allow these adult learners the opportunity to become educated, or to continue their education through online learning.

An often-heard comment from the Baby Boomer generation (Americans born between 1946-1964) is one of regret about not taking advantage of the chance to pursue a college education in their younger years. For various reasons, many Baby Boomers did not follow the traditional college student pattern—graduate from high school and attend college the same year with financial support provided by parents, graduate from college, and begin a career. Now as working adults, they realize the value of an education and would like to reclaim the opportunity for further learning. However, due to responsibilities and demands in their adult lives, they are unable to quit their jobs to attend school full-time. Another generation that has demands on its time is Generation X, the 40 million Americans born between 1965 and 1978. Although almost 45% (Center for Teaching and Learning, 1999) of Generation Xers have some college education, this generation has more in student loans and credit card debt, is less likely to own a home, and is just as likely to be unemployed. Generation Xers battered by the dot-com boom and bust are now looking to education to update their skills and knowledge.

Who are the working adults?

Baby Boomers and Generation X currently make up the group identified as "working-age adults." According to the National Center for Education Statistics (NCES) and the U.S. Bureau of the Census (Nontraditional Undergraduates 2002), working-age adult learners are defined as "24- to 49-year-olds enrolled part-time in some type of postsecondary education (see Figure 1)." In the year 2000, 24-year-olds were those born in 1976 (Generation Xers), and 49-year-olds were those born in 1951 (Baby Boomers). In 2004, the youngest Generation Xer will be 26, and the youngest Baby Boomer will be 40 (see Figure 1).

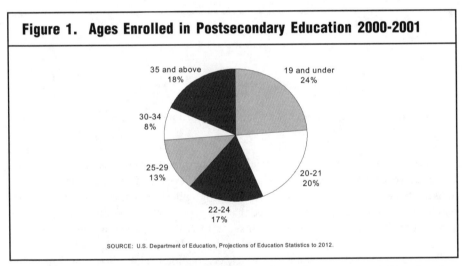

Figure 1. Ages Enrolled in Postsecondary Education 2000-2001

SOURCE: U.S. Department of Education, Projections of Education Statistics to 2012.

During the 2000-2001 school year, 24% of the undergraduates were ages 19 and under; 37% were 20-24 year olds; 39% were older than 25 (see Figure 2).

Of the students enrolled in a postsecondary school in 2000-2001, almost two-fifths (39%) were over the age of 25.

During the 20th century, the demand for college degrees has increased. In 1900, approximately 3% of Americans in the workforce had a college degree and about 2% of Americans from the ages of 18 to 24 were enrolled in a college (Herrnstein, 1994). Near the end of the century, more than 60% of this age group were enrolled in four-year and two-year colleges. In 2002, approximately 27% of U.S. adults held bachelors or higher degrees (U.S. Census Bureau, 2003).

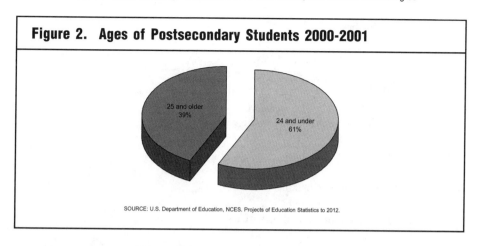

Figure 2. Ages of Postsecondary Students 2000-2001

25 and older
39%

24 and under
61%

SOURCE: U.S. Department of Education, NCES. Projects of Education Statistics to 2012.

According to the Department of Education (NPSAS 2000) during the 1999-2000 academic year, 80% of the total undergraduates were employed either full-time or part-time (see Figure 3).

Undergraduates who were employed identified themselves either as students who were working their way through school (48%) or as employees who were taking classes part-time (32%). Working adults identify themselves primarily as employees (full-time) who enroll in school (part-time). Because many are not willing or cannot afford to quit their jobs and attend college on a full-time basis, working adults usually attend school part-time. They pursue learning through education part-time for varying reasons:

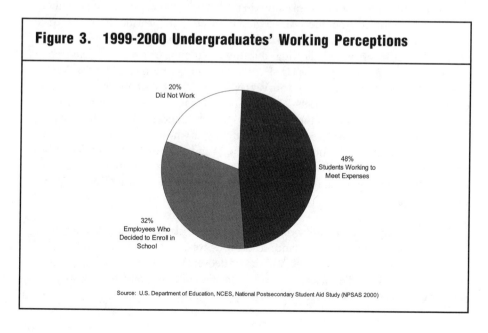

Figure 3. 1999-2000 Undergraduates' Working Perceptions

20%
Did Not Work

48%
Students Working to
Meet Expenses

32%
Employees Who
Decided to Enroll in
School

Source: U.S. Department of Education, NCES, National Postsecondary Student Aid Study (NPSAS 2000)

- Personal enrichment

- Curiosity in a specific area of interest

- Additional education or training to maintain their current position at work

- Necessary knowledge to advance in their job or career

- Classes needed for promotion

- Updating of knowledge or skills

- Personal fulfillment in graduating with a degree or certificate

Working adults lead demanding lives. Compared to the younger traditional students, they are financially independent. Although some may receive loans or grants to assist in paying for their education, working adults are self-supporting, working at least 35 hours per week. Many have dependent children. Others have aging parents requiring attention. When faced with a problem or crisis, the working adult assumes responsibility for making decisions. A number of working adults also volunteer their time and talents for community service. Whether married or single, the working adult must juggle financial obligations, family responsibilities, and time demands with the desire to pursue lifelong learning.

What is Online Education?

Like many businesses and organizations in the latter part of the 20th century, higher education took advantage of the technological innovations to provide alternate ways for sharing information and meeting market demands. Learning opportunities expanded beyond the "classroom walls," allowing education or training courses to be delivered to off-campus sites. According to the U.S. Department of Education's NCES 1999-2000 National Postsecondary Student Aid Survey (NPSAS: 2000), 8% of undergraduates took distance education courses in 1999-2000, and 10% of graduates and first-time professional students took them. Of the total of working adult undergraduates, those who worked full-time and considered themselves employees who study, participated at a 14.7% rate in distance education courses. In the 24 and older category of undergraduates enrolled in higher education courses, almost 10% were enrolled in a distance education course. Of the undergraduate students under age 24, only 6% of the total enrolled in distance education.

Whereas traditional students come to the campus for classes, distance learners have information sent out to them. Distance-learning delivery methods include online programs delivered via the Internet (Web-based delivery), videoconferencing, prerecorded television or audio packages, teleconferencing, computer conferencing, and satellite transmission (see Figure 4).

Figure 4. 1999-2000 Distance Education Undergraduate and Graduate/First Professional Students' Methods of Delivery

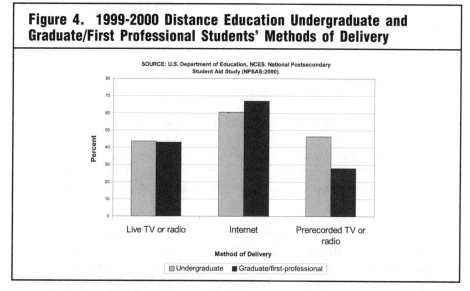

SOURCE: U.S. Department of Education, NCES. National Postsecondary Student Aid Study (NPSAS:2000).

A majority (60%) of all students enrolled in distance education classes participated in Internet classes. Initially, higher education institutions targeted their distance education efforts to three types of students: (1) part-time students, (2) students who could not travel easily to campus, and (3) graduate students. However, higher education institutions gradually expanded their course offerings to provide a wider range of programs, including undergraduate distance education degree programs, and thereby increased the number of course offerings at postsecondary institutions. A survey conducted by the NCES using the Postsecondary Quick Information System (PEQIS) (NCES 2003-017) found that in the fall of 1995, 39% of two- and four-year degree-granting institutions offered distance education courses; in 1997–98, 44% offered distance education courses; and by 2000-2001 56% offered distance education courses. By increasing distance education course offerings, educational institutions have created more opportunities for individuals who want access to higher education and/or training courses.

In 2003, 133 million U.S. adults, or about 67% of the adult population had access to the Internet. Because of the popularity of online education, the phrase "e-learning" evolved. E-learning appeals to many working adults because they are able to,

- attend class at their own convenience,

- study at home, at work, or in the library,

- access learning resources online 24/7,

- learn from subject-matter experts, and

- stay current without radically altering their lifestyles.

E-learning also appeals to physically challenged individuals, allowing them access to educational opportunities. Educationally, the e-learning student benefits by

- developing self-discipline,

- learning new information through secondary research, and

- experiencing how technology can be used as tool to advance learning.

Due to the popularity of the Internet, its wide usage by all ages, and the fact that more information is now available online (online banking, online shopping, online entertainment), it is easy to link online learning users with instructors, other students, and course material.

In distance education, the instructor or teacher becomes a facilitator. According to the National Business Education Association (NBEA) Policy Statement 61, ("This We Believe about the Delivery of Business Education"), business educators are defined as "...the primary facilitators of learning both for and about business." Facilitators analyze the needs of the learner, decide how the material should be presented, choose the appropriate teaching strategies, provide feedback to the learner, and enlist the support of others in the learning process.

Distance Education vs. On-Campus Education—Which Will the Adult Learner Choose?

Although online learning is not for everyone or for every institute of higher education, it is appropriate for some individuals and schools, as well as specific types of learning or training. Most of the students surveyed by the U.S. Department of Education (NPSAS, 2000) were satisfied or more than satisfied with the quality of instruction in their distance education courses (see Figure 5).

The survey reports that approximately 70% of undergraduates participating in distance education were more satisfied or equally satisfied with the quality of instruction in distance education relative to classroom-based instruction, whereas graduate students participating in distance education showed 73% were satisfied or equally satisfied (see Figure 6).

Reasons students are not successful. Unfortunately, approximately 30% of e-learning students' experiences are not successful. Surveys show that the dropout rate for online higher education courses is about 20% higher than for traditionally delivered courses and can sometimes reach as high as 50% or more at community colleges (Is Distance Learning for Me? n.d.). Reasons students do not do well in online classes include the following:

Figure 5. 1999-2000 Undergraduate Distance Education Students' Satisfaction with Quality of instruction in Distance Education Relative to Classroom-Based Courses

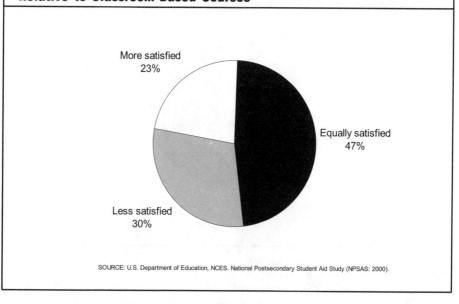

SOURCE: U.S. Department of Education, NCES. National Postsecondary Student Aid Study (NPSAS: 2000).

- The belief that online courses are easier than on-campus courses
  (Online courses require as much time as on-campus classes for attending and completing assignments.)

- Unrealistic expectations of what is required in an online learning environment
  (The e-learning student must be comfortable with technology. E-learning students must feel confident in their ability to use the Internet and with basic computer skills, such as word processing, Internet browsing, and e-mailing. In addition, if a student is new to the online learning environment, he/she must learn how to use the classroom management software, as well as learn the course material.)

- A puerile attitude for not assuming personal responsibility for their own learning
  (For learning to occur in an online course, individuals must be self-motivated, have enough self-discipline to be able to work independently, be tenacious, and work well on an individual basis.)

- A lack of basic communication skills needed to succeed in an online course
  (Students must have good reading and writing skills, as well as basic English (grammar) skills to effectively communicate to the instructor that learning has occurred.)

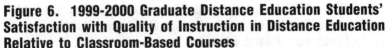

Figure 6. 1999-2000 Graduate Distance Education Students' Satisfaction with Quality of Instruction in Distance Education Relative to Classroom-Based Courses

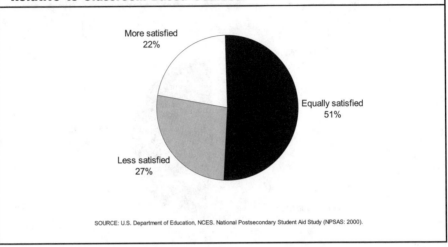

SOURCE: U.S. Department of Education, NCES. National Postsecondary Student Aid Study (NPSAS: 2000).

- Lack of face-to-face interaction
  (Less interaction among peers, as well as from the teacher, can create feelings of isolation. Many instructors feel these types of feelings associated with low levels of interactivity can lead to a decrease in motivation resulting in poor academic performance or quitting completely.)

- Ineffectiveness of online classroom management
  (If the online course is not thought out and well-planned, frustration with the design of the course can be an excuse for students to quit trying. Well-designed online courses encourage students to focus on the content. Ineffective online course organization hinders the learning process. Effective classroom management remains a cornerstone for learning to occur.)

Addressing and resolving these issues before a student embarks on an online learning journey creates an environment in which students are more likely to succeed.

Educational accountability. Educational institutions must be held accountable and responsible for offering quality e-learning experiences. Online courses designed and presented in the exact same manner as on-campus courses are doomed to failure. Instructors' educational preparation for effective online classroom management and facilitating are vital for a solid e-learning strategy. Many colleges and universities have designed and encouraged professional development opportunities for online instructors, including providing certification to teach online, offering online courses on campus, providing mentoring opportunities, and enabling instructors to attend online conferences.

When all the technology is working correctly, e-learning can be a pleasant experience. However, if the resources are not available, or if students' technical questions are not answered in a timely fashion, the learner experiences frustration. Technical support for the students, as well as the faculty, must be in place before offering online courses. If a student cannot access the course information online, submit work due to technical problems, or receive assistance because no help desk is available, he/she may eventually quit trying. This becomes a barrier to offering quality learning materials through the Internet. Timely, high-quality technical information is crucial to assure a successful e-learning experience.

Online learning must be supported by the administration. Many school administrators perceive online learning as a way to lower costs by reducing facility requirements. However, this savings may need to be reallocated to other costs, such as personnel time, money for equipment, and training of faculty and support staff. The administration must also address the faculty's reservations about the impact of faculty job security and morale. In order to ensure a successful online learning experience, the school must commit resources to it by maintaining and updating technology essential to quality distance education, by training and compensating appropriately to the needs of the faculty, and by providing online instructors the opportunity to participate in key decisions affecting online courses. Successful e-learning institutions must involve all key personnel—administrators, technical support personnel, and instructors.

Future of e-learning. While the Internet is playing a major role in distributing information globally, some believe that it will make classrooms obsolete. Management guru Peter Drucker in 1997 predicted that the residential university would be defunct by the year 2027. A better bet is that traditional higher education will change, not disappear. Just as typing reports using the typewriter has become obsolete, not using technology in the learning process will become obsolete. Digitally accessed software will become part of every teacher's lesson plan.

According to the U.S. Department of Education Pocket Projections (2002), degree-granting postsecondary education institutions will see an increase in enrollment (see Table 1).

It is also projected that by the 2011-12 school year, there will be a 34% increase in postsecondary students who are older than 25.

Table 1. Projected Enrollment Increase in Postsecondary Education

Age	Percent Change 2000-01 to 2011-12
19 years and under	17
20-21 years	20
22-24 years	10
25-29 years	19
30-34-years	11
35 years and over	4
Average Percent Change	14

The increase in the demand for online education will continue because of the affordability of owning a personal computer; the accessibility of the Internet from home or abroad; the continuous improvement of technology, such as wireless; and the appeal of enrolling and attending a class at one's convenience. According to BusinessWeek Online (The E-learning Explosion, 2001), enrollment in online courses at postsecondary institutions will grow from 2 million in 2001 to about 5 million in 2006.

Generation Y, Americans born between the years of 1979-1994, is the next generation of adult workers. Growing up during the media explosion, they are "cyberliterate" and are comfortable with technology. Integration of technology in the learning process is expected. The e-learning experience will incorporate more than just text. It will also include computer animation, wireless communication, and just-in-time information. The ability to access distance-education courses anytime and anywhere through personal digital assistants will become a part of our society (*m-learning*, for mobile learning). The next generation is depending on higher education institutions' embracing this fast growing, on-demand e-learning. Faculty must learn new communication techniques and creative ways to facilitate their coursework with students online. The next generation is depending on us.

REFERENCES

American Distance Education Consortium. (2001, April 9). *ADEC and Virtual Universities.* Retrieved February 26, 2003 from http://www.adec.edu/vuniv/place1.html.

Armour, Stephanie. (2003). Classrooms filled with returning adults. [Electronic version] *USA Today.* Retrieved July 25, 2003, from http://www.usatoday.com/money/economy/employment/2003-06-12-backtoschool_x.htm.

Chenoweth, J. & Mausehund, J. (2003). The wireless classroom: Planning for new challenges. *Business Education Forum.* 57(4), 40-42.

E-Learning. (2003, April 10). U.S. News. Retrieved April 10, 2003 from http://www.usnews.com/usnews/edu/elearning/elhome.htm

Fox, M. (2002). Keeping the blended promise: What does it take to make e-learning really pay off? *E-learning.* (3)(3) 26-30.

Giving it the old online try. (2001, December 3). [Electronic version]. *Business Week.* Retrieved April 7, 2003 from http://www.businessweek.com/magazine/content/01_49/b3760072.htm

Glenn, J. (2003). E-learning e-volution: Your (digital) future awaits. *Business Education Forum.* 57(4), 8-14.

Herrnstein, R., & Murray, C. (1994). *The Bell Curve.* Chicago: The Free Press, p. 31. (Division of Independent Publishers Group).

InnoVisions Canada, 2003. *Distance Education.* Retrieved April 7, 2003 from http://www.ivc.ca/part10.html.

Is Distance Learning for Me? Questions You Should Ask Before Going Online. (n.d.). Retrieved September 14, 2003, from http://distancelearn.about.com/library/weekly/aa091102a.htm

Lewis, S., & Blair, R. (2003). Reflections of a first-time online teacher. *Business Education Forum.* 57(4) 52-55.

Lorenzo, G. (May/June2002). E-ArmyU and the future of distance learning. *Technology Source.* Retrieved April 13, 2003 from http://ts.mivu.org/default.asp?show-article&id=998.

Mulrine, A. (2002, October 28) *Special report: E-learning online education: It's in the army now.* Retrieved April 10, 2003 from http://www.useic.ru/dl/article-09.htm

Snider, A. (2002). Find a winning blend: A real-world guide for your e-learning initiative's success. *E-learning.* 3(3) 22-25.

The E-Learning Explosion. (2001, December 3). [Electronic version]. *BusinessWeek.* Retrieved October 7, 2002 from http://www.businessweek.com/magazine/content/01_49/b3760073.htm

U.S. Bureau of the Census. (2003). *Educational Attainment in the United States: March 2001 and March 2002.* Retrieved Setember 14, 2003 from http://www.census.gov/Press-Release/www/2003/cb03-51.html.

U.S. Bureau of the Census. (2002). *Current Population Survey, October 1999 Supplement.* State-level data provided by Pinkerton Computer Consultants, 2002.

U.S. Department of Education, NCES (2002a). *The condition of education 2002* (NCES 2002-025). Washington, D.C.: U.S. Government Printing Office.

U.S. Department of Education, NCES (2002b). *Digest of education statistics 2001* (NCES 2002-130). Washington, D.C.: U.S. Government Printing Office.

U.S. Department of Education, NCES (2002). Fall Enrollment Survey, 1999–2000. Unpublished tabulation provided by Tom Snyder at NCES, U.S. Department of Education, Washington, D.C.

U.S. Department of Education, NCES, (2002). *National postsecondary student aid study, 1999-2000.* (NPSAS: 2000). Washington, D.C.: U.S. Government Printing Office.

U.S. Department of Education, NCES (2002). *Nontraditional undergraduates: Findings from the condition of education 2002* (NCES 2002-012). Washington, D.C.: U.S. Government Printing Office.

U.S. Department of Education, NCES (2002). *Pocket projections: Projections of Education statistics to 2012.* (NCES 2002-033) by William J. Hussar and Debra E. Gerald. Washington, D.C.: U.S. Government Printing Office.

U.S. Department of Education, NCES (2002). *Profile of undergraduates in U.S. postsecondary institutions: 1999-2000.* (NCES 2002-168). Washington, D.C.: U.S. Government Printing Office.

U.S. Department of Education, NCES, (2003). *Distance education at degree-granting postsecondary institutions: 2000–2001.* (NCES: 2003-017). Washington, D.C.: U.S. Government Printing Office.

U.S. Department of Education, NCES, (2003). *A profile of participation in distance education: Postsecondary education descriptive analysis reports, 1999-2000.* (NCES: 2003-154). Washington, D.C.: U.S. Government Printing Office.

What research tells us about Generation X. Center for Teaching and Learning. Retrieved September 14, 2003, from Western Michigan University Web site: http://www.wmich.edu/teachlearn/winter1999/teaching/genx.html

E-Commerce Programs: What's Right for the Times?

Jo Ann Oravec
University of Wisconsin, Whitewater
Whitewater, Wisconsin

Tasks that ought to be simple—such as arranging a meeting with colleagues from partner companies and automatically updating every attendee's calendar—are a nightmare. Productivity is one of the main casualties. Solving such problems is the key challenge for the next generation of the Internet. —Bill Gates, 2001

Electronic commerce (e-commerce) introduces a wide spectrum of new choices—and new hazards—into everyday consumer experiences. It is also providing organizations with new means of doing business with other businesses (B2B or BtoB), linking suppliers with manufacturers and manufacturers to retailers in more efficient ways. As reflected in the quotation in the epigraph, businesses are no longer content with e-commerce applications that do not increase productivity and organizational effectiveness. E-commerce programs and related curricula are developing new facets as the scope and extent of these initiatives expand. Given the ubiquitous nature of the Internet, students can do much more in e-commerce programs than just read about e-commerce and engage in occasional online "field trips." Rather, classroom settings can provide a place for application development, consumer research, and critical analysis of various e-commerce services and approaches. Businesses often welcome students as interns in e-commerce positions, since they have advanced technical skills that businesses need. Educators and students can also serve as consumer advocates in these realms, helping to mitigate some of the current and potential hazards associated with e-commerce and playing effective roles in public policy debates.

Many questions still remain about what e-commerce constitutes, what programmatic structures best support it, and how specifically instructors can integrate it into curricula. This chapter contends that many kinds of business-related topics can have merit for students, if programs are rigorous and constructed to emphasize skills of analysis and criticism. Even critical studies of the pencil can illuminate important business issues (Petroski, 1992), although this chapter is obviously not recommending "pencil studies" programs. Grouping courses in e-commerce programs provides a ready platform for integrated exercises and stimulating, in-depth treatment of topics. The "packaging" of the program is often more important to potential employers and participants than it is to educators, who have worked toward construction of cohesive and intensive courses of study. As described in this chapter, e-commerce provides a venue for many kinds of hands-on projects that can be tightly integrated across various disciplinary areas (such as marketing, management, and information technology). E-commerce has thus developed beyond the "fad" stage to become a significant form of international economic exchange, as well as a major emphasis in many business schools. It can indeed provide an appropriate anchor for demanding and well-aligned program approaches.

Included under the rubric of "e-commerce" today are such activities as online marketing and purchasing, as well as an expanding number of forms of consumer research. New forms of electronic currency exchange are being designed, as both businesses and consumers find it more convenient to use electronic rather than paper means to exchange money. Online distribution of various digital information products (such as music, video, e-books, and newsletters) is also a major aspect of e-commerce. Many businesses use e-commerce capabilities to expand their communication with other public and private sector organizations, exchanging product information and purchase orders with such technologies as XML (eXtensible Markup Language, described later), along with older standards such as EDI (Electronic Data Interchange). Consumers are themselves utilizing new e-commerce strategies to exchange information among households and with consumer advocacy groups about the quality of the products and services they receive. Organizations can learn about consumer preferences by "listening in" on these established consumer forums or conducting their own surveys and focus groups online.

Since many aspects of e-commerce blossomed so quickly, high schools and postsecondary institutions often found themselves short of both the human and material resources to deal with its technical and business dimensions (Mitchell & Strauss, 2001). As a result, a myriad of approaches have been developed, largely linked to the existing strengths of the institutions involved—as Novitzki (2002) found in research on a selected group of AACSB (American Association of Collegiate Schools of Business) institutions. Some departments emphasized e-commerce to the exclusion of the "basics" or "fundamentals" of business, while others scrambled to infuse e-commerce into programs in more piecemeal fashion. An assortment of influential textbooks and curricular materials emerged in the late 1990s to support faculty members in introducing e-commerce in the classroom and to provide some direction for e-commerce efforts. A pioneering text that emphasizes the technological dimensions of e-commerce is Daniel Amor's (1999) *The E-business (R)evolution*. Some less technical but comparably influential early texts include

Kalakota and Robinson's (1999) *e-Business: Roadmap for Success* and Shapiro and Varian's (1999) *Information Rules: A Strategic Guide to the Network Economy*. A textbook that attracted a growing general audience is Laudon and Traver's (2002) *E-commerce: Business, Technology, Society*. Such popular books as *Smart Mobs* by Howard Rheingold (2002) have been used as supplemental texts. Rheingold presents some of the innovative and futuristic technologies involved in e-commerce in entertaining way—such as the recommendation systems used to recommend books in Amazon.com's Web site. Through these systems, profiles of readers' purchases and item ratings are matched so that the recommendations rendered have some statistical grounding.

A major drawback of many e-commerce materials developed before the late 1999 dot-com failures and the terrorist attacks of September 11, 2001, is that they often reflect a misplaced euphoria. Many privacy, security, and economic issues have changed greatly in character since these events. In 2001, the Dean of Arizona State University's College of Business, Larry Penley, expressed worries that downturns in the high tech economy would stall the needed infusions of technological content and instructional technology into business schools (Datz, 2001). Few e-commerce ventures are currently being undertaken without careful scrutiny by all parties involved (including their financiers and their customers). Case studies and exercises that include accounts of eager venture capitalists need to be put into context for today's students, many of whom are finding it difficult to obtain employment or obtain business start-up loans (Fisher, 2002). Books such as *dot.bomb: My Days and Nights at an Internet Goliath* by J. David Kuo (2001) can help provide background on this bygone era for students. One of the most effective ways for faculty to introduce concerns brought on by dot-com failures is possibly the most entertaining: the documentary *Startup.com* (2001, directed by Jehane Noujaim and Chris Hegedus) portrays the lifespan of GovWorks.com, a start-up initiated in 1998. *Startup.com* won many film industry awards for its demonstration of how people-related factors as well as large-scale economic and competitive forces can affect the adoption of business innovations. Other comparable documentaries of companies that emerged in this era include *Dot.com: A Case Study*, produced by ABCNews in 2001 (currently available through the Films for the Humanities & Sciences). These documen-taries provide strong lessons in how technological euphoria can override business common sense.

The downturns in economic markets have obviously not stalled e-commerce entirely. Estimates of the size of the markets for e-commerce vary greatly, depending on what is construed as being "e-commerce" (or "e-business"). Many analysts project that soon e-commerce will be so closely integrated into everyday business practices that distinguish-ing it in some way from "bricks and mortar" activity will be nearly impossible (Levine, 2000). The popularity of expressions such as "bricks and clicks" and "clicks and mor-tars" underscore how many businesses tightly couple electronic and face-to-face interac-tions with consumers—and these couplings will probably become tighter in the decade to come (Min & Wolfinbarger, 2002).

Introducing E-Commerce Offerings in Business Curricula: The E-Commerce Dilemma

Confusion about where to place e-commerce in the full spectrum of business school offerings is mirrored in the puzzling assortment of business e-commerce approaches (O'Hara, 2000; O'Hara & Stephens, 1999; Sendall, 1999). Despite the lack of clarity about what e-commerce constitutes, there are still many academic programs and individual course offerings in higher education that are specifically labeled as "e-commerce-oriented." These include (a) graduate programs (usually at the Masters level); (b) e-commerce undergraduate majors and minors; (c) e-commerce certificates (sets of specific courses, but not a coherent major or minor); and (d) isolated courses, often offered online. Some larger institutions have coupled all four approaches, although this strategy can stretch the resources of smaller schools. The business education departments of a number of high schools have also integrated aspects of electronic commerce into coursework and student organization activity. For instance, the Web site of the McDowell County Economic Development Association in North Carolina was developed in 2002 by the E-Commerce Class of McDowell High School (http://www.main.nc.us/meda/authors.htm).

The decision to segregate e-commerce offerings into a separate program is complex; the "e-commerce dilemma" faced by many institutions involves whether to diffuse or congeal their e-commerce courses and internships. Business schools faced comparable problems in the recent past. For example, a number of "expert systems" and "knowledge engineering" programs were developed in the late 1980s and early 1990s, as excitement about the prospects for expert systems technology grew and students prepared for the profession of "knowledge engineer" (Oravec & Travis, 1992). However, as business enthusiasm for expert systems waned, such programs were often annexed to other programs, combining a number of technologies and emphasizing "knowledge management." Business schools will face comparable decisions in the future, as such innovations as advanced biotechnology become more dominant as economic forces, so the process of deciding how to integrate cutting-edge topics into curricula will continue to be of concern.

The first major US e-commerce graduate program was established in Vanderbilt University's Owen Graduate School of Management in 1996, while economic and social conditions for e-commerce were still highly supportive. By 1997, programs were inaugurated with considerable fanfare at the University of Texas-Austin, Fuqua School of Business at Duke University, Sloan School at MIT, Stanford University, the University of Michigan, and the University of Rochester. The program at the University of Pennsylvania has a focus on developing CEOs and senior managers equipped to deal with e-commerce issues (Lee, Chen, Barmes, & Hsieh, 2003). Many community colleges developed e-commerce programs in the late 1990s as well, such as Gloucester County College (Conway, 1999); such programs made e-commerce careers more approachable for returning adult students. Subsequent economic downturns in high tech industries have brought some sobriety to discussions of e-commerce in education. Some of the most highly rated business schools have reportedly adopted a "back to basics" position in regard to e-commerce offerings, introducing them when essential, but emphasizing the more traditional topics and approaches (Merritt, 2002). In 2000, the Web site of UC-Berkeley's Haas School boldly declared that e-commerce programs are akin to programs dealing with the telephone (Durlabhji & Fusilier, 2002), and hence should not displace more traditional offerings. Armour (2001) provides the following interview segment:

> Anytime you find students chasing a trend, it's dangerous," says Carl Zeithaml, dean of the McIntire School of Commerce at the University of Virginia in Charlottesville, which has shied away from offering an e-commerce degree. "It's important to give students a broader variety of skills (p. 16).

Accounts of the decision processes behind the institution of e-commerce initiatives are helpful in understanding the problems of conceptualizing and justifying new academic programs. Miller (2001) provides a useful discussion of the specific decision procedure that Philadelphia University undertook in developing its pioneering e-commerce approach. The school created a university-wide committee to coordinate its efforts in creating and supporting an E-Commerce Major. New courses created for the major include "Survey of E-commerce," the capstone course, "Building an E-business," and an advanced database course. The broadly based committee was able to bring the campus together to obtain resources and create the needed courses quickly (and with a minimum of rancor).

Another e-commerce program success story is from Creighton University in Omaha, Nebraska. It started a Masters of Science in E-commerce and established an e-commerce research center with the help of a $1.5 million gift from alumnus Joe Ricketts, Chairman and CEO of Ameritrade Holding Corp. (headquartered in Omaha). The center helps local and national businesses create partnerships and develop specialized educational programs. Students thus have a wide range of internship and job placement options. Arizona State University (ASU) took the following strategy:

> Recognizing that changes were needed in ASU's business curriculum, an e-business task force of ASU faculty and high-tech vendors recommended that students be given more hands-on experience working with business applications, such as supply chain management and customer relationship management software. As a result, ASU students get to play around with enterprise software from companies such as Manugistics and J.D. Edwards in order to better understand how it works. —Datz, 2001

Utah State's approach was developed with the help of an advisory board (Bartholome & Olsen, 2002), which encouraged overall industry involvement.

Despite these upbeat examples, many campuses have not faced the e-commerce dilemma head on or have provided only partial solutions. Infusion of e-commerce into business education curricula has been incomplete according to a survey conducted in

2001 by Morrison and Oladunjoye (2002). They claim that "business educators are not infusing e-commerce topics sufficiently into curricula to prepare their students for roles in companies in which e-commerce is an integral part of operations" (p. 295). The rapid pace of change in e-commerce itself is one of the factors behind this situation. Mitchell and Strauss (2001) contend that e-commerce itself is a "moving target"; educators must constantly reassess what is relevant, a task that is especially difficult in higher education, where programmatic change processes can be lengthy.

The case of XML (eXtensible Markup Language) provides examples of how business curricula need to be updated and reviewed on a regular basis to accommodate e-commerce advances. XML first emerged in real-world business contexts in 1996, so many instructors who received their educations in the early 1990s (or in previous eras) may not have been trained in it. It provides content-oriented markup that allows for the transfer and easy analysis of vast quantities of business data via the Web, and thus can be very useful for a wide variety of B2B exchanges. Many of today's Web sites are pro-grammed in HTML (hypertext markup language), and even high school classes often provide a smattering of HTML to students. HTML is relatively friendly as a language; the Internet browsers that interpret HTML to produce Web pages are somewhat "forgiving" (most errors are not fatal). On the other hand, XML requires much more strictness in coding, and a minor error can produce devastating results for students who are not comfortable with testing and debugging programs (Festervand, 2002).

A number of business forecasters project that XML will soon displace EDI (Electronic Data Interchange) as a major platform for B2B interactions (as discussed in Scott & Comer, 1999; Chen, 2003). Organizations such as Microsoft are integrating XML into their Web strategies (Taft, 2003), including .NET, with Sun Microsystems and others following suit. Bill Gates (2001) contends that XML is a "lingua franca" for the Internet age, helping to "break down the distinctions between the Internet, standalone applications and computing devices of every kind." However, developing XML applications can be very different from working with HTML for nontechnically oriented students (although they are both "markup languages") and business schools need to adapt their curricular approaches accordingly. The rigor required for XML and related extensible markup languages such as XHTML and ebXML may indeed be disheartening for many students (and instructors) who are used to the relative friendliness of HTML; the many emerging varieties of markup language are adding confusion as well. Shifting business curricula so that XML instruction is provided will consume a large share of the limited institutional resources devoted to e-commerce, an adjustment that programs must make to remain current. Wide assortments of new technologies such as XML are emerging that can profoundly influence e-commerce, so programs must be flexible to accommodate them.

Emerging E-Commerce Themes and Approaches

Approaches to e-commerce instruction are likely to vary as society itself struggles to balance electronic with other forms of commercial activity (including paper-based and face-to-face). Today, most individuals and businesses can make strategic choices as to whether to utilize electronic transaction mechanisms—nonelectronic alternatives are

105

often still available. For example, most taxes can be either filed online or by postal mail using paper. Soon such choices may not be available as society stabilizes on a particular transaction mode (or modes). Lee et al. (2003) found that successful programs start with an analysis of potential students and their needs, followed with a survey of university stakeholders (including employers) about economic conditions, possible career paths, and other critical aspects.

Analyses of the kinds of content that e-commerce courses encompass help to illuminate discourse on these matters (as demonstrated by Schneberger, Parent, & Haggerty, 2000 and Surendra, 2000). Whitten & Stephens (2001) reviewed the e-commerce offerings of the top business schools in university settings (according to *Business Week's* rankings). They found the following topics covered in the syllabi of beginning e-commerce courses of eighteen of the top thirty graduate-level programs: business models, strategy, infrastructure, technology, programming languages, privacy and security, payment, advertising, pricing, auctions, and legal issues. Some of the academic perspectives that focus on e-commerce emphasize technical matters such as network architecture and programming language nuances. Information technology (IT) educators worldwide have struggled to define a place for e-commerce among the other, more traditional computer science topics (Pedro, 2001). Other academic perspectives tightly couple technical with business concerns. For instance, such matters as bandwidth availability and the choice of programming languages have business as well as technical aspects.

Many of the programs within business schools that include e-commerce offerings purport to (a) outline the history of e-commerce, for example, examining the origins of the legacy systems that are still a factor in business; (b) explore advanced technical innovations in both business-to-business (B2B) and business-to-consumer (B2C) commerce; (c) emphasize user friendliness and human factors, along with modes of education of both business people and consumers; (d) explore international aspects of B2B and B2C approaches; (e) examine the economic dimensions of e-commerce (especially the online delivery of various information products); (f) expand students' use of the Internet as a business reference tool; (g) investigate new consumer research trends, including the growing range of C2C (consumer to consumer) communications, as individuals exchange information about products and services as well as utilize cooperative buying strategies; (h) predict the future of e-commerce using such methodologies as scenario development and trend projection, as well as highlight how innovations are developed and disseminated; and (i) emphasize consumer advocacy in such issues as privacy, security, and fraud prevention. The sections below expand the above topics.

Historical approaches toward e-commerce. Current circumstances in e-commerce have many parallels with situations early in this century in retailing. Retailers had the problem of how to acquaint shoppers with the realm of mail order products; subsequently, many home economics and business education teachers helped to introduce mail order channels to young consumers. Some early writings also had an influential role in consumer advocacy: for example, *Your Money's Worth* by Chase and Schlink (1927) provides specific strategies for consumers in how to avoid fraud and wasteful spending. Consumers needed to be informed about the specific procedures for making mail order purchases. They also needed to be encouraged to form new kinds of relationships with the companies with which they were doing business: they had to learn to evaluate their trustworthiness from a distance, then establish and maintain relationships with them. Similarly, in the early days of e-commerce, shoppers had little help in dealing with the growing number of choices (as well as hazards) that they faced (Bayne, 1997).

Emphasizing historical considerations in technical discussions of e-commerce also involves describing the "legacy systems" that still exist and have continuing value for organizations. For example, the fact that the pioneering computer language COBOL is still used for many critically important business applications was underscored by the "Y2K problem," in which programmers had to labor to correct potential date-related problems before January 1, 2000 (Oravec, 1999). Students who believe that businesses readily jettison older systems in favor of the new should study what happened during this traumatic period in business history.

Current advances in e-commerce. Recent advances in e-commerce are expanding the models and notions of commerce itself and are providing an ever-increasing range of activities and products for consumers. Wireless devices and "M-commerce" (mobile commerce) are delivering services to various locations (Oravec, 2001). Rather than just duplicating what can be done in traditional modes of commerce, developers are experimenting with new means to connect potential buyers with sellers. Modes through which e-commerce advances can be introduced into business classrooms are also expanding in kind and number. Students can participate directly in storefront development, online shopping, and other e-commerce activities with little or no expenditure (except for basic Internet access). Often, students will have utilized such systems in their everyday lives but only explored a few of their features, or perhaps did not use them successfully.

Attracting the attention of consumers is often the first step in establishing a buyer-seller relationship; with thousands of Web sites pertaining to various products, businesses must take steps to distinguish themselves. Some online marketers are directly paying consumers to do surveys or view particular online promotions. There are also many contests in which various sums of money can be earned by Internet surfers. Other services make it easier to compare prices for computer equipment and other products on the Internet. For example, MySimon.com and Pricewatch.com compile billions of prices from retailers in the United States and Canada, updating them regularly. Yahoo's Stores is a free service on the Web that gives users access to special deals, (as well as help in locating suitable gifts), simply by entering search terms such as keywords or name brands.

Many consumers are also using online services that have built-in "recommender systems" to obtain information from each other about products in a way that resembles "word-of-mouth" interaction. In this strategy, consumers construct profiles of their needs and interests through completing online surveys. The profiles are then matched with those of other consumers. Information about the likes and dislikes of the consumers whose profiles match are subsequently shared, and people with similar interests are linked. Many new online consumer options are indeed complex and may require proactive educational efforts on the part of designers and promoters. Faculty can create exercises so that students can experiment with such online services in laboratory settings, comparing results with each other and critiquing the overall "user friendliness" of the systems (as described in the next section).

User friendliness and human factors, along with modes of consumer education. Many academic programs that focus on e-commerce integrate consumer research strategies as well as "usability" and "accessibility" concepts (Chan, Wolfe, & Fang, 2003). These efforts involve examinations of how individuals use technologies, as well as how technologies can be improved so as to increase the "fit" between them and their users. In order to reach the everyday consumer for a larger range of buying decisions, e-commerce must be made easier to participate in and more enjoyable. Individuals with special needs for visual or auditory assistance must be accommodated as well, with various state and federal laws as incentives (Oravec, 2002). Information overload is becoming a problem for nearly all consumers, and "Internet addiction" is emerging as a problem for some users as well (Young, 1998). Developers of e-commerce systems are focusing on ways to make the kinds and number of choices consumers are given more manageable and to reduce the potential for ill effects of computer use. They are also trying to make these choices more attractive in order to capture the audiences that currently utilize malls, catalogs, and television to make their everyday purchasing decisions. Such notable figures as Donald Norman (2001) and Jacob Nielsen (2000) have championed everyday users and provided strategies for developing interactive technologies and media that are more intuitive. Examining these strategies can provide challenging classroom activities in both high school and college settings. E-commerce advances also open new social and political issues that are being discussed in classrooms, including privacy concerns, consumer fraud, identity theft, and the manipulation of children and the unwary.

International aspects of B2B and B2C approaches. Exploring e-commerce and information technology opportunities based in other countries, as well as studying how those countries are dealing with their related social issues, can aid students in gaining perspective on international business concerns (Karakaya & Erdener, 1995; Pedro, 2001). International perspectives are critical in nearly all e-commerce considerations because of the global nature of the Internet. Nations are dealing with these issues in various ways; for example, privacy issues are being focused on very heavily by the European Union (Rodger, 1998) and online pornography and gambling are major concerns of many other countries.

Economic dimensions of e-commerce (especially the online delivery of various information products). Students can gain experience in starting and advertising businesses online, building free (or relatively inexpensive) Web sites through the facilities provided by GeoCities, Angelfire, or other hosts. Geocities has provided reliable service to both schools and amateur Web site builders for a number of years (Quittner, 1998).

Teams of students can build complete online storefronts; the more technically oriented students can design shopping carts, while the students who are gaining expertise in marketing can design and advertise the sites. There are many dimensions of e-commerce besides just developing a Web presence, however. Most students are aware of the availability of "free" (illegally available) online products exchanged through peer-to-peer systems such as Kazaa and Morpheus; however, fewer students are cognizant of the kinds and extents of copyright legislation that pertain to the distribution of these items. Many e-commerce programs tackle these complex intellectual property issues. Out of all these efforts, critical and reflective programs can help students draw larger principles concerning entrepreneurship and business practices (Gundry & Kickul, 2003).

The Internet as a business reference tool. The Internet and computer networking in general have been beneficial tools in the classroom in the past decade, allowing access to reference materials and other resources that would be hard if not impossible to locate in a timely fashion. With the growing capabilities of search engines such as Google, online business research efforts can be even more effective while helping individuals to avoid "information overload." Web sites such as www.searchenginewatch.com can be used in classrooms to alert students to search engine advances.

New consumer research capabilities. E-commerce is also providing new ways to research consumer activity. Marketers are interested in why people shop online and what activities they engage in when they are at particular sites (Wolfinbarger & Gilly, 2001). Many customers are finding effective means online for obtaining information about products as well as communicating with sellers. Customers with questions can readily query organizations via e-mail, providing a new channel for feedback about products and services. These advances in marketing research are not without drawbacks, however. Information collection about consumers on the Internet has raised a number of important issues, especially when the collection of information from children is involved. Groups such as the Center for Media Education long contended that children who surf the Internet are being drawn into revealing information about their households by marketers (Pasnik, 1997). A number of countries are considering legislation to protect households from these and other hazards. In the US, legislation has been passed (the Children's Online Privacy Protection Act of 1998, or COPPA) but is under challenge in the courts (LaRochelle, 2001).

Futuristic approaches to e-commerce using such methodologies as scenario development and trend projection. Exploring how e-commerce advances are developed and disseminated can equip students to analyze the business dimensions of various innovations as they emerge. Such professional forecasting firms as the Gartner Group and Forrester Research release trend projections in hopes that businesses can be prepared for various technological advances. Some businesses also release futuristic accounts so that consumers can envisage their future homes and shopping patterns (Oravec, 1996). For example, Bill Gates' *The Road Ahead* (1998) provides such scenarios of home and community life. Intel's Andy Grove (1996) projected how developments in networking would change basic business processes and strategies. Students can develop their own futuristic scenarios either in written or video form, as well as explore the prognostications that business leaders construct.

Consumer advocacy in such issues as privacy, security, and fraud prevention. Establishing trust is an important element in the advent of e-commerce; issues of trust and integrity are especially complex online, given the international scope of the Internet and thus its expansion beyond the reach of any particular legal system. In each of their online interactions, consumers must evaluate the likeliness that the companies or individuals with which they are doing business will deliver the products or services they ordered. However, they must evaluate how trustworthy these companies are to handle their personal information (such as credit card numbers) with privacy and security. Consumers must also watch out for scams and for potential security breaches. Business educators (along with their students) can also serve as "consumer advocates" in this new electronic realm, helping to identify and publicize problems before the average consumer is harmed by them. Some of the discussion and debate techniques outlined in Settle and Berthiaume (2002) can be of help in classroom treatment of these issues.

Scams are indeed growing in variety and number on the Internet as consumers spend considerable time and money in online stores and auction sites. Mannix (1997) declared in *US News and World Report* that "a new generation of hucksters has made the Internet the latest tool for carrying out all sorts of schemes" (p. 59)—and the problem has only escalated since this statement was made in late 1990s. One of the organizations that has tackled the issues of consumer fraud on the Internet and provided useful information to teachers is the Internet Fraud Complaint Center (IFCC), which is a partnership between the US Federal Bureau of Investigation (FBI) and the US National White Collar Crime Center (NW3C). It organized a clearinghouse for information about e-commerce fraud (http://www1.ifccfbi.gov) and also helps to investigate particular consumer complaints.

Can We Locate E-Commerce Program Success Factors?

Determining the "success factors" for e-commerce initiatives in real-world business contexts can be difficult, in part because of rapid changes in the technologies involved (Vijayaraman & Bhatia, 2002). Similarly, distilling success factors for the wide assortment of e-commerce educational programs can be problematic for comparable reasons. Exposure to e-commerce notions can often be of assistance to many students in finding immediate employment, despite recent economic downturns. However, this fact by itself is not sufficient to ensure its prominent placement in business curricula at the undergraduate and graduate levels (and especially in high school contexts). Because class time is limited in all of these venues, introducing e-commerce or any other topics necessarily displaces other vitally important material. Thus, students should obtain some substantial educational value from e-commerce studies other than just exposure to trendy business concepts. In the years to come, most likely other technologies besides the Internet will be driving business growth, and programs that prepare students to conceptualize all business concerns in terms of a limited range of current technologies may not be useful in equipping them to deal with those advances. Along with the decisions that colleges and universities have to make in this regard, students and employers have choices as well. Students must decide whether degrees with the label "e-commerce" and transcripts full of Web -related courses will best fill their long-term needs. Employers will be determining whether individuals with e-commerce program backgrounds are the best equipped to face future business problems. The fact that many e-commerce programs are delivered online or have significant technology mediation further complicates this analysis, since it is very difficult to distill "best practices" for such forms of education (Gemeinhardt, 2002).

Students who enter e-commerce programs should not be under any illusion that what they are studying is somehow stable or enduring; however, the skills they acquire can be readily transferred to other business environments. The question of what e-commerce technologies and approaches will have longevity looms large for the development of curricula. However, critical and reflective approaches to e-commerce that integrate an assortment of the dimensions described in the previous section can help students to gain value from their educational experiences as well as become effective "change agents," whatever approaches and technologies ultimately succeed in the marketplace. Students trained to be critical thinkers will be better equipped to introduce these advances in their future organizations and work to minimize potential problems. Business classrooms (both at high school and postsecondary levels) are ideal settings for evaluating e-commerce technologies and assessing their associated social and economic issues. Whether or not they will be directly employed in e-commerce enterprises, many of today's business students will soon be faced in their working lives with the problem of how to present innovative services to consumers, as well as how to participate in the development of new ones. In their roles as consumers, they will also be dealing with e-commerce concerns in such everyday matters as online shopping and airline ticket purchases. Hence, whatever societal roles students play, being able to assess and project creative uses for new e-commerce applications will be useful in ensuring their future success.

SUMMARY

E-commerce has expanded beyond the experimental stage to the point at which it is part of the everyday lives of many consumers as well as the day-to-day operations of most businesses. Integrating e-commerce into curricula is itself extending beyond the "hype" or "gee whiz" stage to one in which the advances are framed in meaningful and intellectually challenging ways. The advantage of a coherent program focusing on e-commerce or other important business themes is that students can better engage in sustained and well-integrated critical analysis in cases and projects, often focusing on their separate disciplines but needing to deal with various aspects of the problems they face. Through placing today's e-commerce developments in context with the history of business computerization and the larger picture of business operations, instructors can empower students to project the future more adequately and be better prepared for the changes to come. The Internet can be the center of a broad range of hands-on classroom activities in business curricula, as students and teachers both sell and shop (or at least "window shop") in markets worldwide and utilize innovative means for locating items and making purchasing decisions. In order to increase their effectiveness, business educators can bring guest speakers into the classroom and relate details from their own consulting experiences and continuing education (O'Connor, 2002; Phillips & Phillips, 2002).

In order to avoid hype and prepare students for an uncertain future, e-commerce advances are best presented in a critical and reflective manner. In learning skills of criticism and reflection, students will benefit however business conditions evolve. For example, students should engage in discussion and written review and analysis of various e-commerce activities after their participation in a way that encourages them to integrate their knowledge into other classroom content. Students' observations and insights often have immediate business value as well. Many of the e-commerce systems students encounter in classrooms are under continuous improvement, and consumer input is generally welcomed by developers. For example, some of the online travel services have complex options that consumers may overlook in their haste to book an airline ticket.

Students can also learn a great deal about human factors and accessibility issues in their examinations of these new systems, concepts that have ramifications for the full spectrum of technological issues. E-commerce applications that are not accessible to those with limited eyesight and various other impairments can shut out an increasing segment of the population, which is inappropriate both in its social and business dimensions (Oravec, 2002). Accessibility concerns are best addressed through practical experience. In general, internships are especially useful in the e-commerce realm, since students have real skills they can share with businesses (especially small businesses), skills that the businesses often do not have the means to acquire in other ways. For example, many businesses and not-for-profit organizations need Web sites, Web site upgrades, or e-marketing campaigns, and students can often make substantial headway on these projects during a semester- or year-long internship.

Although e-commerce is growing rapidly, it is still in its infancy. Business educators have a unique opportunity to participate with their students (and with others worldwide) in the development and fine-tuning of new modes of conducting business. An expanding array of technically-oriented activities can be brought directly into classrooms, from building an e-commerce Web site to testing applications for usability. These exercises can serve to enhance students' overall understanding of both business and technology. Students can also have first-hand exposure to e-commerce through designing and implementing online consumer surveys and focus groups as well as participating in internships. E-commerce, like life, is a participation sport—and students can become more competent individual performers as well as team members through direct involvement.

REFERENCES

Amor, D. (1999). *The e-business (r)evolution*, Englewood Cliffs, NJ: Prentice-Hall.

Armour, S. (2001, January 1). Degrees in e-commerce seem less dazzling. *USA Today*, p. 16.

Bartholome, L., & Olsen, D. (2002). A practical approach for implementing e-commerce programs in business school. *Communications of the ACM, 45*(1), 19-22.

Bayne, K. (1997). *The Internet marketing plan.* New York: John Wiley & Sons.

Chan, S., Wolfe, E., and Fang, X. (2003). Issues and strategies for integrating HCI in masters level MIS and e-commerce programs. *International Journal of Human-Computer Studies, 59,* 497-520.

Chen, A., LaBrie, R., & Shao, B. (2003). An XML adoption framework for electronic business. *Journal of Electronic Commerce Research, 4*(1), 1-14.

Chase, S., and Schlink, F. (1927). *Your money's worth; A study in the waste of the consumer's dollar.* New York: Macmillan.

Conway, T. (1999, August 8). E-commerce grows as an academic pursuit. *Philadelphia Business Journal,* 1.

Datz, T. (2001, August). Are b-schools e-schools? *Darwin Magazine.* Retrieved October 31, 2003, from http://www.darwinmag.com/read/080101/buzz_schools_content.html

Durlabhji, S., & Fusilier, M. R. (2002). Ferment in business education: E-commerce master's programs. *Journal of Education for Business, 77*(3), 169-177.

Festervand, T. (2002). The role of XML in preparing students for a career in e-commerce. *Journal of Internet Commerce, 1*(2), 77-88.

Fisher, A. (2002, December 9). I'm not shedding tears for dot-commers facing reality. *Fortune, 146*(12), 244.

Gates, B. (1998). *The road ahead.* New York: Viking.

Gates, B. (2001, June 18). Why we are building .NET technology. Microsoft Press Pass. Retrieved February 1, 2003, from http://www.microsoft.com/presspass/misc/06-18BillGNet.asp

Gemeinhardt, G. (2002). Best practices in technology-mediated learning in American business education. *Educational Technology & Society. 5*(2), 39-46.

Grove, A. (1996). *Only the paranoid survive.* New York: Doubleday.

Gundry, L., & Kickul, J. (2003). *E-commerce entrepreneurship: Emerging practices, key challenges, and future directions.* CEAE Coleman Foundation. Retrieved October 31, 2003, from http://www.colemanchairs.org/files/documents/19/gundrykickul.pdf

Kalakota, R., & Robinson, M. (1999). *e-Business: Roadmap for success.* Reading, MA: Addison-Wesley.

Karakaya, F., and Erdener, K. (Eds.). (1995). *Utilizing new information technology in teaching of international business : A guide for instructors.* New York: Haworth Press.

Kickul, J., & Kickul, G. (2001, Spring). Implementing e-learning innovations and technologies: Test of an integrated model within a university setting. *Business, Education, & Technology Journal,* 7-14.

King, C., Frank, S., & Platt, R. (2001). E-commerce courses: Overview of nature and content. *Journal of Education for Business, 76*(6), 332-337.

Kuo, J. S. (2001). *Dot.bomb: My days and nights at an Internet goliath* New York: Little, Brown, & Company.

LaRochelle, M. (2001). Online privacy update: Enforcing COPPA. *Consumers' Research Magazine, 84*(9), 43-44.

Laudon, K., & Traver, C. 2002, *E-commerce: Business, technology, society.* Reading, PA: Addison Wesley.

Lee, H., Chen, K., Barmes, C., & Hsieh, C. (2003). A mission-based and student-oriented strategy for e-commerce curriculum development. Decision Sciences Institute Southwest Region, March 6-8, 2003.

Lee, H. G., and Clark, T. H. (1997). Market process reengineering through electronic market systems: Opportunities and challenges. *Journal of Management Information Systems. 13*(3), 113-136.

Levine, A. E. (2000). The future of colleges: Nine inevitable changes. *The Chronicle Review, XLVII*(9), B10-B11

Mannix, M. (1997). Have I got a deal for you! *U S News and World Report. 123*(16), 59-60.

Merritt, J. (2002, October 21). The best b-schools. *Business Week, 3804*, 84, 10.

Miller, A. (2001). E-Commerce education: A university's quick response. Retrieved October 31, 2003 from http://www.abe.villanova.edu/proc2000/n041.pdf

Min, S., & Wolfinbarger, M. (2002). Do early movers, clicks and mortars, and generalists prevail in e-Commerce, submitted to *Journal of Business Research*, August, 2003.

Mitchell, T., & Strauss, J. (2001). Practitioner and academic recommendations for Internet marketing and E-commerce curricula. *Journal of Marketing Education, 23*(2), 91-103.

Morrison, J. L., & Oladunjoye, G. T. (2002). E-commerce infusion into business education: Encompassing the realities of an emerging business model. *Journal of Education for Business, 77*(5), 290-296.

Nielsen, J. (2000). *Designing Web usability: The practice of simplicity.* New York: New Riders Publishing.

Norman, D. (2001). *Invisible computing.* New York: Basic.

Novitzki, J. (2002). E-business education: A comparison of graduate programs and curricula. *Informing Science/InSITE Conference June 2002 Proceedings*, 1187-1196. Retrieved October 31, 2003, from the World Wide Web : ecommerce.lebow.drexel.edu/eli/2002Proceedings/toc.htm

O'Connor, M. C. (2002). The role of technology in learning marketing and management concepts. In Ann Remp (Ed.), *Technology, Methodology, and Business Education, Yearbook 2003* (pp. 148-163). Reston, VA: National Business Education Association.

O'Hara, M. (2000). A survey of electronic business and electronic commerce degree programs. *Proceedings of the 15th Annual Conference of the International Academy for Information Management* (pp. 60-69). Brisbane, Australia.

O'Hara, M., & Stephens, C. (1999). The required IT management course in AACSB curriculums: A comparison of the undergraduate and MBA course. *Proceedings of the 14th Annual Conference of the International Academy for Information Management* (pp. 264-273). Charlotte, NC.

Oravec, J., & Travis, L. (1992). If we could do it over, we'd... Learning from less-than-successful expert systems projects. *Journal of Systems and Software, 18*, 113-122.

Oravec, J. (1996). *Virtual individuals, virtual groups: Human dimensions of groupware and computer networking.* New York: Cambridge University Press.

Oravec, J. (1999). Learning from Y2K. *Ivey Business Journal, 63*(2). 20-25.

Oravec, J. (2001). Adopting teaching strategies to encompass new technologies, *Business Education Forum, 56*(2), 52-54.

Oravec, J. (2002). Virtually accessible: Empowering students to advocate for accessibility and support universal design. *Library Hi Tech, 20*(4), 452-461.

Pasnik, S. (1997). Caught in the Web : How online advertising exploits children. *Principal, 76*(3), 24-25.

Pedro, F. (2001). Transforming on-campus education: Promise and peril of information technology in traditional universities. *European Journal of Education, 36*(2), 175-188.

Petroski, H. (1992). *The pencil.* New York: Knopf.

Phillips, C., & Phillips, A. (2002). Helping business students bridge the gap with the real world. *Proceedings of the Allied Academies International Conference* (pp. 65-69). Nashville, TN.

Quittner, J. (1998). Levittown on the Web. *Time, 151*(15), 22-23.

Rob, M. (2003). The rise and fall of an e-commerce program. *Communications of the ACM, 46*(3), 25-26.

Rodger, W. (1998). AmEx, EDS may face European privacy lawsuits. *Inter@ctive Week, 5*(25), 8.

Schneberger, S. L., Parent, M., and Haggerty, N. (2000). Teaching e-commerce: A multidisciplinary approach. *Journal of Informatics Education and Research. 2*(2), 1-8.

Scott, M.. & Comer, P. (1999). The strategic importance of XML applications. *International Journal of e-Business Strategy Management,* 1(2), 1-10.

Sendall, P. (1999). A survey of electronic commerce courses. *Proceedings of the 14th Annual Conference of the International Academy for Information Management* (pp. 119-128). Charlotte, NC.

Settle, A., & Berthiaume, A. (2002). Debating e-commerce: Engaging students in current events. *Journal of Information Systems Education, 13*(4), 279-285.

Shapiro, C., & Varian, H. (1999). *Information rules: A strategic guide to the network economy.* New York: McGraw-Hill/Harvard Business School Press.

Surendra, N. C. (2000). Designing and teaching an e-commerce course: Two principles and a case study. *Journal of Informatics Education and Research. 2*(2), 9-13.

Taft, D. K. (2003, January 6). Microsoft boosts focus on XML-based services. *eWeek, 20* (1), 11.

Vijayaraman, B. S., & Bhatia, G. (2002). A framework for determining success factors of an e-commerce initiative. *Journal of Internet Commerce,* 1(2), 63-73.

Whitten, D., & Stephens, C. (2001). Development of an e-commerce model curriculum, *Proceedings of the International Academy of Management,* December, 2001, 85-86.

Wolfinbarger, M., & Gilly, M. (2001). Shopping online for freedom, control and fun. *California Management Review, 43*(2), 34-55.

Young, K. (1998). *Caught in the net: How to recognize the signs of Internet addiction-and a winning strategy for recovery.* New York: John Wiley & Sons

E-Commerce Degrees: Are They Merely a Fad or Academically Sound Initiatives?

Richard Clodfelter
University of South Carolina
Columbia, South Carolina

In recent years, entire industries have been reshaped and some have even been eliminated by e-commerce and the Internet. College graduates must be prepared to work and compete in this ever-changing world; however, the question remains of how best to prepare them. E-commerce degrees have emerged as a nationwide trend at many business schools as a means of providing that education and training.

Some experts believe that e-commerce degrees will soon be as common as computer science degrees and that no college will be without one; but, others believe that e-commerce degrees will disappear in five years. What does the future hold? In an attempt to determine if e-commerce degrees will be merely a fad, this chapter will first examine projections for e-commerce and identify the reasons for growth in e-commerce degrees. Arguments in support of e-commerce degrees as well as arguments critical of the degrees will be presented. Different types of e-commerce degrees, along with descriptions of several e-commerce programs, will be described. Issues facing e-commerce degrees will then be analyzed, and the future of e-commerce degrees will be discussed.

INTRODUCTION

There is no question that e-commerce is a hot topic at colleges and universities across the country. Jay Kridel, director of professional development for AACSB (Association to Advance Collegiate Schools of Business), a nonprofit organization that works to promote and improve higher education in business administration and management, stresses that, "It seems to be as big of a topic in higher education as business globalization was in the early '90s" (Ramirez, 2000). For example, eight years ago Vanderbilt's Owen

Graduate School of Management launched the country's first d-commerce (digital commerce) concentration—with one student. Today half the school is pursuing the subject, and the program has grown to include a dozen professors, 19 courses, and a center devoted to e-research (Lord 2000). What are the opportunities for these graduates?

Despite the downturn in Internet stocks and some dot-coms going bankrupt, e-commerce activity continues to grow. Although several online retailers closed their operations in 2001, total online retail sales still grew to $36 billion, representing 1% of total retail sales (Yen 2002). In 2002, online retail sales in the United States increased to $45.6 billion, and the *Internet Retailer* (2003) reported that this figure is expected to grow to 2.5%, or $110 billion by 2006. Through June 2003, total retail sales grew 6.9% while online sales grew 13%, and average weekly sales in the first half of 2003 were $875 million, compared with $775 million a year earlier (Peters 2003). Worldwide, e-commerce is projected to reach $6.8 trillion in 2004, growing at an annual rate of 68%. Moreover, the Internet already accounts for 3.8 million jobs, and demand for new workers is expected to continue to grow for the foreseeable future (Lawson, 2000).

Now that many of the harebrained schemes and weaker players have been eliminated, e-commerce has finally begun to find its niche. In fact, 42 of the top 50 companies in the U. S. are multichannel businesses—firms that have a strong presence both on the Web and in brick-and-mortar stores and/or catalogs (Yen, 2002). Most of these firms, however, are facing a critical shortage of professionals that understand how to use technology in business processes, and how to leverage business strategy based on this technology to add value to their firms.

As the evidence indicates, e-commerce continues to grow, and e-commerce degrees have been one of the fastest-moving educational trends to rattle the ivory tower in recent years. Yet, students wanting to obtain further training in e-commerce should prepare themselves for a world that is as unsettled as e-commerce itself. Programs range from undergraduate and graduate degrees, to certificate programs, to MBA programs with concentrations in e-commerce. These programs also differ in their emphasis. They can range from a heavy business focus to the hands-on approach of master-of-science programs, but they all have several characteristics in common—these programs have been cobbled together in record time, they are evolving by the minute, and they have been popular with students.

REASONS FOR GROWTH IN E-COMMERCE DEGREES

Demand has been one of the major reasons for growth of e-commerce degrees. "There has been a tremendous demand coming from all sides—students, recruiters, even faculty," says Michael Shamos, codirector of the Institute for E-Commerce at Carnegie Mellon University in Pittsburgh. In fact, more than 180 students competed for 35 available slots in the inaugural year of the Carnegie Mellon program (Dobbs 1999).

Another reason for the growth of e-commerce degrees is the change occurring in the business world. E-commerce is already taken seriously by nearly every size business. All businesses that want to increase their business efficiencies are examining possible uses for e-commerce technologies within their firms. Since almost every industry is being affected by the Internet, e-commerce is a necessary tool for people entering the workforce.

The rapid expansion of technology sectors associated with the Internet has led to a marked increase in the demand for graduates with relevant skills and qualifications, and the demand for experienced workers is rapidly outpacing supply. The new digital economy will require appropriately-trained personnel—not just those who have learned by trial and error. The growth and projected growth of e-commerce requires graduates who understand current and future trends in technology and are prepared to manage the analysis, design, implementation, and operation of e-commerce systems. These e-commerce professions will need skills in multiple disciplines, including computer science, economics, human factors, industrial engineering, management, and marketing.

Many companies that have embraced e-commerce have reinforced their market position; however, this will *not* continue to occur unless there is a supply of skilled graduates able to develop systems that are well-structured, reliable, and usable. The challenge for colleges and universities lies with the development of courses, programs, and degrees specifically aimed at filling this gap in the market.

In creating these programs and degrees, however, colleges and universities are facing some tricky questions. Potential students and employers must weigh the offerings based on how schools answer these questions:

- What exactly makes up an e-commerce degree?

- Should training concentrate on the technology behind e-commerce or on the business decisions required from implementing the technology?

- Should programs concentrate on some combination of these two components?

- Can both business and technology concepts and skills be fit into a single program of study?

Many academic institutions are betting that e-commerce training will meet the high demand for Web-conversant executives, but critics of the trend of e-commerce degrees think universities are exploiting its popularity, when what students really need is on-the-job training or a basic grounding in business.

ARGUMENTS IN SUPPORT OF E-COMMERCE DEGREES

Almost all proponents of e-commerce degrees stress that universities are simply responding to the needs of the business world. In fact, Cindy Claycomb, associate professor of marketing and entrepreneurship at Wichita State University believes that, "E-commerce is so important it ought to be taught in almost every class," (Mazzullo, 2002). Many other educators agree with this assessment. Proponents of e-commerce degrees assert that colleges that do not embrace e-commerce degrees will turn out unprepared students. With nearly every industry racing furiously to develop and implement e-commerce initiatives, the demand for experienced workers is wildly outpacing supply. Melissa Davis, marketing director for printing giant R. R. Donnelley & Sons Co., describes job candidates who combine information systems and e-commerce knowledge with an MBA degree as "golden." She even goes on to describe them as "hot commodities" (Baeb 1999).

Carnegie Mellon, which has long enjoyed a stellar reputation in both business and technology, strongly defends its masters of science in e-commerce. "What they learn is not possible in an MBA program," says Carnegie's Mukhopadhyay, referring to the intense focus on e-commerce and the hands-on experience that students receive from completing industry projects.

ARGUMENTS CRITICAL OF E-COMMERCE DEGREES

Not everyone in the field is as supportive of e-commerce degrees, however. "There's clearly some controversy," says Frank Wert, executive director of the Association of Collegiate Business Schools and Programs, an accrediting organization. "It's still not settled whether e-commerce is something new or unique, or if it is the fundamental principles of marketing, just in a different medium" (Armour, 2001).

Heather Biancalan of Streffco Consulting, a Denver recruiting firm that specializes in high-tech positions, believes that most companies want to see a candidate who has taken some e-commerce and technology classes—someone who has studied the most recent ideas. But, she adds that, "Everything is moving so fast that I don't think a complete degree program is necessarily the answer" (Dobbs 1999).

Because the academic picture is still unclear, some educators doubt that dividing e-commerce from the rest of business education is the best way to train the leaders of the new digital economy. While few schools dispute that e-commerce needs to become part of business school curriculums in some way, many educators think a more solid way to introduce e-commerce to students is to serve it as a side dish—as part of a concentration, rather than the main course.

The rush of colleges and universities offering e-commerce degrees and programs is also coming under more scrutiny as dot-com companies have fizzled and Internet business models have struggled in recent years. While supporters argue that academia must embrace e-commerce to stay current, critics say the topic has been overemphasized by colleges looking to raise money and shore up flagging enrollments. These critics say educators have put together slapdash e-commerce programs that may leave students at a competitive disadvantage.

According to Roy Moore, director of the Baccalaureate/Graduate Degree Commission of the Association of Collegiate Business Schools and Programs, an accreditation association for business education, schools are using the e-commerce hype to line their wallets rather than thinking carefully about what students need. "E-commerce is being blown up to be more than it is," he says. "I'm not sure it deserves a separate discipline. I see it more as a money-making gimmick" (Mitchell, 2000). In 1999, for example, graduate schools were receiving at least $24.3 million in revenue from tuition paid by students in e-commerce master's programs, according to a study conducted by *Electronic Commerce World* (Armour, 2001).

Detractors also say schools are straying from their mission of providing a broad educational foundation. "Anytime you find students chasing a trend, it's dangerous," says Carl Zeithaml, dean of the McIntire School of Commerce at the University of Virginia in Charlottesville, which has shied away from offering an e-commerce degree. He believes that, "It's important to give students a broader variety of skills" (Armour, 2001).

Robert Nason, chair of the department of marketing and supply chain management at Michigan State University, also speaks bluntly of the emergence of e-commerce courses. He believes these are fad programs. "The best programs," he says, integrate the changes e-commerce is bringing to the business world into existing degrees rather than slicing them out of the wider business context" (Mitchell 2000).

Outside academic circles, there are others who are skeptical of the e-commerce degree trends. Dave Happe, president of Ecrutiers.net, an executive search company that specialized in Internet technology and e-commerce, thinks that these degrees are *not* getting at the heart of what is needed today. He reports that his clients would take a young talent with six months' worth experience at an Internet start-up company over a graduate with an e-commerce degree (Mitchell 2000).

One side effect of the failed dot-com economy has been that many degree programs in e-commerce are facing an enrollment decline. For example, at the Illinois Institute of Technology in Chicago, only 10 students enrolled in the school's e-commerce program in 2001—compared with 29 the previous year, resulting in school administrators suspending future admissions. At Chicago's DePaul University, no students enrolled in the school's e-commerce program the first semester it was offered (Svetcov, 2001).

TYPES OF E-COMMERCE DEGREES
Universities have scrambled to turn the study of electronic commerce into majors and degrees. Some business schools have added a concentration in e-commerce as an option for MBA candidates. Other colleges and universities now offer majors, certificates, or degrees in e-commerce. Many of these degrees are collaborative programs between business and information sciences departments.

Research has shown that businesses are looking for a particular profile in e-commerce graduates, says Rob Nickerson, director of the Center for Electronic Commerce in the College of Business at San Francisco State University. They want people who can bridge the gap between the technology specialists and executives and manage the development of e-commerce sites and projects. Nickerson's school offers a Master of Science in Business Administration with a concentration in e-commerce. The program requires the same eight business courses as the MBA in the first year, but the second year is nearly all e-commerce.

Despite the uncertainty, some schools have already inaugurated various forms of e-commerce education. These degrees typically run one year and combine some business courses with courses in subjects like database management, computer security, and supply chain management. The idea is that while students do not learn how to create a database or fix a network, they learn how to communicate with the people who can—the link between business and technology that has become a crucial part of doing business today. If these degrees are lighter on business topics than a typical MBA, they certainly are heavier on technology.

Students at Carnegie Mellon e-commerce program typically enter the e-commerce program with degrees in engineering, computer science, or business. They usually have an average of seven years of work experience in areas like Internet business development, consulting, MIS management, and Web development (Mitchell 2000).

At Boston University's Metropolitan College, the master's degree in e-commerce, which launched January 2000, combines classes from BU's administrative sciences and computer science departments. The degree is geared toward both local working professionals and full-time international students. Program administrators feel they are probably attracting people who thought the MBA was not specialized enough (Mitchell 2000).

At Wichita State University there is not a degree dedicated to e-commerce, but students can get a business administration degree with an emphasis in e-commerce. A representative of the school indicates that there is no rush at this point to start an e-commerce degree because so many classes discuss it and have some applications of it (Massullo, 2002).

At MIT's Sloan School of Management, approximately 80 students participate in a discussion in an amphitheater-style class entitled *Proseminar in Electronic Commerce and Marketing*. Approximately one quarter of the class is female, nearly one-third are from countries other than the United States, and most students are in their twenties (Melymuka, 2000). E-commerce is a track rather than a separate program at MIT. Despite MIT's reputation as a top technology university, the school's approach to e-commerce is all business. "You don't need to know the details of the technology. How the technology interacts with the business model and the environment is what's important," says Melinda Rothstein, a second year student in the e-commerce track (Melymuka, 2000).

The MBA-with-a-specialization approach is typical of many schools, including Loyola University in Chicago, where the expectation is that eventually e-commerce studies will be absorbed into business classes. Nearly one-third of the 800 students in the MBA program are specializing in e-commerce, making it the school's most popular specialization.

A quite different approach is being taken by the Master of Science in E-Commerce program at the School of Business Administration of the University of San Diego. North Carolina State University also strikes an interesting middle ground between business and technology. The school offers an e-commerce concentration in its master's program in management; yet, the program is more technology-focused than most other business programs (Melymuka, 2000).

Michigan State University has dubbed its two-year e-commerce curriculum the Marketing Technology program and is housed in the Eli Broad College of Business and Graduate School of Management. Admission to the program is open only to students with undergraduate degrees in engineering or science.

OVERVIEW OF SEVERAL E-COMMERCE PROGRAMS

Carnegie Mellon was among the first of an estimated dozen U. S. schools to start offering specialties, certificates, or majors in e-commerce in 1999. Its master of science program is considered by many the most in-depth in the country. Students pay $38,000 to spend one year studying everything from fundamentals of Web programming to Internet marketing. The program, which consists of the equivalent of 14 semester courses, was designed to enable students to create and maintain a company's online business (Dobbs, 1999). Most other schools' curricula are less intensive.

At LaSalle University in Philadelphia, for instance, any student can qualify as an e-commerce "fellow" by completing two courses, a research paper, and a 40-hour internship. At the University of Florida in Gainesville, students can earn an e-commerce certificate as part of a two-year MBA program by attending seven courses; topics include Internet economics and online marketing. These programs are more condensed, but graduates still enter the work force with e-commerce portfolios (Dobbs 1999). Regardless of the program's depth, school administrators say graduates with any kind of academic credentials in e-commerce are highly sought.

Many colleges and universities are offering e-commerce concentrations as part of MBA programs. Many educators are eschewing this approach in favor of an actual master of science degree in e-commerce. The MBA approach is directed toward business students, not techies. This kind of focus helps a technical person see the big picture in terms of e-commerce applications and their implications for business.

Old Dominion University's College of Business and Public Administration in Norfolk, VA, has introduced a bachelor's and a master's degree in e-commerce. The university is one of only five in the country to feature an undergraduate degree in the discipline. Both degrees provide students with extensive training and education in all facets of using technology to manage a business. Both degrees consist of core technology courses, such as supply chain management, information systems, and programming with C++, plus courses in major business components of e-commerce, including legal issues, data mining, marketing on the Internet, and economics of e-commerce. "Our programs will teach students to apply business principles to this new frontier technology," says J. Taylor Sims, dean of Old Dominion's College of Business and Public Administration. "Through these courses and degree programs we will provide students with the knowledge they need to keep pace with the revolutionary changes that are happening in the business world." (Press Release, 2001, n.p.).

The University of South Alabama in Mobile is another school that has launched a bachelor's of science in e-commerce, as has Texas Christian University in Fort Worth. In its first year, eight students enrolled in the Texas Christian program with many more students on a waiting list (Armour, 2000).

Clemson University is offering South Carolina's first e-commerce degree at the master's level. The e-commerce master's program is the result of an interdisciplinary effort that involved key departments in both the business and engineering colleges. Courses in the degree include computer science, economics, industrial engineering, management, marketing, and psychology. The school decided to concentrate the e-commerce degree at the master's level because many existing undergraduate programs at the university had already incorporated e-commerce concepts into their curricula— meaning a basic knowledge of e-commerce was already a part of many undergraduate courses of study. The Master of Electronic Commerce degree program requires 30 semester hours. Entering students typically have an undergraduate background in economics, finance, marketing, and computer science. Students who do not have this background must complete these areas as corequisites (Lawson, 2000).

ISSUES FACING E-COMMERCE DEGREE PROGRAMS
So which type of degree is better? Academic insiders (Mitchell 2000) believe there is indeed a difference between students graduating with an MBA and those students holding a focused e-ecommerce degree. Although these programs are still too new to categorize definitively, it is fair to say that the master's degrees in e-commerce attract students with more of a technology bent who have some interest in learning the business basics, while MBA degrees with e-commerce concentrations attract students who wish to dig deep into the business aspect and learn enough e-commerce technology to give those business lessons some context.

New approaches must be taken in teaching "the moving target of e-commerce" at the college level. Implementing an entirely new degree is not an easy feat to accomplish. It is costly and requires lots of time. Changing a university's curriculum is never an easy task, and universities are not known for their agility. Now that many schools are ready to try to keep pace with business, they face hurdles in faculty, budget approval, and time.

Since a textbook on e-commerce would likely be outdated quickly, most e-commerce courses rely heavily on case studies of Internet start-up companies and older companies that have successfully implemented e-commerce initiatives (Baeb 1999). Students at Carnegie Mellon are put to work on real-world problems furnished by the business world.

Other challenges facing schools implementing e-commerce instruction are the shortage of qualified instructors and the lack of up-to-date course materials. One challenge is to find professors who know the subject better than the students who walk into their classes, and then somehow to keep those professors abreast of the myriad new developments in technology each month. The University of Pennsylvania's Wharton School of Business, which began offering an e-commerce major in 1999, already has 50 faculty members teaching or researching e-commerce to keep the course content up to date. Meanwhile, Carnegie Mellon's Michael Shamos, co-director of the Carnegie Mellon Institute for E-Commerce, says he and his colleagues will have to alter their entire course schedule nearly every semester because Internet business models are changing so rapidly. "I can't teach the same course twice," he says. "I can't even repeat the same lecture I gave a few months ago. The preparation is very time-consuming." (Dobbs 1999).

Because the academic picture is still unclear, some educators doubt that dividing e-commerce from the rest of business education is the best way to train future leaders for the new economy. Few schools dispute that e-commerce needs to become part of business school curriculums in some way, but more feel that offering it as an MBA concentration is the most appropriate approach. That might mean that these MBA students get the best of both worlds—a solid grounding in business and enough e-commerce to be able to speak the language of the new economy to those who do the technology work. Typically, students taking this approach spend two years in a program, take core courses in standard MBA fare, such as financial accounting and statistical analysis, and then add course in areas like channel management, electronic commerce management, and Internet marketing.

THE FUTURE OF E-COMMERCE DEGREES

Debate continues to swirl around the best way to integrate e-commerce into the college curriculum. No clear consensus has yet been reached. While e-commerce degrees may not be serving students the way that everyone wants, they are still attracting attention. Some experts predicted earlier that e-commerce degrees would disappear in five years; yet, they still survive, and many colleges are now adding them to their curriculum. However, it probably is too early to determine which types of e-commerce degrees best prepare students for the changing workplace. Intensive follow-up efforts are needed with graduates of these programs. College faculty, students, and employers need to carefully examine the components of these programs of study, and what benefits—if any—will emerge for companies hiring graduates with e-commerce degrees.

Colleges and universities must also provide programs to serve nontraditional students. The greatest unmet need is among a very large group of business professionals who received their degrees prior to the e-commerce revolution and who find themselves lacking the technical knowledge needed for professional advancement. Certificate programs may be the most appropriate response for this audience.

There will be a dire need for better educated e-business managers—graduates with an understanding of *both* online and offline business systems. Students can learn Web design techniques, such as JAVA and Flash, easily and less expensively with specific courses. However, education for e-commerce must involve more. Such education must draw on the experiences and lessons already learned from bricks-and-mortar companies and demonstrate to students how to put these lessons into action in e-commerce environments. The future looks good for college students taking this approach, and armed with such credentials, they will be highly desirable in the job market. At colleges providing this kind of preparation, e-commerce degrees will not be a fad and will continue to grow.

SUMMARY
As e-commerce education ages and becomes more mainstream, *it will change*. Many experts believe that over time the "e" part will probably vanish and simply become a standard part of all business degrees. Moreover, no matter how many times colleges and universities put "e" in front of their degree programs or certificates, the fact remains that the basic tenets of business are not vanishing anytime soon. To be successful, businesses still have to turn a profit, acquire new customers, manage growth, and keep up with changing times. In fact, integrating e-commerce concepts into traditional business courses instead of creating new ones may be the best approach because they work hand-in-hand.

REFERENCES
Armour, S. (2001, January 16). Degrees in e-commerce seem less dazzling. *USA Today*, p. D1.

Armour, S. (2000, February 23). "New major: e-commerce, *USA Today*, p. A1.

Baeb, E. (1999, August 23). Internet's ivy league: More biz schools tout e-commerce classes, degrees. *Crain's Chicago Business*, p. 4.

Barker, J. (2001, September). Old Dominion is among first in country to offer e-commerce degrees. *Old Dominion University Press Release*.

Dobbs, K. (1999, December). New rage on campus: E-commerce degrees, *Training*, 36 (12).

Lawson, E. (2000, November 29). Clemson University to launch e-commerce degree program, *CLEMSONews*.

Lord, M. (2000, April). Suddenly, e-commerce is the hot new specialty, *U. S. News and World Report*, 28 (14).

Mazzullo, L. (2002, January 28). E-commerce becoming key part of curriculum for universities, *Wichita Business Journal.*

Melymuka, K. (2000, November 20). Mastering e-commerce by degrees, *Computerworld.*

Mitchell, M. (2000, September 11), Are e-commerce degrees just a fad? *CIO.* Retrieved September 11, 2000, from http://www.cnn.com/2000/tech/computing/09/11/ecommercedegrees.idg/index.html

Online sales grew 27% last year, the commerce department reports (2003, February 24). *Internet Retailer.* Retrieved February 24, 2003, from http://www.internetretailer.com/dailynews.asp?id=8701

Peters, K. (2003, August). State of the industry, *Internet Retailer.* Retrieved August 21, 2003, from http://www.internetretailer.com/article.aspid=9871

Press Release (2001, January 13), Old Dominion University. Retrieved November 13, 2002 from http://www.odu-cbpa.org/ecomm.htm.

Ramirez, C. E. (2000, April 25). MSU e-commerce program quietly gains fans, grad students, *The Detroit News.* (n.p.)

Svetcov, D. (2001, November 11). E-commerce degrees: Fight or flight?" *New York Times Education Life Supplement.*

Yen, J. (2002, August 16). E-commerce is here to stay. *Forbes.com.* Retrieved March 12, 2003 from http://www.forbes.com/2002/08/16/0816sf.html

International Business Courses: Partnering with Overseas Students

Lila Waldman
Bloomsburg University
Bloomsburg, Pennsylvania

Reaching students through distance learning can be traced back to the 1700s, when correspondence courses were first taught in the United States. The evolution of the Internet is revolutionizing distance learning, especially when it crosses international borders. The continuing expansion of high-speed broadband Internet service will create an even greater global impact in the years to come (Government of Canada, 2000). Business educators who wish to expand their distance learning offerings to overseas partners need to be aware of many cultural and practical considerations.

Although it is difficult to know the precise number of institutions involved with international distance education (DE), a variety of sources list several institutions. In 2003, Athabasca University's Centre for Computing and Information Systems listed 12 virtual campuses, 27 open and distance learning institutions, 23 DE departments within conventional institutions, and 14 distance learning networks. These 76 institutions were based in 16 different countries. The Open University of Hong Kong's Electronic Library of Distance Education Institutions (1997) listed 48 institutions on five continents. Peterson's Internet guide (2003) listed 25 U.S. institutions offering international distance learning. Hoyle (2002) listed 24 international colleges and universities in ten countries on his Web site, "Distance Learning On the Net." The Japanese organization, Cross-Cultural Distance Learning (2002), listed 15 institutions "with the aim of mutual understanding and foreign language acquisition" in 12 countries—one in Hawaii. Marshall (1999) listed 19 distance education institutions in Africa.

INTERNATIONAL DISTANCE EDUCATION MODELS

Granger (1988) offered three models for the delivery of distance education courses: (a) courses offered through an independent institution dedicated to distance learning; (b) distance learning courses offered through a conventional institution/university—called dual mode universities by Dhanarajan (2001); and (c) distance learning made available by combining the resources of a number of institutions. Examples of each of these models are presented below.

Distance Learning Offered Through Independent Institutions

Although the best-known distance learning institution in the world is the Open University (OU) of Britain, the first independent institution dedicated to distance learning was the University of South Africa, founded in 1951 as a correspondence university (Willis, 1994). In 2000 it was announced that Britain's OU was to begin working with several British universities to launch an "e-university" consortium (Carr, 2001; MacLeod, 2000). The Swedish government announced in 2001 the establishment of its Net University with course offerings entirely through the Internet (Bollag, 2001b).

Other countries utilizing the open university model include Bangladesh, China, India, Indonesia, Israel, Korea, the Netherlands, Pakistan, South Africa, Sri Lanka, Taiwan, Tanzania, Thailand, Turkey, and Zimbabwe (Cross-Cultural, 2002; Dhanarajan, 2001; Murphy, 1989; The Open University, 1997). The African Virtual University serves an entire continent. Unsuccessful attempts to develop open universities have been made in Venezuela and Brazil. Despite some failures, this model is rapidly becoming the mode for developing countries, where open-university courses are offered under the umbrella of the country's government (Dhanarajan, 2001).

Distance Learning Offered Through Conventional Institutions

Programs based in or offered through conventional institutions or universities abound, especially in the United States. In large, sparsely populated countries like Canada and Australia, universities have for years been meeting the challenge of widely dispersed student populations by adding distance education to their conventional course offerings. International correspondence courses were offered through universities as early as the 1850s (Lewis, Levin, & Greene, 1999). Lee and Do (1997) wrote about an international distance education model offered to Korean students through Michigan State University.

Related to this are the large number of cooperative programs among established institutions, such as the one between the University of British Columbia (Canada) and Monterrey Institute of Technology in Mexico (Yawan, 2000). Lin-Liu (2002) wrote about the efforts of Chinese universities to cooperate with overseas institutions to develop distance business education offerings in that country. Howard-Vital and Rosenkoetter (1999) described the University of North Carolina's virtual university partnership with four universities in Japan. Private companies are increasingly gaining a role in the offering of distance education. In 2000, for example, the Partnership in Global Learning announced that "a collaborative effort between Bell Labs and universities in Brazil, Mexico, and the U.S. was being funded" (Lucent, 2002).

Tahach and Murphy (1994) described a continuum of collaboration in distance education. Their macro level was institution-to-institution collaboration, where different institutions worked together to offer complete degree programs to students at distance sites. They offered several examples of this type of collaboration, which they felt was increasing. Cited were a masters degree program in Library Science at the University of Arizona, which was offered via satellite to distant locations and collaboration efforts between the State University of New York, the Moscow Institute of Electronics, Tufts University, and Moscow State University.

Distance Learning Offered through Combined Resources

Granger's third model for international distance education combines the resources of a number of institutions; this can be accomplished in a variety of ways. Utsumi, Rossman, and Rosen (1988) proposed the idealistic Global Electronic University, "a worldwide electronic network and educational partnership of universities and businesses; of governmental, nongovernmental, and community organizations; of students, workers, and individual citizens" (p. 57). Some developments have already been made in that direction. The World Bank's Global Development Learning Network (GDLN) was launched in 2000. This network established partnerships with 31 distance learning centers in six world regions—Africa, East Asia and the Pacific, Europe and Central Asia, Latin America and the Caribbean, the Middle East and North Africa, and North America (Lorenzo, 2002). Taylor and Sharma (2002) advocated the collaboration of distance learning facilities in seven South Asian countries. They discovered overlapping course offerings and concluded that collaboration could produce "economies of scale" and shared resources, both items of importance in countries with strained economic re-sources.

Traditional distance education programs have been offered through networks or alliances for many years. The South African Committee for Higher Education, for example, has worked for over 30 years to offer courses through a consortium of international institutions, including the University of London (International Centre). China Radio and TV Universities have "formed close ties with many distance and open learning institutions" (Yawan, 2000).

Another way to combine the resources of a number of institutions is the selling and buying of courses. Rumble (2000) explained that this is sometimes done through franchising arrangements, a method more likely to be used by commercial institutions than by universities.

CONSIDERATIONS IN DEVELOPMENT AND IMPLEMENTATION OF INTERNATIONAL DISTANCE EDUCATION

Because of inherent differences between the traditional classroom and distance education, several considerations need to be taken into account in the development and implementation of distance education courses and programs. This is especially impor-tant in international distance education.

Learning Styles

Individuals learn in different ways. This is important to remember in courses of all types. Some of the problems with learning stem simply from the nature of learning at a distance, where students learn in isolation, away from instructor and classmates. International distance education, however, requires the additional consideration of the dimensions of culture and language. As Wilson (2001) stated, "The displacements in time and place that have traditionally defined distance education have now been joined by a third one: cultural distance" (p. 52). Granger (1995) listed seven "distances" to be navigated in distance learning programs: knowledge, prior skills, language, culture, context, learning patterns and styles, and learning goals and motivations; but language and culture were listed as most important in international distance learning.

Cultural and Language Differences

Heredia (1999) defined cultural learning styles as "those learning styles of an individual that are the product of his or her cultural background and upbringing." Therefore, no discussion of learning styles in international distance education can be complete without a discussion of cultural and language differences. Widely quoted in discussions on cultural differences is Dutch researcher Geert Hofstede. His 1986 article focused on cultural differences in teaching and learning. He stated that differences in teacher/student and student/student interactions can be anticipated in four dimensions:

1. Individualism versus collectivism (large versus small)

2. Power distances (strong versus weak)

3. Uncertainty avoidance

4. Masculinity versus femininity

International-Business-Center.com (2003) offered a brief summary of these four dimensions: *individualism versus collectivism* focuses on the degree that a society reinforces individual or group achievements and interpersonal relationships; *power distance* focuses on the degree of equality, or inequality, between people in a country's society. *Uncertainty avoidance* focuses on the level of tolerance for uncertainty and ambiguity in a society; and *masculinity versus femininity* focuses on the degree to which a society focuses on the traditional masculine work role model, which emphasizes achievement and power.

Hofstede's (International-Business-Center, 2003) fifth dimension, *long-term versus short-term orientation*, was added after later research. This dimension focuses on the degree of importance a society gives to long-term commitments and tradition, perhaps affecting distance learning, in that new methods of learning may not be as readily accepted in a society with a long-term orientation.

The first four of these dimensions will be discussed, as they relate to international distance education. Two additional cultural dimensions affecting international distance education are *oral versus written traditions* and the importance of *personal relationships* in a society.

Individualism/collectivism. In collectivist societies, the group is of more importance than the individual. This dimension is reflected in an educational setting by the behavior of students. Haulmark (2002) referred to this dimension in her research of Thai students who had participated in an online course from an American university. She pointed out the importance of individual student autonomy in most American online learning courses and stated that Thai students needed to adapt to the more self-directed, active learning style of individualistic cultures. Dunbar (1991) stated that Indonesian society was strongly heteronymous; he defined heteronomy: "The will of the individual is almost always subordinated to the domination of others and subsumed by the collective will of the group" (p. 176). In this society, learning is a communal activity, and learners are taught from primary school to "avoid behaviors or statements which may be construed by others to be expressions of personal autonomy" (p. 169), making them not prepared for the independent nature of distance education.

Power distance. Another of Hofstede's cultural dimensions, power distance, is also significant in a learning environment. Murphy (1989) stated that, in countries with a large power distance, learners are accustomed to "somewhat authoritarian face-to-face educational programs" (p. 3). This contributes to their being unprepared to learn independently because they do not have access to the forms of motivation that Western instructors normally provide. For example, distance learners in Turkey must make a transition from the traditional teacher-centered form of education to one in which they must function independently. Bates (2001) pointed out that "There is a tendency in 'western' cultures . . . to encourage critical thinking skills, debate and discussion, where student views are considered important and where the views of teachers can be legitimately challenged and student dissent is even encouraged" (p. 129). This idea is alien to students from large power distance cultures and can be evident in their unwillingness to perform in online forums.

In Asian countries with a Confucian heritage, students are taught to show "deference to teachers, unquestioning acceptance of grades, reluctance to express opinions," and a motivation to learn because they think they should, "rather than an intrinsic desire for knowledge" (Wilson, 2001, p. 54). Japanese students are accustomed to situations "where the teacher usually motivates through pressure on the students, who work together to support each other" (McCarty 1999). In Turkey, "Islamic tradition emphasizes rote learning and memorization" (Murphy 1989, p. 18).

Uncertainty avoidance. In societies with strong uncertainty avoidance, "students feel uncomfortable in unstructured learning situations" and "teachers are expected to have all the answers" (Hofstede, 1986, p. 312). In a study of Japanese students who participated in a distance education course with an American instructor, differences in lecture structure were noted. The students expected a discourse course structure, even though the course was text-based. The students were also unaware that key prompts were given at the beginning of the lecture; these types of structures are not used in the Japanese language (Wilson, 2001).

Masculinity v. femininity. Although the dimension of the masculinity/femininity extends beyond the roles of men and women in a society, the literature reflected some information about the role of distance education related to the role of women. Distance learning can aid in the education of women in cultures where they are not allowed to be directly taught by male instructors (Willis 1994). Women in many developing countries may be barred from traditional educational opportunities for a variety of reasons, including overwhelming child-rearing and domestic responsibilities; distance education can offer them opportunities to pursue education (Shrestha, 1999).

Oral/written traditions. "Cultures rooted in an oral tradition are likely to express themselves in terms of practical situations rather than in abstract terms" (Murphy, 1989, p. 18). Verbal (the use of words) behavior is more highly valued in Western cultures than Eastern cultures (Elliot, Scott, Jensen, & McDonough, 1982; Lee & Do 1997). The exclusive use of text in many distance education environments can cause problems for students from cultures with an oral tradition, such as Indonesia, "which emphasizes oral communication, in a society with a continuing oral tradition" (Dunbar 1991, p. 166)... Serious reading and writing are widely unpopular and not highly valued as a means of gaining or communicating knowledge" (p. 168). Turkey, a predominately Islamic culture, is rooted in an oral tradition (Murphy 1989). The island countries of the Maldives and the Solomons "went rapidly from an oral culture to modern electronic communications, without establishing a literary culture" (Meacham & Zubair, 1992, p. 3-4). Their indigenous languages are spoken languages. Therefore, the island nations faced the additional challenge of having to teach English to students so they would be able to take distance learning courses.

Personal relationships. Thai students taking an online course from an American university expressed concern about not having an established relationship with the professor; they wanted to be able to meet the person face to face (Haulmark, 2002). Japanese culture is "traditionally a face-to-face social system" (McCarty 1999). There is "strong emphasis in Turkey on social interactions, or their need for affiliation"; therefore, face-to-face interactions are very important (Murphy 1989, p. 12).

Language. Finally, language is an important consideration in the development and teaching of international distance education courses and programs. Today, English is the most predominant language used in the delivery of distance education (Bates, 2001). There is a natural tendency when developing courses and programs to use terminology that reflects cultural values. This can cause an "understanding gap" if the student does not have sufficient knowledge of the host country's culture. Instructors and developers need to refrain from using such phrasing or provide a glossary of definitions (Soefijanto, 2001). A "cultural discontinuity" can exist when instructors use content examples drawn from their own cultures (Wilson, 2001). As Bates (2001) pointed out, there is a natural tendency for instructors and course developers to do this. Even styles of writing may be a cultural barrier.

Language barriers for Thai students taking an online course from an American university were especially problematic when attempting to obtain technology support (Haulmark, 2002). McCarty (1999) stated that the "language barrier will continue to be the most intransigent obstacle to using the Internet" for Japanese. Bates (2001) also mentioned the problem of uneven workloads because of student differences in language fluency. Japanese students participating in the University of North Carolina virtual university reported that they found participation in discussion difficult because it was conducted in English (Howard-Vital & Rosenkoetter, 1999). Bates (2001) presented another view in his description of a collaborative online program between the University of British Columbia and Monterrey Institute of Technology: "The asynchronous nature of online teaching allows students to take their time in composing responses in another language, whereas in classroom contexts often the conversation moves on before they have crafted an appropriate intervention" (p. 129). This can be a benefit, especially if mastery of another language is a secondary function of the distance education course.

Appropriate Learning Materials

Researchers (Dunbar, 1991; Rumble, 2000) have pointed out how purchased DE programs designed for one cultural group often are not successful when used in another culture. Howard-Vital and Rosenkoetter (1999) warned that when it originates in the U.S., "distance education to other countries usually comes as a by-product of a distance education program designed primarily for American students" (p. 1). Therefore, the authors (Rumble, 2002; Simonson, 1999; Wilson, 2001) agreed that distance education instructors need to ensure that the learning materials are appropriate, both in culture and language, for the individuals who will use them.

Kenney-Wallace (2002) pointed out the problems that can result when educators view electronic learning as "just technology and infrastructure" (p. 49). Items as seemingly insignificant as colors and designs on Web pages and print media can cause cultural conflicts. She also recommended the blending of different approaches for teaching as a method for more effectively reaching culturally different students. Bates and Escamilla (1997) described a Web-based course designed for students from Mexico and Venezuela; they "deliberately kept the design simple and avoided the use of unnecessary graphics to ensure fast speed access" (p. 56). Soefijanto (2001) suggested that designers of electronic learning pages "allow learners to individualize their own pages." Hawkridge, Jaworski, and McMahon (1990), in their book *Computers in Third-World Schools*, wrote about the need to "nationalize" computer software and hardware for the country in which they will be used. They suggested such modifications as displaying the national language on the screen, right-to-left screen displays for Arabic languages, and language-specific keyboards. Another concern was avoiding cultural bias in educational software—often written in the English language.

O'Shea (2001) addressed another issue with the development and distribution of international distance education course materials: cultural values reflected in course materials that are either offensive or illegal in some societies. Developers of learning materials also need to be aware of the perception of many that such materials might be perceived as a means of infusing Western values in countries throughout the world. This is another aspect of culture that needs to be considered.

Of course, quality is important as well. Dhanarajan (2001) stated that a poor quality "commercially driven distance education" in Africa over 30 years ago had caused "perceptions of noncampus-based education as [too] second rate and second class to continue to persist" (p. 63).

Technology Access

Beyond the aspects of technology involved with course design, the major concern in many international distance education programs is student access to the technology. Many (McCarty, 1999; Of Haves, 2001) have written about the world technology gap or the "IT divide," the division of the world population into the "haves" and "have-nots," as related to information technology access and skills. If distance education is only delivered via the Internet, only those with access to the technology will be able to participate. Many of the poorest countries, where education is most desperately needed, have limited access to the necessary technology (Bates, 2001; Bollag, 2001a; Dhanarajan, 2001; Rumble, 2000; Ruth & Shi, 2001).

Educators in the Western, "technology-have" countries need to remember that there are many modes for the delivery of distance education. Lee and Do (1997) grouped distance education technologies into media types: print, audio, video, computer assisted and computer mediated. Lewis et al. (1999) classified the technologies into four generations:

- First Generation (Predominately one technology)

- Second Generation (Multiple technologies without computers)

- Third Generation (Multiple technologies including computers and computer networking)

- Fourth Generation (Multiple technologies including the beginning of high-band width computer technologies)

While distance education course developers and instructors may desire the latest technology available, they cannot dismiss the earlier generations when considering international distance education offerings, especially in less-developed areas of the world, where many people are still without access to electric or telephone service. Distance learning has been successfully offered for over 200 years through print media; it is still a viable method of instruction today, although even this method depends on a reliable delivery system and literacy. Dhanarajan (2001) stated, "A naïve faith in the new technologies to solve all of the problems of educational deprivation around the world is misplaced" (p. 64). He listed the following problems related to technology in developing areas: lack of access, lack of skill to use it, and the cost of providing the necessary infrastructure.

As pointed out by Ruth and Shi (2001), even in regions of the world where fourth generation technology is available, not all have access to the service. Therefore, until sufficient technology is available to all potential students, the earlier generations of technology will need to be considered.

Practical Considerations

With any distance education initiatives, different institutional methods of operation are required beyond those involving the teaching or development of the courses. Those practical considerations that are impacted when distance education courses are offered to other countries will be discussed.

Marketing. The first area affected when internationalizing distance education is the marketing of distance education courses. Too often universities utilize the same marketing techniques for international courses as they do for domestic distance programs. When Fitchburg State College entered into a program to provide their master's in education degree to teachers in Bermuda, for example, the school discovered that its traditional methods of marketing were not working. It learned that in the Bermudan culture, word-of-mouth was more effective than other, more expensive forms of advertising (Bohrer, Colbert, & Moran, 1998). Providers at the University of Oklahoma, after unsuccessful attempts at marketing distance learning programs to potential students, discovered that they had been targeting the wrong individuals and finally decided to hire a professional advertising agency (Beesley & Cavins, 2002). As with any successful marketing campaign, appropriate marketing research can help to ensure that the courses to be offered will meet the needs of the prospective students (Bohrer et al., 1998; Yawan, 2000). Bollag (2001a) quoted India's Secretary of Education, who stated that advertising for distance education had increased in India. "The problem is that the student has no way of knowing if the ads or the tall claims are true," (p. A30) he said. Problems of this type will eventually lead to more government regulation of distance education course offerings.

Student support services. Student support is important in any successful educational effort. Students from certain cultures, as stated earlier, prefer some human interaction to enter into the learning process. The Open University of Britain provides local student support through study centers in locations where sufficient student numbers make it economically feasible (Rumble, 2000). With the advent of advanced technology in distance education, students will require more support in learning how to use and troubleshoot the equipment. The key to success in international distance education will be necessary technical support (Perraton, 2000).

Currency exchange issues. Whenever money (e.g., course tuition) crosses international borders, the potential for problems arises. Problems that any international business must deal with are "…exchange rate fluctuations; restrictions on foreign exchange and the export of money from the country of operation to pay for services sourced from another jurisdiction; political turmoil, civil unrest and war" (Rumble, 2000). Bates and Escamilla (1997) related a situation in which an international online student had to deal with two different offices on campus to pay course fees and purchase course materials. Not only did the bookstore refuse to ship the books until all payments had cleared, but also sent the books through regular mail and did not track them. Consequently, the student was at a disadvantage from the start of the course.

Distribution of course materials. A department or office should be designated to coordinate the production, acquisition, and distribution of the print materials required in international distance education courses (Perraton, 2000). As mentioned earlier, there is a lack of technology access in many regions of the world. Unfortunately, other infrastructure problems, such as poor mail and shipping services, can make even first generation distance education problematic (Meacham & Zubair, 1992; Rumble, 2000). In addition, "the cost of accessing academic materials within developing countries is usually so high that students … have great difficulty acquiring books and journals" (Shrestha, 1997). This makes a cyclical argument for offering distance learning via electronic means, which, of course, is dependent on the availability of technology.

Customs present another challenge in the distribution of course materials. In the collaborative program between a Canadian and a Mexican university, course materials were at times held up in customs (Bates & Escamilla, 1997).

Copyright issues. Because of problems in the distribution of course materials and other factors such as the cost of the materials, copying in violation of copyright laws is commonplace in the international distance education environment. Technology has made this practice much easier, and many countries' copyright laws, if they exist, are not as stringent as those in the U.S. An additional challenge with electronic course material is the limitation of access, providing some means whereby only registered students are able to access it (Rumble 2000).

Registration and credit issues. Perraton (2000) wrote about the need for new practical arrangements, including registration procedures for off-campus students, when institutions make the transition toward distance learning courses. Alosh (2001) posed the following questions that need to be considered by all institutions desiring to move into international distance education:

1. Can students in other countries register for courses offered without going through the regular formal admission process?

2. If they can, does this imply that they are eligible for a student visa?

3. If students can register without getting a student visa, can they enroll in courses leading to a degree?

4. If so, how can they satisfy a degree residency requirement? (p. 353)

Thach and Murphy (1994) suggested that a distance education coordinating office could be helpful in facilitating some of the practical problems described above. They also recommended institutional policy changes to eliminate some of the duplication of effort and unneeded bureaucracy in dealing with international distance education students.

Role of Government

As evidenced by the development of its Global Development Learning Network and its financial support of the African Virtual University, the World Bank considers distance education an important player in global development (Bollag, 2001a).

Many governments around the globe have recognized that distance education is an affordable, practical means to educate a broader section of the population, "a way to educate more people for less money" (Bollag, 2001a, p. A29). The education of teachers is especially important in the development of a country. Therefore, this population is often the first to be considered for any opportunities in higher education. In response to government requests, a number of Asian open universities have run programs to upgrade teachers (Perraton, 2000). Meacham and Zubar (1992) reported that in the Solomon and Maldives islands the major clients for distance education were, or would be teachers, in the hope that "their additional training will permeate further" (p. 7).

Perraton (2000) stated that most governments support education, but that they do so for a variety of reasons "…because education is a human right, because it brings social and economic benefits, because of public demand" (p. 177). She assessed governmental education policy concerning investment in unconventional methods of education, such as open and distance learning, and found three major reasons for this support: ideology, economy, and politics. Idealistic reasons included social equity, empowerment of poor and disadvantaged people, and narrowing the distance between privilege and poverty. Economic reasons were mainly labor-related, meeting market needs and a better educated workforce. Public demand for distance education was the main political reason.

Another international distance education issue is what role governments play in it. As expected, national governments want to be in control of education in their respective countries. For example, Britain's e-University is being developed by the British government. Institutions wishing to offer distance education in another country need to be cognizant of the governmental regulations within that country. This explains why so many open universities operate within a single country. Litto (2002) blamed the "top/down model of control over education" (p. 4) in Brazil for halting the formation of that country's open university. Thirty different attempts to create an "Open University" had met with failure. McCarty (1999) pointed out that institutions wishing to offer distance learning in Japan must seek accreditation from a governmental agency. Bollag (2001a) stated that because of the false advertising claims and often poor quality of many distance education programs offered in the past, "all foreign universities that want to offer distance education in India will soon have to register with the government" (p.A30). Meacham and Zubair (1992) reported that "without the support of Atoll Chiefs in the Maldives and local politicians and government officials in the provinces of the Solomons, distance education is unlikely to succeed" (p. 7).

STRATEGIES FOR SUCCESS IN INTERNATIONAL DISTANCE EDUCATION

The strategies needed for success in any distance education program also apply to international distance education programs in business education. In addition to these, the following recommendations, compiled from seven sources (Bohrer et al., 1998; Dunbar, 1991; Meacham & Zubair, 1992; Rumble, 2000; Ruth & Shi, 2001; Shrestha, 1997; Yawan, 2000), are offered.

1. Remember that methods used in marketing distance education programs in one country will not necessarily be effective in another country. Learn as much as you can about effective marketing practices through partners within the country or marketing professionals with experience there. Consider the development of a partnership with an institution in the country.

2. Ensure that government regulations are followed and that relevant political structures are taken into consideration. Develop good working relationships with any decision makers in the hierarchy of the country's government.

3. Manage the activities of all institutional departments that must interact with international students to ensure that practical issues such as currency exchange, customs, and infrastructure are not hindering international distance education.

4. Offer the appropriate level of technology based on availability, learner abilities, and student needs. Consider all types of distance learning technologies, not just the most popular or most "high tech." Remember that cultural differences need to be considered in the development of learning materials.

5. Consider offering courses in languages other than English, translating course material into other languages, or providing the necessary support for those students for whom English is not a first language. Remember that using culturally specific examples and explanations can cause confusion for students from other countries.

6. Take cultural differences into consideration when developing and teaching international distance education courses. Hofstede's cultural dimensions of individualism versus collectivism, large versus small power distances, strong versus weak uncertainty avoidance, and masculinity versus femininity need to be taken into consideration. In addition, many cultures place a priority on face-to-face personal

interaction. Consider the inclusion of this type of interaction if at all possible. Consider offering a variety of instructional strategies. If international distance learning students come from a culture with a tradition of oral communication, expressing themselves in writing will not be as easy as it is for students from Western cultures.

SUMMARY

The March 2001 issue of the National Business Education's publication, *Keying In* (Online, 2001), gave examples of secondary and postsecondary business educators involved with international distance learning. In 2003, Peterson's Internet guide listed 18 institutions where a business education degree could be earned online. In 2002, the National Business Education Association (see "Institutions" in Peterson) listed 96 institutions with business teacher education programs; of those, 21 (22%) offered a distance learning program. The number of such programs is likely to increase in the future.

Business educators who intend to partner with overseas students should take into consideration the advice given in this chapter. They should determine which model of distance education is best suited to their course or program and the students that they wish to serve; the best option may be to offer courses through their own institutions or to develop programs of cooperation with other institutions.

When developing and implementing courses and programs, business educators need to realize that international distance learning is different from distance learning in which the students are located within their own country. Cultural and language differences need to be considered and accommodations made as needed. Educators should ensure that learning materials are appropriate and of good quality. They should select the level of technology that will be most appropriate for students in the country or region where the students are located, remembering that the latest technology will not always be the most appropriate.

Too often educators fail to take into consideration the many practical things that can make an international distance learning program successful. When programs are expanded to other countries, issues such as currency exchange, distribution of materials, and the role of government become considerations. Awareness of such differences and the strategies that can help alleviate problems can help ensure success when partnering with overseas students in international business courses.

REFERENCES

Alosh, M. (2001, July-August). Learning language at a distance: An Arabic initiative [Electronic version]. *Foreign Language Annals, 34*(4), 347-354.

Athabasca University Centre for Computing and Information Systems (n.d.). R.I.D.E.: Distance education organizations. Retrieved March 20, 2003, from http://ccism.pc.athabascau.ca/html/ccism/deresrrce/ride/Institut.xml.

Bates, A. W. & Escamilla, J. G. (1997, January 1). Crossing boundaries: Making global distance education a reality [Electronic version]. *Journal of Distance Education, 12*(1-2), 49-66.

Bates, T. (2001). International distance education: Cultural and ethical issues. *Distance Education, 22*(1), 122-136.

Beesley, A. D. (2002, Summer). Marketing distance learning with an ad agency. *Online Journal of Distance Learning Administration, 5*(2).

Bohrer, G. F., Colbert, R., & Zide, M. M. (1998, February 1). Professional development for Bermudian educators. Paper presented at the Association for Teacher Educators Annual Conference, Dallas, Texas.

Bollag, B. (2001a, June 15). Developing countries turn to distance education. *The Chronicle of Higher Education, 47*(40), A29-30.

Bollag, B. (2001b, October 5). The Swedish government has submitted a bill to Parliament that would create a nationwide virtual university [Electronic version]. *The Chronicle of Higher Education, 48*(6), A36.

Carr, S. (2001, August 17). With national e-university, Britain gets in the online-education game [Electronic version]. *The Chronicle of Higher Education, 47*(49), A27.

Cross-cultural distance learning (n.d.). Retrieved October 15, 2002, from https://ccdlsrv.project.mnc.waseda.ac.jp/ccdl/static/top_eng.html.

Dhanarajan, G. (2001) Distance education: promise, performance, and potential. *Open Learning, 16*(1), 61-68.

Dunbar, R. (1991). Adapting distance education for Indonesians: Problems with learner heteronomy and a strong oral tradition. *Distance Education, 12*(2), 163-174.

Elliot, S., Scott, M. D., Jensen, A. D., & McDonough, M. (1982). Perceptions of reticence: A cross-cultural investigation. *Communication Yearbook, 5*, 591-602.

Government of Canada announces commitment to bringing high-speed broadband Internet services to all Canadian communities. (2000, October 16). Retrieved November 11, 2002, from http://www.ic.gc.ca.

Granger, D. (1988). U.S. higher education and international distance learning. *The American Journal of Distance Education, 2*(3), 80-88.

Granger, D. (1995). Supporting students at a distance. *Adult Learning, 7*(1), 22-23.

Haulmark, M. (2002). Accommodating cultural differences in a Web-based distance education course: A case study. Paper presented at the 9th Annual International Distance Education Conference.

Hawkridge, D., Jaworski, J., & McMahon, H. (1990). *Computers in third world schools.* London: The Macmillan Press.

Heredia, A. (1999, October). *Cultural learning styles* (Digest No. 9999-10). ERIC Clearinghouse on Teaching and Teacher Education. Retrieved October 29, 2002, from http://ericcass.uncg.edu/virtuallib/diversity/1036.html.

Hofstede, G. (1986). Cultural differences in teaching and learning. *International Journal of Intercultural Relations, 10*, 301-320.

Howard-Vital, M. R., & Rosenkoetter, M. (1999, April). International distance education: The digital communities project. (ERIC Document Reproduction Service No. ED429504)

Hoyle, G. (n.d.). Distance learning on the Net. Retrieved November 11, 2002, from http://www.hoyle.com/distance/colleges_int.html

Institutions offering degrees or licensure in business education. (2002, October). *Business Education Forum, 57*(1), 61-64.

International-Business-Center.com. (2003). Geert Hofstede Analysis. Retrieved August 16, 2003, from http://www.cyborlink.com/besite/hofstede.htm

International Centre for Distance Learning. (2002). SACHED. Retrieved November 11, 2002, from http:// www-icdl.open.ac.uk/instResult.ihtml?inst_id=5901&p=1

Kenney-Wallace, G. (2002, April 16). Further education: Rostrum: E-learning is booming but the UK still lags behind, says Geraldine Kenney-Wallace [Electronic version]. *The Guardian, 14.*

Lee, I., & Do, J. (1997, October). *Principles and practices of international distance education. Global Distance Education Initiative.* Michigan State University. Institute for Public Policy and Social Research.

Lewis, L., Snow, K., Farris, E., Levin, D., & Greene, B. (1999, December). *Distance education at postsecondary education institutions: 1997-98.* Retrieved from the National Center for Education Statistics Web site: http://nces.ed.gov/pubs2000/2000013.pdf.

Lin-Liu, J. (2002, May 17). Chinese universities and overseas institutions work together on distance programs [Electronic version]. *The Chronicle of Higher Education, 48*(36), A39.

Litto, F. (2002, January). The hybridization of distance learning in Brazil: An approach imposed by culture [Electronic version]. *International Review of Research in Open and Distance Learning, 2*(2), 1-14.

Lorenzo, G. (2002, March). World Bank's global development learning network: Sharing knowledge electronically between nations to "fight poverty" [Electronic version]. *USDLA Journal, 16*(3).

Lucent Technologies. (2000, March 9). *Lucent grants $1.5M for distance learning in S. America.* Retrieved November 11, 2002, from http://www.bell-labs.com/news/2000/march/9/1.html

MacLeod, D. (2000, February 22). E-uni quest for best of British ambitious plans for an international web-based UK university are credible but can only succeed if resources are pooled as quickly as possible [Electronic version]. *The Guardian, 12.*

Marshall, S. (1999, November 19). Africa: Educating communication and development. Retrieved November 6, 2002, from http://communicationculture.freeservers.com/institutions.htm

McCarty, S. (1999, May/June). Japanese culture meets online education [Electronic version]. *Educom Review, 34*(3).

Meacham, D., & Zubair, A. S. (1992, November). Models of distance education for developing island states. Paper presented at the World Conference of the International Council for Distance Education, Bangkok, Thailand.

Murphy, K. L. (1989, March 1). A study of motivation in Turkish distance education. Paper presented at the Annual Meeting of the American Educational Research Association, San Francisco, California.

National Business Education Association. (2001, March). Online learning: A digital revolution. *Keying In, 11*(4), 1-2, 5. Reston, VA: Author.

Of haves and have-nots. (2000, January 21). [Electronic version]. *Asiaweek, 26*(2).

O'Shea, T. (2001, July 3). Education: Higher education: How to please all the people: The e-university is gaining credibility but faces acute cultural and practical dilemmas, warns Tim O'Shea [Electronic version]. *The Guardian, 13.*

Perraton, H. (2000). *Open and distance learning in the developing world.* New York: Routledge.

Peterson's: Distance learning internationally. (2003). Retrieved March 20, 2003, from http://www.petersons.com

Rumble, G. (2000, Winter). The globalization of open and flexible learning: Considerations for planners and managers [Electronic version]. *Online Journal of Distance Learning Administration, 3*(3).

Ruth, S., & Shi, M. (2001, May/June). Distance learning in developing countries: Is anyone measuring cost-benefits? Retrieved November 12, 2002, from http://www.icasit.org/ruth/distance%20learning%20in%20developing%20countries.pdf

Shrestha, G. (1997, April). A perspective on cultural and linguistic problems associated with distance education in developing countries. United Nations Development Programme. Retrieved October 30, 2002, from http://www.undp.org/info21/text/public/pb-pers6.html

Simonson, M. (1999, November). Equivalency theory and distance education. *TechTrends, 43*(5), 5-8.

Soefijanto, T. (2001, Spring). Culture in distance education. Retrieved November 6, 2002, from http://people.bu.edu/totok/culture.html

Taylor, J., & Sharma, M. (1990). Distance education in South Asia: Towards regional co-operation. In M. Croft, I. Mugridge, J. S. Daniel, & A. Hershfield (Eds.), *Distance Education: Development and Access,* 312-316. Caracas: the International Council for Distance Education.

Thach, L., & Murphy, K.L. (1994). Collaboration in distance education: From local to international perspectives. *The American Journal of Distance Education, 8*(3), 5-21.

The Open University of Hong Kong. (1997). Electronic library: Distance education institutions. Retrieved November 12, 2002, from http://www.lib.ouhhk.edu.hk/dli/home.htm.

Utsumi, T., Rossman, P., & Rosen, S. M. (1988). The global electronic university. *The American Journal of Distance Education, 2*(2), 57-67.

Willis, B. (1994). *Distance Education Strategies and Tools.* Englewood Cliffs, NJ: Educational Technology Publications.

Wilson, M. S. (2001). Cultural considerations in online instruction and learning. *Distance Education, 22*(1), 52-64.

Yawan, L. (2000). *Experiences and perspectives of international co-operation in China: Open and distance education.* Retrieved November 12, 2002, from the University of South Australia Web site: http://www.com.unisa.edu.au/cccc/papers

Opportunity with a Capital E: The New E-Technologist

Sue Stidham
Pittsburg State University
Pittsburg, Kansas

Brenda Frieden
Pittsburg State University
Pittsburg, Kansas

The integration of theory and practice has never been more critical than it is today in the e-marketplace. E-business is shaking the foundation of what worked well for businesses as little as three years ago. E-business affects all levels of the organization; a lack of an effective e-strategy negatively affects the profitability, and thus, the future of the company. Employers no longer have the luxury of allowing their information specialists to become immersed in the culture of the company through time-honored traditions of assimilation. Information specialists, who are now called business technologists, have emerged as the pivotal axis to companies' success as they switch from their pre-Internet days to Web-based marketing. The computer experts of the past often lived in an isolated digital cubical, where computers and computer specialists addressed specific technological problems that needed to be solved without person-to-person interaction. The strategic thinking essential in this e-marketplace has changed the organizational flowchart; now the business technologists will be sitting at the conference table with the top executives in an intense one-on-one approach to strategizing. These specialists must work at the confluence of business, basically at warp speed because time, temperature, and distance have all become moot points in e-commerce. The partnership between business leaders and business technologists must continually be focused on the changing architecture of the company, so that the focus will be on where the company is going, not where the company has been.

WHY E-COMMERCE IS IMPORTANT

Electronic commerce is important for several reasons, but two very important ones are its dramatic growth and its growth potential. According to Norton & Crook (2003), the adoption speed of e-commerce is unprecedented. While "electronic data interchange between large companies has developed steadily over the last fifteen years, there has recently been an explosion of growth in retail e-commerce and in transactional use by small business. Industry forecasts have consistently underestimated e-commerce growth" (Norton & Crook, 2003, ¶3). The following illustrates that growth:

> In the U.S. business-to-business e-commerce is now expected to reach $1 trillion by 2003. Similarly, business to consumer e-commerce is thought to have reached $7 billion in 1998 and to be on track to reach between $40 billion and $80 billion by 2002 (Norton & Crook, 2003, ¶3).

This pattern suggests that dramatic growth is being maintained and the potential for future growth has yet to be totally tapped.

E-BUSINESS CHALLENGES

Technology optimization challenges business technologists to perform under the demands of the warp speed of e-marketing, e-strategy, and e-commerce. Just as these three terms caused businesses to ask and address a completely different set of questions in their search for product growth and development, the same basic questions apply to the business technologist. According to Hoque and Gulbin (2001), the four main concerns an executive management team or CEO has are growth, effectiveness and efficiencies, leveraging intangibles, and using technologies. The e-technologist will be expected to address the fourth, technologies; but contrary to past assumptions, she or he will be expected to positively affect the other three areas as well. In the quest for the e-technologist, the first question might be to ask to ask what qualities are needed, and the second might be to ask where technologists with these skills can be found. As Hoque and Gulbin (2001) explain, technologists "typically speak only the language of applications, processes, and technology—they are, after all, technologists. But in this brave new world, technologists must teach business executives how they can use technology to create better business"(p. 1). Experts warn, however, that without "service skills [such] as how to listen, understand and communicate, the programming and product knowledge are useless; with these soft skills, it becomes much easier to learn and to satisfy customers" (Maccoby, 1999, p. 1). Basing her detailing of soft skills on research, Block (2003) defined those skills as follows: "...has verbal and written communication skills; has problem solving ability; has emotional maturity; has leadership attributes; has a willingness to embrace new ideas; has an eagerness to learn; has good manners; has responsiveness; has listening skills; has respect for others; and has teamwork competence." (p. 51)

Before the e-marketplace, the combination of computer technologist and individual with good soft skills was an oxymoron. However, in the brave new world, e-technologists must enhance their hard skills with soft skills. Companies are now seeking people "...with leadership, communication, influencing skills, ethics, political savvy, negotiation skills, and ability to manage competing demands, team building, decision-making and, of course, business knowledge" (Garner, 1997, p. 2).

The e-technologist needs "the political smarts to deal with high-level business colleagues, the business acument to understand why they want what they want, and the drive to get it done now" (Garner, 1997, p. 2). Obviously, bridging the electronic gap between the traditional and the new has created the need for the new breed of e-technologist. According to Bill Gates, the successful businesses of the future will be "those that not only use information technology in all the ways most of us have come to take for granted but in new ways that will provide them immediate, in-depth knowledge of their customers—and their needs" and "the winners will be the ones who develop a world-class digital nervous system so that information can easily flow through their companies for maximum and constant learning" (Casto, 1999, p. 1). Creating a digital nervous system that connects suppliers, partners, customers, employees and stakeholders requires a high level, holistic approach.

E-BUSINESS AND THE FUTURE

David Foote's prophecy is that "Seven to 10 years from now, there will be no information technology organization as we know it today" (Engler, 1998, p. 1). Experts agree that this prophecy is quickly materializing. Targeting online customers can be elusive. The first step in targeting an audience is to learn more about the who, what, when, and where of these customers. According to Scarborough & Zimmerer (2003), the baby boomers will spend approximately 5 ½ years online; current college-age students will spend almost 10 years online; and the secondary and elementary school populations will spend approximately 23 years online. This knowledge directly impacts e-marketing, and as a result, four minimum baseline technology requirements have been established.

1. Customers must be able to transact business that empowers them with choices and self-sufficiency.

2. When customers do interact with an organization online, they should have an experience that leaves them with the impression that the organization is an industry leader.

3. Partners, supplies and external stakeholders must work seamlessly to enjoy the benefits of a connected value chain.

4. And finally, this must be in real time. To the customer or partner, that means getting the right information and the right product or service, anytime and anywhere. (Hoque & Gublin, 2001, p. 4)

Thus, companies are now seeking e-technologists who are also visionaries, who can combine business skills and analytical thinking, and who can demonstrate an ability to master multiple specialties (Garner, 1997). The key word is seeking. The baseline question continually emerges: Where do we find such individuals?

For the world of engineering, Tompkins (2002) formulates a successful approach for "future-capable" companies of any kind. They must respond to change by being flexible, modular, upgradeable, adaptable, selectively operable, and automation supportive. He further states that the prospective successful company has a handle on the following factors:

1. Cost

2. Customer Service

3. Global

4. Speed

5. Certainty/Change

6. Control

7. Balance

8. Quality

9. Maintenance

10. Human Capital

11. Continuous Improvement

12. Synthesis (pp. 1-2)

Each of the requirements for a successful business can be applied to e-business and to the emerging e-technologist. In the changing world of the chemical industry, "uncertain business conditions and employee demographics will compel future leaders to develop more sophisticated skills to deal with both rapid change and the expectations of younger employees" (Van Arnum, 2002, p. 1). Further conclusions suggest that "top executives will increasingly have to become master strategists, leaders of persistent change, relationship builders and talent developers" (Van Amum, 2002, p. 1). When the e-technologists are placed within that setting, the same conclusions can be surmised—e-technologists must become master strategists, leaders of persistent change, relationship builders, and their own talent developers.

INFORMATION TECHNOLOGY IN E-BUSINESS AND THE IMPLICATIONS FOR EDUCATORS

The following skills in e-business have been identified by employers as indicators for success: clear communication, current technology, quality human relations, and good work attitudes. Schools must "…incorporate today's technology into their instructional programs and use whatever is available to enhance student learning" (Mansfield & Echternacht, 1998, p. 46). The business educator must develop and deliver a comprehensive business program with a broad curriculum and high standards, to teach diverse students about business and prepare them for business careers.

Information technology impacts the business world and greatly enhances the global presence of e-business. Business educators need to incorporate IT into the curriculum, making it a vital part of the educational process at all age levels. In order for students to understand how information supports every discipline and the ethical and social issues related to the use of technology, the Wisconsin Department of Public Instruction (2002) has established the following list of what students should know and be able to do in order to effectively relate e-business to information technology:

1. Access, navigate, and use online services.

2. Identify and use productivity software.

3. Use the integration features of word processing, spreadsheet, database, and graphics software.

4. Analyze spreadsheet data and database reports.

5. Identify and use communication software, such as fax, e-mail, and voice mail.

6. Design and produce documents using desktop publishing techniques.

7. Describe emerging hardware and emerging programming languages (p. 4).

The Department has also created an information technology scope and sequence for e-business: Grades Pre-K-4 keyboarding; Grades 5-8 computer application and keyboarding; Grades 9-12 computer applications, desktop publishing, e-business, information processing, multimedia applications, and word processing/keyboarding (Wisconsin, 2002, p. 3). By building business skills and standards into the curriculum, Wisconsin students will be better prepared for an e-business future.

Internship, Cooperative, and Work-Study Programs

Although internship programs, cooperative programs, and other work-study programs have been instrumental in producing the "pure" technologists of the past, these programs must now bridge the gap between conceptual and applied knowledge, and allow students to apply book knowledge to reality. Just as the rules have changed in e-business, the rules have changed for programs that serve as the training ground for future e-technologists. These programs must not only address the new technology that drives the changing needs of business, but also must prepare the "people with the vision to say what the next step will be in how we use the Internet for business purposes and to act first and ask permission later" (Garner, 1997, p. 1). While such programs have remained relatively conservative in the past, the warp speed electronic changes drive more aggressive approaches to this real-time dilemma. New careers, new titles, new job descriptions, all based on e-business needs, must be central to preparatory programs, which are charged with producing the diplomatic liaisons between the information technology departments and the noninformation technology departments (LaPlante, 1997).

Critical thinking must be the core of these preparatory programs. Brown and Keeley (2001), Nosich (2001), Paul (1995) suggest that critical thinking involves (a) an understanding of critical elements, issues and questions that lead to the pragmatic answers; (b) an understanding of which questions to ask; and (c) having the internal drive to address issues and questions for resolution. For e-technologists to face anytime, anywhere changes, highly developed critical-thinking skills must be in place.

Consortium Approach

The consortium approach to grooming future e-technologists has merit. In this setting, the education provider in the academic setting creates a partnership with a small group of noncompeting companies for the purpose of developing leaders in e-technology. These companies strategize to "tailor the curriculum to meet their company-specific needs" (Lawler, 2000, p. 1). The education and the provider select employees who have the potential to enter this specialized training. Paul Palermo, director of human resources at Perkin-Elmer Corporation echoes the success of this venture: "We recognize that the program provides a traditional overview, but we also recognize that individuals experience something on a personal level as far as gaining self-confidence, being able to lead teams, and being exposed to the combination of classroom learning, practical team experience, company presentations and case studies" (Lawler, 2000, p. 2). Beyond the obvious advantages, "employees selected to attend know that they're valued by their organization and that they're being groomed for greater roles. It also improves the overall quality of the consortium program because it means that you have a select group of people attending" (Lawler, 2000, p. 2). The success of a consortium program "stems from high-quality customized curricula, high-quality participants, and a highly interactive experience" (Lawler, p. 3). This model, according to Harry Safstrom from Dow AgroSciences, has value over the open-enrollment program for five reasons:

1. I'm assured of the quality of the content, because I have a chance to guide it.

2. I'm assured of the quality of the instructors because consortia tend to attract the very best.

3. I'm assured of the quality of the participants because we establish guidelines that we all collectively adhere to.

4. I'm assured that the content reflects current issues because we adjust it every year to keep up with changing times.

5. The content is more focused than it would be in an open-enrollment course because we know who the population is. (Lawler, 2000, p. 5)

This type of interaction, which leads to success, can only be gained through partnerships between education and business, working in a true interdependent circle.

BUDDY, TEAM, CONSULTANT, AND REVERSE MENTORING APPROACHES

Different types of mentoring relationships can be optimized, as long as the bottom line is enhancing the personal and professional growth of another. Gregg (1999) differentiates between four types of mentoring.

1. The 'buddy' system: New hires often benefit from being shown the ropes by peer mentors who have similar day-to-day responsibilities. This one-to-one interaction can supplement formal training and orientation programs, accelerating newcomers' productivity and fostering a sense of belong.

2. Team mentors: Although mentoring traditionally has involved a relationship between two people, some firms encourage their employees to work with multiple mentors, each of whom provides assistance in a specific area. Others establish formal mentoring teams composed of department managers, human resources representatives and senior partners, each of whom plays a role in coaching a group of selected candidates.

3. Consultant mentors: When there's no one in a company who has a specific skill set or the range of expertise needed, businesses sometimes seek the expertise of consultants to prepare middle managers to take on a new or expanded role....Mentoring provided by professional consultants should be balanced by mentoring from the inside.

4. Reverse mentors: While there's no substitute for the wisdom born of experience, some firms have discovered the value of infusing their corporate strategies with a different kind of knowledge—the savvy of their youngest employees. People just beginning their careers can provide fresh perspectives on new products and services and younger markets that can prove invaluable (pp. 1-2).

For e-technologists, mentoring from all four perspectives can be advantageous because each approach provides an opportunity to gain knowledge from a different perspective, thus increasing a broader overall perspective. Gregg (1999) cautions that "No matter what the structure a mentoring program adopts, its success depends on the quality of the matches made between mentors and protégés. Although a sense of trust is a critical ingredient in creating a mutually rewarding bond, real learning cannot take place if both individuals are not challenged" (p.2). Such an investment in the future, born from the marriage of a successful company and its top-notch employees, may provide a partial solution for finding and nurturing the new-age business technologist.

IMMERSION PROGRAM

In assessing the efficacy of the mentor model, a useful question might be, "What companies are using the mentoring approach and is it working?" Unlike many corporate executives, who move from one business to another, healthcare executives, like government employees, enter the business and then move within its ranks. This self-contained environment, while it has some advantages, can be problematic because of the lack of an external pool of qualified applicants. In a recent survey by Modern Healthcare, 75% of the CEO respondents said that they agree or strongly agree that executives miss or ignore opportunities to mentor effectively (Tieman, 2002). Sixty-seven percent of respondents said that healthcare executives create short-term management roles—but not career paths—for promising future leaders (Tieman, 2002). One possible answer is being addressed by a nine-hospital Memorial Hermann Healthcare System in Houston, where 110 employees are enrolled in a year-old program to groom them to move up in the organization (Tieman, 2002). Doug Beckstett, vice president of Memorial Hermann, says that while it's too early to have proven success, "...five years down the road we'll have 60 to 70 people better prepared to assume greater leadership roles than we have today" (Tieman, 2002, p. 2). Even with such efforts, the question continues to be raised as to whether or not the next generation of healthcare leaders will have the training and ability to effectively run tomorrow's hospitals (Tieman, 2002). Two earlier examples (Fisher, 1996) were Federal Express Corp. and J.P. Morgan and Co., Inc. According to Rick Nordtvedt, senior manager of development services in FedEx's Information and Telecommunications division, the combination of business and technology are critical to FedEx's success.

The new recruits learn about the products and services the IT division provides, and then they get a lesson on capital expenditures, budgets, and expenses. To drive home the point, they're asked to wear uniforms and assigned to ride with couriers in the company's rumbling white delivery trucks...Afterward, a trainer sends them off to 'The Hub,' the company's massive facility that sorts about 900,000 packages a night; then it's on to the customer service center to watch the call center agents in action, followed by a trip to the invoice processing center. Along the way, the technologists are encouraged to watch how the couriers, package handlers, and call center agents interface with computers. (Fisher, 1996, p. 1)

J. P. Morgan & Co., Inc. also believes in business training for their technologists. Their immersion program is similar in design to that of Federal Express. They want their employees to be immersed in the financial industry, learning about financial instruments, economics and accountings. Their approach is described by Fisher (1996):

> Hands-on exposure to the high-pressure financial world comes on the trading floor. Morgan assigns and develops spots on trading desks, handing out stints that last from a few weeks to a few months, so they can get a bird's eye view of the action and help out as they can. While traders bark out buy-and-sell orders, programmers create tactical applications on the fly. (p. 2)

Such hands-on exposure in the midst of real-time business transactions has proven effective for J.P. Morgan and other companies as well. A combination of the hard and soft skills can enhance the potential success of such an immersion process.

Tailor-made mentoring programs. Other companies have established mentoring programs and some believe that the best programs are tailor-made. For example, Travis Wolff, an accounting firm in Dallas, developed a "mentoring program whereby each new employee is assigned to a senior staff member on the first day of employment. The two-year mentoring relationship is designed to assimilate employees into the firm's culture and provide ongoing professional development of staff to help them advance within the firm" (Gregg, 1999, p. 1). Applicants, in a survey commissioned by RHI Management Resources, inquired more about benefits and corporate culture during job interviews than any other issues (Gregg, 1999). When promising applicants are weighing one company against the other, mentoring programs can be the deciding factor. Mentoring can be approached differently, depending on the need of the company and the new recruit. The following are examples of different approaches: the buddy system, multiple mentoring, consultant mentoring, and reverse mentoring.

The buddy system. The buddy system can be called by several names, but the intent is basically the same. As companies continue to try to find the appropriate solution for training the e-technologists, some benefit most from the buddy system model, as described by Gregg (1999):

> New stories [hires] often benefit from being shown the ropes by peer mentors who have similar day-to-day responsibilities. This one-to-one interaction can supplement formal training and orientation programs, accelerating newcomers' productivity and fostering a sense of belonging (p. 1).

Companies like PricewaterhouseCoopers use this technique but go one step further; they align the newcomers with a peer mentor who explains basic in-house issues such as where supplies are and how to solve computer programs. Then, after about three months, the newcomers are reassigned to a more senior mentor for the purpose of career objectives and higher-level organizational skills (Gregg, 1999). New employees can benefit from peer mentors who have experience and a proven record of approaching the company's future proactively.

Multiple mentoring. Another system that works effectively for companies is the multiple mentoring approach. In this approach, instead of assigning newcomers to one mentor each (the buddy system), the newcomers are assigned multiple mentors for the purpose of establishing expertise in specific areas. Other companies organize their mentoring into teams of department managers, human resources representatives, and senior partners, where each coaches a group of selected newcomers (Gregg, 1999). With this approach, new employees have a layer of mentors from whom to glean knowledge, which allows better balancing of the company's different facets.

Consultant mentoring. Consultant mentors serve a similar purpose, but the mentoring comes from outside the company. These mentors are hired from consulting firms when there is no one in the company with a specific type of expertise. While this type of mentoring can be quite effective, experts recommend balancing outside mentors with inside mentors simultaneously (Gregg, 1999). This type of consultant mentoring can be time and cost efficient and is often the foundation of multimillion-dollar businesses.

Reverse mentoring. Some companies recognize that newcomers offer fresh insight and approaches to the existing business. Therefore, they choose to use reverse mentoring, in which those who are just beginning their careers provide a fresh and youthful approach to new e-market audiences. Gregg (1999) cites the following example:

> A company with a product geared toward young adults may rely on reverse mentoring from employees who are recent college graduates and closely match the firm's targeted demographics. Acting as a 'focus group,' these individuals participate in meetings with more senior employees to provide them with firsthand knowledge of the trends and buying habits of younger consumers. Companies that create formal structures for this kind of information exchange consider what they learn particularly significant (p. 2).

By valuing the fresh approach of new employees, companies have learned that they can stay more competitive and reach a larger audience, which equates to higher profits.

BUSINESS LEADERS, EMERGING LEADERSHIP, AND JUNIOR ACHIEVEMENT

Some business partners and companies realize that partnerships between established business leaders and emerging leaders can be fostered proactively, rather than reactively. These leaders choose to build future leaders from very early ages through a visionary organization called Junior Achievement (JA), which has evolved to 158 affiliates, and reaches nearly four million U.S. students each year in cities, suburbs, and rural areas (Mavromatis, 2002). An additional 108 nations around the world are also involved ("Fuqua exports American dream," 2001, p. 1). This voluntary program consists of businesspeople, college students, and retirees who strive to bridge the gap between business and their own school communities. JA programs promote entrepreneurship and economic savvy, while giving young people the playing ground to develop skills for our global economy. The mission statement is that every child in America has a fundamental understanding of free enterprise. Jim Hayes, president of JA, said that the organization is a "positive, constructive message of great relevance to our nation's youth. It is a message that can be a powerful force reconnecting large numbers of our kids to the splendid realities and opportunities of life in the United States" (Hayes, 1999, p. 2). These reconnections are linking students in all levels of public schools to such opportunities.

While JA programs began in 1978 for both lower and upper elementary grades, the new program integrates themes for kindergarten through sixth grade. Mark Deion, president of business development firm Deion Associates & Strategies, Incorporated, gave the following example of how elementary students participated in JA activities in Providence, Rhode Island (Mavromantis, 2002):

> One of the things that they really like is looking in the Sunday classifieds and picking out a job they'd like to apply for. They can fictionalize their credentials. We'll have an interviewer and an interviewee and we'll do the interview in front of the class. The kids can dress up. The class watches the interview and critiques both the interviewers and the applicants (p. 1).

A similar implementation approach was enhanced when The Service Corps of Retired Executives teamed up with Junior Achievement to bring SCORE's business coaches into schools with a curriculum of reading, writing, and entrepreneurship. Some proponents of this combined approach are saying that the next generation of leaders may begin from the playground of American schools.

Such approaches led to a 1994-95 study which indicated that JA's educational approach had impacted the students. The research indicated that in each grade level in which the JA approached was used, students had greater comprehension of economic principles than comparison group students. Among sixth graders, the JA students scored 27% higher than the other students in basic economic understanding (Mavromatis, 2002). In another study at the high school level in 1992, JA students significantly outranked their peers in the Test for Economic Literacy (Mavromatis, 2002). JA's interaction among business leaders, schoolteachers, and students has proven far more successful than learning about jobs from books. As JA continues to grow and more students are positively impacted each year, businesses can expect a more highly skilled labor pool in the future.

Junior Achievers, who won the eighth-team national JA Titan, competed by creating an interactive computer simulation, in which students serve at the helm of a virtual cyber pen company. The simulation involved students managing everything from hiring to pricing, to investing, to marketing. Their virtual company strategy was high production and low cost (Kooser, 2001). By building such leadership at the high school level, companies can only benefit when these students reach their first real-time careers.

JA established a three-phase evaluation plan for formative, summative, and longitudinal studies, and the results can be valuable to existing and future businesses. One such study indicated a gender issue does exist. According to a recent poll, nearly two out of three boys think they will make at least $1 million by age 40, but only one out of three girls believe they will do so. Approximately 24% of girls believe they will make less than $50,000 per year by age 40, while only 11% of the boys believe the same thing ("The earning expectations," 2002). These same students indicated a trend that is now awakening some businesses to recruit top applicants differently. The students said that they would be able to get their ideal jobs, but 60% also said that they would prefer jobs that allow them more time for family and fun (The earning expectations, 2000). As a result of these findings, some companies are rethinking their recruitment approaches to make family and time off a significant part of their packages.

SCHOOL-TO-WORK

School-to-work (STW) or school-to-careers programs have similar components to Junior Achievement. These programs tend to "strike the necessary balance of state and local funding with business support and strong partnerships, in order to continue the innovative learning experiences that are working in so many regions" (Cutshall, 2001, p. 3). While the program was initially written to provide seed money for eight states, according to Peggy O'Malley, deputy commissioner and state director for school-to-work in Indiana, federal money is still very important to the programs in her state (Cutshall, 2001). On the other hand, Connecticut's program director, Ann Gaulin, says, "They have been thinking about the issues of sustainability since the outset and find that they will have[the] money [for] their efforts sustained" (Cutshall, 2001, p. 1). O'Malley warns that programs go away and sustainability is critical (Cutshall 2001). While these two states relied on federal dollars, Maine never relied on such dollars as a huge issue.

The programs have extended to the 50 states, and the states successful with these programs have addressed the importance of local partnerships among schools, business, and higher education (Cutshall 2001). One coalition, the National Employer Leadership Council (NELC) is composed of leaders from the National Alliance of Business, the National Association of Manufacturers, the U.S. Chamber of Commerce, the Committee for Economic Development, and the American Business Conference Council of Growing Companies (Cutshall, 2001). Hawaii approached STW metaphorically by comparing the canoe to their island (Hickcox, 1998). Students are encouraged to learn to work together as a team to prepare for their transition into the "adult community—acting responsibly, thinking critcally and creatively, valuing [the self] positively, working productively, learning effectively, communicating clearly, and working cooperatively" (Hickcox, 1998, p. 1). The entire core curriculum is integrated to address five competencies: resources, interpersonal, information, systems, and technology (Hickcox, 1998, p. 2). Together, teachers and business leaders have helped Hawaiian students to dream of a better tomorrow for Hawaii and have necessary life skills to be a part of that vision. Such coalitions are critical to the future success of STW, since sustainability rests largely local businesses from both the private and public sectors buying into the program. With workable coalitions of students, communities, and businesses, everyone will benefit, as both hard and soft skills—the curricular foundation of such programs—improve among the students.

E-BUSINESS RESOURCES FOR STUDENTS

Just as in business, comprehensive business educational programs need the integration of support groups throughout their curriculums. The following student organizations are examples of coalitions of business educators and students working together to build leadership skills, community awareness, recognition, and personal growth:

1. The Ewing Marion Kauffman Foundation supports youth entrepreneurship through grants, reports, and resources. (www.emkf.org)

2. Future Business Leaders of America (FBLA) is an association of students preparing for business and business-related careers. (www.fbla-pbl.org)

   The association has four divisions:

   a. FBLA for secondary students

   b. FBLA Middle Level for junior high, middle, and intermediate school students.

   c. Phi Beta Lambda (PBL) for postsecondary students

   d. Professional Alumni Division for businesspeople, educators, and parents, who support the goals of the association

3. The National Coalition for Empowering Youth Entrepreneurs, Inc., provides resources such as newsletters and online resources for young entrepreneurs, ages 13-21. (www.ncey.org)

4. The National Foundation for Teaching Entrepreneurship teaches entrepreneurship to low-income young people, ages 11-18, so they can become economically productive members of society by improving their academic, business, technology, and life skills. (www.nfte.com)

5. The Rural Entrepreneurship through Action Learning provides entrepreneurship education and training curricula for youth and adults in schools, postsecondary institutions, and community-based organizations. REAL provides hands-on experience in starting a business (www.realenterprises.org) (Inland Northwest, 2003, p. 1).

With this combination of strong leadership, universal resources, and a continued investment in today's youths, the future of free enterprise can only be enhanced.

STATE INITIATIVES

Some states have started their own initiatives. The Texas Scholars Program was begun as a joint venture between business and education in hopes of encouraging high school students to become interested in business. Businessmen can either support the program financially, give their time, or both. Lionel "Skip" Meno, former commissioner of the Texas Education Agency said that the "Scholars/Recommended High School Program initiative has caused more change in Texas schools than any other reform introduced in recent years" (Johnson, Johnson, Randolph, & Schmitz, 1998, p. 3). The program, he says, "is not a 'fix-all'" but "it is an excellent first step to building community support for world class schools" (Johnson, et al., 1998, p. 3). Postsecondary education has demonstrated success with similar initiatives. Obviously, one of the primary benefits of a state initiative is that real-time education can be immediately impacted because the layering between a state program and a state school system can be seamless and interchangeable.

Co-op Programs

Co-op Programs, like all other programs, depend on the foundational plan, the key players, and the win/win approach for all participants, especially for technology-based students. The paradox for new graduates is often that they can't get a job without experience, and they can't get experience without a job. Co-op programs and internships have helped to solve this dilemma. Co-op programs have been recorded as existing as early as 1906 and now total about 1,000 (Thiel & Hartley, 1997). One of the primary functions of the early co-ops was to help students with their educational expenses. Those financial benefits are still a part of many programs; additional benefits to students from co-op programs include work familiarization, self-evaluation, improved field position, broadened vocational vision, networking, knowledge, compensation, credentialing, confidence building, and positive change (Tobias 1996). Multiple benefits to companies come in the forms of

> ...recruitment leverage, pick of the crop, leveraging the student connection, easier access to faculty services, curricular benefits, value from the co-op student's work, useful insight into educational trends, knowledge from periodic reviews and the exit interview, keeps tabs on industry practices, good community and industry public relations, part-time teaching jobs for qualified employees, serving the institution's educational objectives, professional placement objectives, and competitive position. Additionally, enrollment benefits increase to the pool of qualified students (Tobias, 1996, p. 2).

Some schools use this same learning environment to improve intergroup relations among diverse student groups. One of the most "innovative widely prescribed strategies to manage and build upon the strength of the increasing diversity found in classrooms is the use of cooperative learning techniques" (Slavin, 1995, p. 1). When the students, the companies, and the school commit to the same quality objectives, with measurable outcomes, regardless of the approach, then co-op programs can serve all three populations as e-business paradigms shift.

CONCLUSION

Since research substantiates that the process for training e-technologists can begin as early as elementary school and transition through the upper grades and college, an all-inclusive approach must be used to prepare for this pivotal and critical position. Each approach, whether internship, consortium, mentoring, company training, or partnership, has strengths and weaknesses. E-business and educators must strategize to extract the best of each of these approaches and combine them into one seamless, effective long-term, preparatory program. Key players in this "anytime, anywhere" e-marketplace must commit to "growing their own" e-technologists, and there is no short cut. E-businesses no longer have the luxury of CEOs using past successes to make all the decisions that impact their companies. The warp speed of e-marketing, e-strategizing and e-commerce allows little time for reflection of what worked in the past, but requires a targeted balance between technology optimization and the changing needs of the electronic customer. The need for the e-technologists will only become a larger divide between companies that maintain their profitability and thus continue to secure their futures in the Web-based environment and those that do not. Simply said, e-technologists will be the driving force between the haves and have-nots of future e-business survivability.

REFERENCES

Block, B. (2003, February). Soft skills. Are you a walky-talky? *Business Education Forum*, 57(3), 51-53.

Brown, M.N., & Keeley, S. (2001). *Asking the right questions, a guide to critical thinking*. Upper Saddle River, NJ: Prentice Hall.

Casto, J. E. (1999, May 29). Bill Gates' way to high-tech heaven. [Electronic Version]. *Editor & Publisher, the Fourth Estate*, 132(22), 36-7, 2 pp. Retrieved January 3, 2003, from OCLC FirstSearch/BBP199044600.

Cutshall, S. (2001, January). Facing tomorrow: The future of school-to-work funding. [Electronic Version]. *Techniques*, 76(1), 26-8, 2 pp. Retrieved January 4, 2003, from OCLC FirstSearch/BED101000040.

The earning expectations gap between boys and girls. (2002, March). [Electronic Version]. *Techniques*, 77(3), 11(1), 1 p. Retrieved January 3, 2003, from Infotrac Expanded Academic ASAP/A84148556.

Engler, N. (1998, November 16). The new business technologists. [Electronic Version]. *Computerworld*, 106(1), 3 pp. Retrieved March 18, 2003, from Infotrac Expanded Academic ASAP/34892948.

Fisher, S.E. (1996, February 19). Hands-on training. [Electronic Version]. *PC Week*, 13(7), E1(2), 2 pp. Retrieved January 4, 2003, from Infotrac Expanded Academic ASAP/A18015557.

Fuqua exports American dream: J.B. Fuqua has always seen the value in education and it has been at the center of his philanthropic efforts. The most recent example is a $4 million gift to Junior Achievement International (2001, September). [Electronic Version]. *Fund Raising Management*, 32(27), 32(2), 2 pp. Retrieved January 3, 2003, from Infotrac Expanded Academic ASAP/A80542335.

Garner, R. (1997, September 29). Driving forces. [Electronic Version]. *Computerworld*, 32(39), 90(2), 3 pp. Retrieved January 4, 2003, from Infotrac Expanded Academic ASAP/A19817338.

Gregg, C. (1999, November). Someone to look up to. [Electronic Version]. *Journal of Accountancy*, 188(5), 89-91, 4 pp. Retrieved January 2, 2003, from OCLC FirstSearch/BBP199090761.

Hayes, J. (1999, October). Junior achievement: Building communities, changing lives. [Electronic Version]. *Executive Speeches*, 14(12), 13, 3 pp. Retrieved January 4, 2003, from Infotrac Expanded Academic ASAP/A65226118.

Haynes, T. & Bailey, G. (2003 February). Are you and your basic business students asking the right questions? *Business Education Forum*, 57(3), 33-37.

Hickcox, A.K. (1998, May). The canoe is their island. [Electronic Version]. *Educational Leadership*, 55(8), 58-59, 2 pp. Retrieved January 3, 2003, from OCLC FirstSearch/ 03749595.

Hoque, F. & Gilbin, P. (2001, February). Can you solve the business–technology disconnect? [Electronic Version]. *e-Business Advisor*, 19(2), 26, 6 pp. Retrieved January 3, 2003, from Infotrac Expanded Academic ASAP/A70769930.

Inland Northwester Virtual Incubator. (2003). E-commerce resources for youth. Retrieved March 19, 2003, from http://www.invi.tincan.org/services/ young_entrepreneurs/youth_resources.php

Johnson, W., Johnson, A.M., Randolph, J., & Schmitz, M.A. (1998, June). Texas scholars: Investing in the future. [Electronic Version]. *Phi Delta Kappan*, 79(10), 781-783, 3 pp. Retrieved January 5, 2003, from OCLC FirstSearch/03782361.

Kooser, A. C. (2001, May). We have a winner. [Electronic Version]. *Entrepreneur*, 29(5), 16, 1 p. Retrieved January 4, 2003, from Infotrac Expanded Academic ASAP/A74699904.

LaPlante, A. (1997, September 1). Charting new waters. [Electronic Version]. *Computerworld*, 31(35). 6 pp. Retrieved March 18, 2003, from Infotrac Expanded Academic ASAP/34892948.

Lawler, W. (2000, March). The consortium approach to grooming future leaders. [Electronic Version]. *Training and Development*, 54(3), 53-7, 5 pp. Retrieved January 5, 2003, from OCLC FirstSearch/BBP100023533.

Maccoby, Michael (1999, January/February). Find young leaders or lose them. [Electronic Version]. *Research Technology Management*, 42(1), 58-9, 2 pp. Retrieved January 5, 2003, from OCLC First Search/BBP199009170.

Mavromatis, K.A. (2001, May 26). JA: Turning kids on to careers. [Electronic Version]. *Providence Business News*, 15(49), 1, 1p. Retrieved January 3, 2003, from Infotrac Expanded Academic ASAP/A73274737.

Mansfield, J. & Echternacht, L. (1998). *Integrating the internet into the business curriculum*. Reston, VA: National Business Education Association.

Norton, J. & Crook, C., Speakers. (2003). The business/financial dimension of the information revolution. Retrieved March 18, 2003, from http://www.rand.org/publications/CF/CF154/CF154.chap5.html

Nosich, G. (2001). *Learning to think things through: A guide to critical thinking in the curriculum*. Upper Saddle River, NJ: Prentice Hall.

Paul, R. (1995). *Critical thinking: How to prepare students for a rapidly changing world*. Santa Tosa, CA: Foundation for Critical Thinking.

Scarborough, N.M. & Zimmerer, T.W. (2003). *Effective small business management: An entrepreneurial approach*. New Jersey: Prentice Hall.

Slavin, R.E. & Cooper, R. (1999, Winter). Improving intergroup relations: Lessons learned from cooperative learning programs. [Electronic Version]. *Journal of Social Issues*. Retrieved January 3, 2003, from Infotrac Expanded Academic ASAP/A62521561.

Thiel, G. R. & Hartley, N.T. (1997, Summer). Cooperative education: a natural synergy between business and academia. [Electronic Version]. *SAM Advanced Management Journal*, 62(3), 19(6), 7 pp. Retrieved January 5, 2003, from Infotrac Expanded Academic ASAP/A20095841.

Tieman, J. (2002, June 10). Take me to your leader. [Electronic Version]. *Modern Healthcare*, 32(23), 10, 1 p. Retrieved March 18, 2003, from OCLC FirstSearch/ BBP102124354.

Tobias, A.J. (1996, September 30). Co-op programs a good deal all around. [Electronic Version]. *Electronic Engineering Times*, 921, 142(3), 3 p. Retrieved January 4, 2003, from Infotrac Expanded Academic ASAP/A18751387.

Tompkins, J.A. (2002, April). Management side of engineering: Improvement builds road to success. [Electronic Version]. *Plant Engineering*, 56(4), 28, 30, 32, 3 pp. Retrieved January 3, 2003, from OCLC FirstSearch/BAST02115125.

Van Arnum, P. & Sauer, P. (2002 June 3). The changing workforce of the chemical industry. [Electronic Version]. *Chemical Market Reporter*, 261(22), FR22, 1 p. Retrieved March 18, 2003, from OCLC FirstSearch/BBP102123699.

Wisconsin Department of Public Instruction. (2002). Program standards for business. Retrieved January 21, 2003, from http://www.dpi.state.wi.us/dpi/dlsis/let/pdf/ busedart.pdf

Collaborative Telelearning: Project Management

Tamra Davis
Tulsa Community College
Tulsa, Oklahoma

Many studies have been completed on the value of *collaborative learning*. These studies have shown that collaborative learning can increase student satisfaction and achievement by increasing student motivation and the perception of value in the learning projects. Collaboration also provides a built-in support network for students. Collaborative learning is an instructional method that allows "students at various performance levels [to] work together in small groups toward a common goal. The students are responsible for one another's learning as well as their own" (Gokhale, 1995, p. 1). Collaborative learning environments provide an opportunity for students to interact and create a synergy that is missing in individual learning environments.

Telelearning, distance learning, online learning, and correspondence study are all terms for the world of electronic learning ("e-learning"), a world that is growing at exponential rates in education. The number of distance learning students grew from just over 700,000 in 1998 to over 2.2 million in 2002 (Moore, Winograd, & Lange, 2001). Simple uses of distance learning can be found in elementary schools and include Internet research, e-mail, and instant messaging. More advanced features of distance learning can be found in secondary, postsecondary, college, and university classrooms, including classes that are delivered 100% online. Many educators utilize telelearning techniques to varying extents in their classrooms. Online learning offers many opportunities "in extending communication and the availability of resources outside of the classroom" (Moore, Winograd, & Lange, 2001, p. 1.3).

The integration of a telelearning component into the collaborative teaching model allows distance learners to collaborate with one another, eliminating the downside of online education—working in isolation. This chapter will discuss the merits of the integration of collaborative learning and telelearning.

WHY COLLABORATIVE TELELEARNING?

According to Wegerif (1998) and referenced by Moore, Winograd, and Lange (2001), "Community in the classroom can be an integral part of the learning process. Students who feel respected and valued by their peers will begin to interact on a deeper, more meaningful level, will be more open to risk-taking in learning and will begin to engage in collaborative learning" (p. 2.5). Research also indicates, "Students learn best when they are actively involved in the process" (Davis, 1993, p. 1).

The question has been raised about how a collaborative learning environment can be built in the online classroom. "Surprisingly, because of its very anonymity and the time that it allows for individual reflection, the asynchronous learning environment can create as strong a sense of community among students as can the face-to-face classroom, especially if the instructor designs the course around collaborative learning activities" (Moore, Winograd, & Lange, 2001, p. 2.6). This is good news for the millions of students entering the online learning environment.

Face-to-face collaboration has been a part of the business community for decades (personal communication, TCC Business Advisory Board, April 2003). As the business world continues to evolve through the use of technology, Internet collaboration will continue to gain importance, especially as businesses continue to expand globally. Minor and Scifres (personal communication, February 2003) stated, "If we combine collaboration with the Internet as part of a regular academic setting, we can give our students that real world experience", that motivates and enhances course value for them. Collaborative learning is not a tool for every learning situation, but is extremely valuable when used appropriately. For collaborative learning to be successful, "teachers must consider the purposes in designing group work and address potential problems of process" (Blumenfeld, Marx, Soloway, & Krajcik, 1996, p. 37). Gokhale (1995) also wrote about the effectiveness of collaborative learning. Simply stated, "For collaborative learning to be effective, the instructor must view teaching as a process of developing and enhancing students' ability to learn . . . This involves creating and managing meaningful learning experiences and stimulating students' thinking through real world problems" (p. 1).

In addition to the synergy that grows from the exchange of ideas between students, the development of critical-thinking skills through interactive assignments will also occur. Regardless of the learning medium, successful learners appear to have four characteristics in common: "They are knowledgeable, self-determined, strategic, and empathetic thinkers" (Tinzmann, et. al., 1990, p. 1). In order to help students be successful, "effective communication and collaboration are essential" (Tinzmann, et. al., 1990, p. 1).

DESIGNING COLLABORATIVE ACTIVITIES

As the instructor, one must complete certain tasks before successful learning can take place. The first task is to design a plan for collaboration, followed by an explanation of how the project will operate and how grades will be assigned. Next, the instructor should provide the students with the needed skills for success, and finally, if appropriate, the instructor should present a written contract (Davis, 1993), spelling out course requirements. The course plan should include an explanation of how the collaborative project will fit into the overall scope of the course. The instructor must determine the nature of the project, objectives to be met, and grading criteria. After planning the project, explain the project to the students. The explanation should include enough detail to provide each team member with the necessary information to complete the assignment. A complete disclosure of how grades will be determined is another imperative to the success of the project. One way to provide a complete description of the grading process is to create a rubric for grading and give the team members a copy. Another requirement for success of the collaboration project is to make sure that the students possess the needed skills for success. As the instructor, determine what these skills are in advance and teach a unit covering them. Finally, if it is determined to be appropriate, prepare and use a written contract with the instructor and among the team members.

According to Barbara Gross Davis (1993), the first step in designing successful collaborative activities is to create a task that requires interdependence. The students need to perceive a "sink or swim" attitude for the task. Next, make the collaboration relevant to the course. Busywork is not an option for successful collaborative activities. Match the assignment to the skills of the students as the third step in designing the successful project, followed by creating a fair division of labor for the task. The fifth step in the design is to create friendly competition between the groups when possible, and finally, consider group tests in which each group member receives the group score.

Organizing Groups

Organization of the group is important. As the instructor, learn the personalities, strengths, and weaknesses of the students. Then select a method for assigning the groups. A few methods of group selection include random group assignments, student choice, and careful selection based upon the individual skills of the students. For projects with large percentages of the overall course grade, the group selection must be more carefully planned.

One method for random group selection utilizes a deck of standard playing cards. Select from the deck an appropriate combination of cards and allow each student to draw a card. If six groups of four students are needed, the instructor selects all of the two through seven cards from the deck. The students are then placed in groups by the face value of the card that they drew. Another random selection method involves mini candy bars. If five groups of three students are needed for the project, place three pieces of five different varieties of candy bars in a bowl. Allow each student to select a candy bar from the bowl. Students with the same type of candy bar become team members. Once the groups are formed, allow the students to enjoy the treat.

Group size is also important. Small groups of three or four students work best for short-term projects, while long-term projects benefit from using the skills of more group members. Groups of six or seven team members should be the maximum size for most projects. Once the groups are formed, it is very important for the instructor to stay in contact with the group. Monitor the group dynamics for conflicts, but avoid changing the group members from one group to another. Learning to work through personality conflicts is an important part of learning to work in a group (personal communication, TCC Business Advisory Board, April 2003). Blumenfeld (1996) stated, "Effective group work requires students to share ideas, take risks, disagree with and listen to others, and generate and reconcile points of view" (p. 38). Another way to provide a real-world work scenario utilizes a "quit and fire" process. If one group member believes that he/she is doing an extraordinary amount of work compared to other team members, then that team member should discuss the problem with the team. The instructor acts as a mediator for the team members. If a compromise is not possible, the team member (as a last resort) can "look for another job" with a different team and "quit" the original team. Along the same lines, a team member who is not contributing to the group can receive job counseling about the productivity issue and can be "fired" if a plan for improvement is not met. The fired member must then attempt to be rehired by the team, find another team willing to hire him/her, complete the entire project alone, or receive a failing grade on the project.

Tools for Collaborative Telelearning

When an instructor first proposes a collaborative telelearning model, some students balk—they seek the freedom of the "learn anywhere, anytime" distance-learning classroom. This initial drawing card for students often turns into a major disadvantage for them. The asynchronous format, very similar to the traditional independent study courses, does not provide the student an opportunity for collaborative learning. In time, students often find that they miss the interaction with other students and/or the instructor when taking asynchronous online classes. Effective, successful distance learning instructors utilize the learning community and encourage interaction between the students.

The use of technology to facilitate group learning defines collaborative telelearning. "Technologies such as e-mail increase opportunities for conversations by enabling large groups of students to exchange data and share observations in asynchronous conversations" (Blumenfeld, 1996, p. 39). Other technologies allow for synchronous dialogue. Many of the telelearning formats record the conversations digitally, providing a record of the dialog for future reference.

Most online delivery platforms include asynchronous learning tools, such as the discussion board or threaded discussions, plus synchronous tools in the form of virtual chat. Three of the more popular classroom management platforms are Blackboard® (http://www.blackboard.com), WebCT® (http://about.webct.com), and eCollege® (http://www.ecollege.com).

Virtual chat. Available through many e-mail services and classroom management tools, chat is a real-time method or synchronous form of communication that allows students and instructors to interact with each other. The main advantages of chat include the opportunity for conversation and feedback. The instructor must be flexible when using this format because of the inherent delay between the student reading a posting and the student response being visible in the chat room. In order to overcome the disadvantage of a time delay, structure is required. It is the instructor's responsibility to provide the guidelines to make the tool work. Hints for success in chat are given later in the chapter. A second advantage of virtual chat is that it simulates real-time conversations. Although the student may not take the time to form complete or accurate responses, the effect simulates the traditional classroom conversation. Students working from dial-up modems, however, are at a disadvantage in virtual chat situations. Chat is often a very large program and may not load successfully on older or slower computers. For some students, chat may load, but it will react so slowly that frustration with the technology counteracts all the intended benefits of the activity.

Hints for a Successful Chat

Limit the chat size. It may be necessary to divide the class into smaller groups. A maximum group size of six or seven participants will allow each student to read and respond to the messages. Most collaborative projects lend themselves well to a similar group size, making this a reasonable limitation of the chat room tool.

Avoid chaos. Do not allow students to make random postings. Instead, provide guidance for participation. Lynna Ausburn, Ph.D., provided the following suggestion. The instructor posts a conversation message starter. Students type an exclamation point (!) when they want to make a comment or a question mark (?) when they want to ask a question. The instructor facilitates the conversation with a "go code". The "go code" is the virtual classroom equivalent of giving a student permission to speak in class. The ! and ? are the electronic versions of students raising their hands to be recognized by the teacher (personal communication, October 2002).

Recognize students by name. Require students to indicate to whom they are responding by name. Also require students to sign their messages if the full name is not a part of their ID for the chat room.

Make the chat safe. Do not allow any participant to respond inappropriately. Utilize instructor controls to remove a student or block a student from participating if needed.

Tips for Enhancing Online Interaction

MacDonald (2003) encouraged the instructor to maintain a presence in the discussion. "Once the dialogue has started, the professor must come back with questions, challenges, comments, and guidance to help continue to shape the conversation" (p. 1). Another important activity of the discussion is the summation by the instructor. MacDonald (2003) continued, "the professor must validate the salient ideas that have emerged in the conversation, bring up ideas that have not occurred in the discourse necessary to advancing the dialogue, point students to each other, and then offer the comments necessary to carry on the conversation" (p. 4).

Discussion Board/Threaded Discussion

Also known as threaded discussion, the discussion board is usually an asynchronous format used for classroom discussion. The instructor can post a "thread," or topic, for discussion. The students then respond to the topic during a specified period of time. Just as in chat, the instructor must monitor the discussion for content and appropriateness. Moore, Winograd, and Lange (2001) stated, "Threaded discussions allow students to post comments to a discussion topic, react to other students' comments, share ideas, and even upload text and graphics files for others to share" (p. 6.9).

The ability to participate at any time in the asynchronous format is just one advantage of the discussion board for students. Another advantage is that students can take the time to formulate responses that are complete and accurate. The instructor can also require the students to create the response in a word processing program where it can be checked for spelling and grammar. Once the message is composed and corrected, it can be copied from the word processing program into the discussion board. Threaded discussions allow the shy students an opportunity to participate fully, because they may feel safer in the electronic environment.

A disadvantage of threaded discussions involves the speed in which the conversation can grow. Students may find it difficult to follow and comprehend the thread contents of large discussions. Students working through a modem connection may also experience a slow-down in the loading of the discussion board items when the discussion grows. A second disadvantage of the discussion board is that it can seem overwhelming to the procrastinator. If a student waits until the last possible moment to enter the discussion, the number of postings can be difficult to read and process. One solution to these disadvantages involves planning on the part of the instructor. To limit the size of the discussion, the instructor should create a discussion topic that is confined to only one subject at a time and require students to post on multiple days instead of allowing all the postings to be made at the last minute.

Another use of threaded discussion utilizes the discussion board in a synchronous format. The advantage of a synchronous discussion board over the virtual chat is in the way that comments are posted. Virtual chat comments become visible as the comments are submitted to the chat room. This means that the response to a comment may be separated from the original comment by several lines. In a threaded discussion, the comment and all of the responses to it are grouped together in outline format.

E-mail As a Collaborative Tool

E-mail provides the opportunity for private conversations between students and the instructor, or for students to communicate privately with other students. E-mail can be used to accomplish the following collaborative tasks:

1. Create distribution lists for your class that allow you to send announcements and updates to the entire class simultaneously or to subgroups within the class.

2. Create replies that load automatically for students, such as "I received your assignment."

3. Create mailboxes or folders for each student and set up the mail program filter to direct incoming assignments or messages into each student mailbox or into an assignment mailbox.

4. Create form e-mails for those messages that are sent routinely, such as student grades, late assignment notices, change of exam dates, etc.

5. Send messages and attach documents and other file types to individual students or to the entire class.

6. Send messages to individual students in order to add a personal touch. (Moore, Winograd, & Lange, 2001, p. 6.5 – 6.6)

E-groups

E-groups can be formed through most classroom management systems and through free systems available on the Internet. One example of a free e-group platform can be found at Yahoo! Groups.

An e-group provides group members with the ability to communicate through e-mail and chat. Utilizing e-groups through a classroom management system provides the instructor with some control, while free e-groups can be created and used without instructor intervention. One rule in creating an e-group outside the classroom management format should be to require that the group always include the instructor.

Instant Messaging

Instant messaging (IM) is a free tool available from the Internet. Instant messages are two-way conversations between two people only. Not the best tool for collaboration, an IM usually does not have recording capabilities, so a record of the communication is not available to all group members.

Online Guest Speakers

Guest speakers in the classroom can expand the learning opportunities for all students. Utilizing online guests requires creativity on the part of the instructor and the speaker. The instructor can invite the "guest speakers to submit audiotapes or short videotapes, still pictures and written minilectures, to take part in chatroom discussions, or to monitor threaded discussions. And their contributions can become a permanent part of your course" (Moore, Winograd, & Lange, 2001, p. 8.7).

Other Technologies

As an instructor, do not forget that the telephone and fax machines are two technologies that provide collaboration opportunities for students. Although the tools are not the latest technologies, both are simple to use and provide quick, easy access to group members.

Network technologies also provide collaboration tools. Many software packages such as Microsoft Office® contain collaboration tools within the software when used on a network.

Although not widely used yet, video chat is available as a collaboration tool. Video chat requires that all users have access to Web cameras (webcams). If all users are connected via webcams, the group can communicate with full audio and video capabilities and the entire session can be recorded to digital videodisc.

An obvious advantage for video chat is that students will have the ability to see and hear the communication, but the disadvantages currently outweigh the advantages. The two major disadvantages for video chat include the fact that not all students own the necessary equipment for video chat nor the bandwidth required to operate the technology.

BEST PRACTICES

With the growth of distance learning, many great instructors have shared their best practices. The following compilation of these time-proven techniques for collaboration in the distance classroom have been provided by instructors from across the United States:

Dorothy Minor and Denise Scifres

The Internet, e-mail, shared files, and discussion boards have already become the "work horses" of collaboration. They are cost effective and provide efficient time management. Minor teaches at Tulsa Community College in Tulsa, Oklahoma and Scifres teaches at Hinds Community College located in Raymond, Mississippi. Both teach online and utilize Blackboard. Minor and Scifres created groups with team members from both of their classes. Blackboard provided the communication tools needed for the interaction. Each group selected a topic to research and conducted the research completely at a distance (personal communication, March, 2003).

Dawn Parton

Each student is assigned a weekly question. Students must research the assigned question, using resources that are made available in the External Links section of Blackboard. Students are not allowed to use other resources. The students write a brief summary to share the highlights of the research question and post the summary in the Discussion Board. Then the other students must respond to the postings of their classmates. Students are allowed to add information and experiences from their personal lives if the experience supports the topic or adds to the discussion. Students provide much of the content for the class, and they take weekly quizzes based upon the research articles, providing the motivation to do their best with the research assignments and discussions (personal communication, March, 2003). Parton teaches in an Oklahoma child development program for Oklahoma Child Care Centers.

Becki Evans, speaking as a student

Speaking from the point of view of an Oklahoma college student, Becki Evans says, "One of my assignments was to read a book and make comments on chapters to the other class members. Using the Internet, I found the e-mail address of the author and I contacted her. Within 15 minutes, she had responded to my e-mail. She gave me her telephone number and I called her. I was able to ask questions to clarify some issues about my assignment and I asked her if she would be willing to talk to my instructor. She agreed. After talking to my instructor, a chat session was scheduled for the entire class" (personal communication, March, 2003).

David Wemhaner

In a social problems class, there is a discussion board area titled "students helping students," where students are graded for passing suggestions on to one another. The computer allows some distance so that the students feel safe in expressing themselves (personal communication, February, 2003). Wemhaner is a liberal arts professor at Tulsa Community College.

Gornie Williams

"In management classes, I have the students introduce themselves with an e-mail sent to everyone in the class. This activity provides a level of accountability that is often missing in the online classes. Students are no longer able to hide behind the technology, but are required to interact with each other" (personal communication, March, 2003). Williams runs classes and is an employee at the Bank of Oklahoma.

Laura Wilson

Wilson uses the Discussion Board area to post knowledge-level questions for exam reviews. Questions are posted and students discuss the issue as a way to prepare for exams. Students are allowed to discuss without intervention unless they need redirecting.

Jennifer Campbell

Campbell pairs students with an industry mentor. The students e-mail the mentor with predetermined questions. Mentors respond to the students and their responses are posted in the Discussion Board for other class members to see. Students can respond to the postings and ask questions that can be relayed back to the mentor for additional information or clarification. Campbell is an "online learning mentor" who teaches in the medical field in Oklahoma.

CONCLUSION

Distance learning is not a fad, but instead appears to be a driving force for the future of education. Although some find the format to be frustrating, more and more students are turning to online learning in an effort to continue school while supporting families and building careers.

Collaboration in the online environment is just another job skill for many of these students, and they embrace it easily. Students can work together, creating a synergy that would be missing without the interaction. Classrooms without walls allow the students to explore the world around them and find the best resources for completing the learning task. By utilizing e-mail, discussion boards, virtual chat, and other tools, the instructors and students create a diverse learning environment.

The online environment requires participation of all students. In a traditional classroom, the shy student can sit at the back of the classroom, but never participate in the discussion. Just by being present in the classroom, the student appears to be learning. This is not true in the online environment. Every student must post comments and submit materials for class discussion in order to be present in the classroom. No longer can the shy student be present for every class meeting, yet never participate. Instead, because a physical presence is unavailable, the electronic presence must be seen and heard.

Businesses utilize collaboration in the workplace, and according to members of advisory committees (personal communication, April 2003), students need to practice collaboration in the classroom in order to prepare for the realities of the workforce. Instructors must carefully design the collaboration projects, providing clear outcomes and expectations for the students. In addition, instructors need to make sure that the students have the necessary skills to complete the group projects. Group selection and organization are important processes for the success of the project. Instructors should create the groups based upon the desired outcome of the project and the weight of the project in the overall course grade.

The tools for collaborative learning include virtual chat, discussion boards, e-mail, e-groups, guest speakers, and other technologies. The most often used technology in a synchronous format is virtual chat, while the other technologies are best suited for the asynchronous classroom.

Virtual chat can be used to simulate real-time classroom discussions. To participate, students need to be online while the chat is occurring. Discussion boards can also simulate classroom discussions, but the students can use the discussion board following the "anywhere, anytime" principle of learning, since the threads are visible for extended periods of time and participation is not limited to a specific time.

E-mail technology is most often utilized for individual communications or communications that need to go to every class member. An effective way for groups to communicate is through the use of an e-group technology. E-groups allow students to communicate in either real-time or through discussions that are visible for extended periods of time. Instant messaging is a real-time tool that is useful for short conversations, but using IM technology will not be effective for actual classroom discussions.

Guest speakers can enhance the online classroom in multiple ways. Just as the guest speaker provides a new dimension to the traditional classroom, a guest speaker can add to the online classroom. Online speakers provide an additional advantage in that the presentation can be preserved in digital format for future classes.

Video conferencing will become a force for future classrooms, but for today, most students do not have the technology to utilize this tool. Finally, never forget the telephone and fax machine as useful tools for collaboration.

As the use of telelearning techniques continue to grow, more and more instructors are going to be adding distance-learning components to their classrooms. Today's students not only expect to see the use of technology in the classroom, they are beginning to demand it. After all, the incoming freshmen for the fall of 2004 were born in 1985, eight years after the first personal computer was sold (Ambrose, et. al., 2003, p. CF 6). Most of the students have had a computer in their classrooms and homes for their entire lives, and they have utilized the computer to communicate with friends and relatives around the world.

REFERENCES
Ambrose, A., Bergerud, M., Busche, D., Morrison, C., Wells-Pusins, D. (2003). *IC3 basics: Internet and computing core certification.* Thomson-Course Technology: Boston, MA.

Blumenfeld, P.C., Marx, R.W., Soloway, E., and Krajcik, J. (1996). Learning with peers: From small group cooperation to collaborative communities. *Educational Researcher*, 25(8), 37-40.

Davis, B.G. (1993). [Electronic version]. *Collaborative learning: Group work and study teams.* Jossey-Bass: San Francisco, CA. Retrieved from on February 21, 2003 from http://teaching.berkeley.edu/bgd/collaborative.html

Gokhale, A. (1995). Collaborative learning enhances critical thinking. *Journal of Technology Education*, 7(1). Retrieved February 21, 2003 from http://scholar.lib.vt.edu/ejournals/JTE/jte-v7n1/gokhale.jte-v7n1.html

MacDonald, D. (2003). Tips to enhance online interaction. Retrieved December 2, 2003, from the University of Maryland, University College Center for Teaching and Learning Web site: http://www.umuc.edu/distance/odell/ctla/resources/enhance_interaction.html

Paradiso, J. (2003). Interact-ion and collaborat-ion online. *Innovation Abstracts*, XXV (3).

Roberson, T.J., Klotz, J. (2002). How can instructors and administrators fill the missing link in online instruction? *Online Journal of Distance Learning Administration.* V (IV). Retrieved February 10, 2003 from http://www.wetga.edu/~distance/ojdla/winter54/roberson54.htm

Tinzmann, M.B., Jones, B.F., Fennimore, T.F., Bakker, J., Fine, C., and Pierce, J. (1990). What is the collaborative classroom? *North Central Regional Educational Laboratory*. Retrieved on February 21, 2003, from http://www.ncrel.org/sdrs/areas/rpl_esys/collab.htm

Wegerif, R. (1998). The social dimension of asynchronous learning networks. *Journal of Asynchronous Learning Networks, (JALN)*, 2(1).

Measuring the Teaching/Learning Process: Technology-Based Courses

Leslie Crair
McDonald Bradley, Inc.
Herndon, Virginia

As technology tools become more common in the business workplace, the business education community is under greater pressure to ensure that these tools are incorporated into the learning environment (Basile & Aquila, 2002; Mariola & Manley, 2002). This chapter will review current research on nontraditional technology media assessments, including (a) deep learning vs. surface learning indicators, (b) common online learning methods, (c) effectiveness of testing instruments, and (d) sources for the evaluation of online course material.

ENHANCING LEARNING: TECHNOLOGY IN THE CLASSROOM

Technology in the classroom is a double-edged sword: online learning allows institutions of higher learning to reach out to a larger and more diversified student base, but the ability to reach that larger audience is a complex task that must be balanced with the needs of business educators. Educators need an understanding of how best to deliver a quality education via nontraditional media to a student population that is increasingly diverse, and how best to assess the educational experience they provide.

Distance learning or other technology-based learning experiences should measure the effectiveness of each section of the core learning triad: student achievement, teacher effectiveness, and course relevance. This, of course, is premised on the rubric of the learning objective.

Defining Deep Learning

To increase the likelihood that students will retain relevant material, instruction and corresponding assessments should be designed to advance and measure *deep learning*, that is, learning that the student will retain and use in the future. In order for this to happen, course content should mirror corresponding tasks in the field; in their learning environments, students should be given the tools, such as software and a set of tasks that he or she will actually use in the workplace, and they should be assessed in a manner similar to one of the workplace.

Problem Solving with Technology-Based Media

Business educators have access to computers and software comparable to those used in the workplace and, therefore, have the opportunity to replicate the workplace environment. The distance learning classroom can be made to strongly resemble the workplace by using standard business software, assigning learning tasks that replicate workplace tasks, and by putting students in teams to work on assignments together. For example, an accounting class would develop teams of accountants to replicate a company's accounting department and provide assignments that students would likely encounter on the job, using standard accounting software such as DelTek, or even Microsoft Excel spreadsheets.

Since more time is spent in the business world solving problems than it is memorizing data, deep learning is a consideration when constructing curriculum and evaluating course success. Curriculum developed to resemble workplace assignments requires a more business-style approach in assessing student, teacher, and course performance. This approach encompasses student self-evaluation, peer evaluation, teacher-to-student evaluation, and student-to-teacher evaluation.

DEEP LEARNING: A TAXONOMY-BASED MODEL

In order to better develop curriculum and assessment to adequately evaluate technology-based learning, it is useful to compare deep learning and its complement, surface learning, to associated learning interactions. Using a standard cognitive taxonomy, tying deep learning and surface learning to learner interaction will provide additional clarification.

Bloom's (Bloom, Engelhart, Furst, Hill, & Krathwohl, 1956) taxonomy of learning is the classic example of a cognitive learning hierarchy. This taxonomy is used to show cognitive activity that parallels either surface learning or deep learning, as in Table 1. Surface learning is necessary but superficial knowledge about a topic associated with recall and recollection, or in Bloom's taxonomy, knowledge and beginning levels of comprehension. Deep learning is the ability to understand the topic well enough to apply the knowledge gained in unique situations. Deep learning occurs in the cognitive domain levels of *application, analysis, synthesis, and evaluation.*

Using multimedia technology to facilitate interaction that meets Bloom's four cognitive activity levels requires an analysis of the interaction between the media and the student.

Learner-media interaction can be described in levels of depth from *passive*, in which the learner only controls the flow of information to highly *interactive*, in which the learner actually creates the media (Ross & Tuovinen, 2001; Tuovinen, 2000). As illustrated below, Table 1 matches Bloom's cognitive learning domain taxonomy to seven of Tuovinen's *learner-media interactions* and to deep learning or surface learning activities.

Table 1. Deep Learning vs. Surface Learning Assessment		
Type	**Bloom Cognitive Taxonomy**	**Learner Media Interaction**
Surface	Knowledge	Passive – learner controls information flow
Surface	Knowledge	Hierarchical choices – menu navigation
Surface/Deep	Knowledge/Comprehension	Information update control – answering questions
Deep	Application/Analysis	Construction with components
Deep	Application/Analysis/Synthesis/Evaluation	Participation in simulations
Deep	Analysis/Synthesis/Evaluation	Navigation of hyperlinked information
Deep	Synthesis/Evaluation	Multimedia creation

In order to create viable measurements of the learning process using technology-based media, the assessments should take into consideration the media and methods used in the classroom environment and should include the virtual classroom. One consideration during course development is to imbed as many opportunities for deep learning into the curriculum as possible. Many of these methods provide assessment opportunities as well (Ross & Tuovinen, 2001).

COMMON ONLINE LEARNING METHODS

There are several activities used in the distance learning classroom to enhance student performance. These include *case-based reasoning, electronic portfolios, threaded discussions,* and *reflective journals.* Each of these activities is designed to promote deep learning by developing students' critical-thinking skills.

Additionally, the use of a *grading rubric* provides guidance to the student on expectations and acts as an advanced organizer. An advanced organizer prepares the learner for new material by providing a bridge to existing knowledge; information is presented from general to specific and provides examples linking to previously learned material (Ausubel, 1967).

Case-Based Reasoning

Case-based reasoning is the assignment of scenario-based tasks designed to engage students in understanding the *why* of learning a task. Research indicates that thoughtful work that incorporates analogous scenarios provides students an opportunity to understand the application value of the assignment to real world situations and promotes deep learning (Kolodner, 1997). "The intention is to provide useful cases and examples to students as they are solving problems to enable them to make useful analogical inferences: to identify issues to pay attention to, to form ideas about how to move forward, and to project the effects of solutions they have come up with" (p. 57), Kolodner explains.

In classes that are geared toward novices or with those who have not had experiences analogous to the topic, the instruction should be designed to assist in guiding the students to make choices beyond their accustomed abilities (Kolodner, 1997).

Electronic Portfolios

Electronic portfolios have the advantage of allowing the student to collect a volume of work over time, just as he or she would in the workplace. This allows both instructor and student to view the skills and knowledge gained over the semester. Creation of the portfolio allows for critical-thinking skills to evolve as well, especially if assignments are designed to present the opportunity to make use of material developed for application to new situations (Bauer & Anderson, 2000).

When students develop a portfolio of work over the course of the semester, clear expectations should be given as to the amount of content and type of content required, and a *grading rubric* provided. Use of peer and self-evaluation can also be a valuable way of providing feedback on the portfolio (Bauer & Anderson, 2000). Portfolios should be reviewed by the instructor and the student at regular intervals to assist the student in refining current and future tasks.

Reflective Journals

Reflective journals are another method for promoting deep learning and providing a course-long assessment of student progress in learning the material. Students can be given latitude over what information to log in their journals; however, some guidance, which can be in the form of a grading rubric, should be provided to collect material that will show student's perceptions of content and technical understanding over the length of the course (Simonson, 2000). For example, if a student decides to keep an outline of key concepts in his or her journal, guidance would be given to expand the concepts to provide tangible examples that show an understanding of the concepts.

Threaded Discussions

Threaded discussions take place in an online bulletin board, which is an area designated for posting comments. This activity provides a group of students a place for exchanging ideas on a selected topic. Threaded discussions can be managed similarly to chat rooms, where students are instructed to participate at a given time with either the instructor or an assigned mediator. Another method of threaded discussions provides a time frame where students post their thoughts, with time for reflection between postings. Generally, the students are given a topic and its related material to review along with a question designed to promote discussion of the material. Students are required to post an opinion, review the relevance of the material, read other students' comments, and respond by evaluating discussion points made. The downside of this method is that threads can quickly get lost, or students may post only the requisite amount of material. If structured carefully, students have the opportunity to analyze, evaluate, and synthesize material.

Grading Rubrics

Grading rubrics provide a criteria and measurement for submitted work. Rubrics equate student expectations for assignments with specific performance outcomes. The level of expectation for a given score is directly stated for the student. An example of a rubric for participation in a classroom threaded discussion might include criteria on viability and quality. Table 2 provides an example of a grading rubric.

Table 2. Sample Grading Rubric

Score	Criteria
5	Provides ample evidence to support positions taken in discussion; comprehends all key concepts and applies knowledge to novel examples given in discussion; effectively evaluates others' comments; participates in more than the required number of exchanges
4	Provides evidence to support position taken in discussion; comprehends all key concepts and occasionally applies knowledge to novel examples give in discussion; evaluates others' comments; participates in the required number of exchanges
3	Occasionally provides evidence to support positions taken in discussion; comprehends most concepts; participates in fewer than the required number of exchanges
2	Does not provide evidence to support positions taken; comprehends some concepts; participates in fewer than the required number of exchanges
1	Does not provide evidence to support positions taken in discussion or does not participate in discussions; shows no significant comprehension of concepts; rarely or never participates in required number of exchanges

EFFECTIVENESS OF TESTING INSTRUMENTS

If the testing instrument is to be considered effective, it should provide indications of deep learning. The assessment should provide students with the opportunity to demonstrate both assimilated knowledge and the skills they have learned, as well as the ability to apply what is learned these to new situations.

All of the assessments described (case-based reasoning, electronic portfolios, reflective journals, and threaded discussions) provide methods geared towards students' comprehending, applying, evaluating, and synthesizing materials.

Additional considerations in developing measurements to assess deep learning include a careful matching of the demonstration of knowledge and skills to expected outcomes. As with all assessments, the instrument must take into account the learning objective, the content, and expected outcomes.

While teaching and testing may evolve to take advantage of new formats brought on by technology, solid development is still key to meeting the learning objective.

Michlitsch & Sidle (2002) conducted a survey of business schools in the U.S. "to investigate frequency of use and perceived effectiveness of methods used in assessment of student learning" (p. 125). The study, while not focused on technology-based learning, indicated a number of assessment methods that translate well to distance learning and promote deep learning.

Eight effective assessment methods found to be statistically significant were the following: 1) case studies assignments; 2) observations of student group process in resolving case studies; 3) item analysis of a series of multiple-choice questions answered by students; 4) analytical scoring of student writing assignments that break down each skill area; 5) observation of student presentations measuring performance by using criteria; 6) computerized simulation assignments; 7) simple questionnaire focused on specific concepts that students will need to know to understand a topic; and 8) completion of a concept map depicting the major idea in the day's lesson (Michlitsch & Sidle, 2002, p.127). Four of these correspond to the common online learning methods discussed earlier:

1 – Case studies assignments (*Case-based reasoning*)

2 – Observations of student group process in resolving case studies (*Case-based reasoning*)

3 – Computerized simulation assignments (*All*)

4 – Completion of a concept map depicting the major idea in the day's lesson (*Reflective Journal*) (Michlitsch & Sidle, 2002, p. 127)

What are student perceptions of technology-based courses? In general, perceptions of technology-based courses as meeting expectations are driven by familiarity with the technology, as well as by the level of communication and participation (Beard & Harper, 2002). Duncan and Wallace (2002) discovered a lack of cohesive and valid research on assessment of online technology-based courses. While there is a need for theory-based online instructional design and assessments, some evidence does purport that a constructivist approach that focuses on replicating problem solving works best in online courses.

One may be able to generalize that the more confident students feel that the business education experience mirrors the workplace environment, the more likely they are to have positive perceptions of technology-driven courses. For example, teaching that employs software that the student is likely to encounter in the business world (for teaching concepts and skills in topical areas) (Basile & Aquila, 2002) may increase student's value perception of the learning experience.

SOURCES FOR EVALUATING ONLINE COURSE MATERIAL
There are three levels of evaluating online material: the course itself and related parameters, the social and psychological environment in which the course exists, and the program itself, as it facilitates the delivery of course material.

Evaluating online learning material brings additional dimensions to the process associated with the technology itself. Along with judging the educational viability of the medium in which the material is delivered, one must take into account the ability to provide student interaction. This evaluation process requires an understanding of the technology used and a judgment about the appropriateness of the medium to the learning objective.

Michigan Virtual University
One source which provides a tool for online education and is likened to the *Consumer Reports* of online learning assessment (Lorenzetti, 2002), is the Michigan Virtual University (MVU). MVU has created a "Standards for Quality Online Courses" and a course evaluator tool (Estabrook & Arashino, 2002). The assessment tool allows the evaluator to assess the online course in four categories: technology, usability, accessibility, and instructional design standards. The Technology Source is published by the Michigan Virtual University and provides informative articles on information technology on the online classroom for educators at http://ts.mivu.org/default.asp.

Distance Education Learning Environment Survey
In order to monitor the learning environment, a new survey tool is available to assess the social and psychological aspects of distance learning. The Distance Education Learning Environment Survey (DELES) was developed by Scott Walker (Jorgensen, 2002). DELES is accessible via a link from the University of North Texas http://insight.southcentralrtec.org. There are three forms of the survey; two for students and one for instructors.

Question Development for Online Surveys

When using a computer-based learning management system such as Blackboard, a student evaluation *template* is generally available for customization. Two areas to consider when developing a student survey include determining the frequency of desired student feedback (i.e., more than once, or only at the end of the course) and structuring questions that reflect on the inclusion of the technology into the entire learning process.

Survey data, for example, indicates many teachers believe students' self-confidence concerning computer use is higher than their actual computer skill levels (Duncan & Wallace, 2002; Perreault, Waldman, Zhao, & Alexander, 2002).

Sample questions for an online learner assessment to focus on are the following: 1) What is the student's perception of knowledge gained? 2) What is the nature of the student's experience with the technology? Questions regarding the instructor should focus on the availability of the instructor—virtual or face-to-face—as appropriate. For example, were there virtual office hours posted, and was the instructor actually available at those times? Was the expected response time for e-mail communication or returning phone calls set up in advance and adhered to?

It is also important to ask questions about students' motivation to complete tasks in the course. Questions should be based both on the material and the medium, as well as on the course's degree of applicability to the workplace (Duncan & Wallace, 2002). Student assessments should be designed to evaluate all facets of instruction and to show both strengths and weaknesses of the course.

The current dearth of research regarding impact of technology-based business training on the workplace indicates a need for additional research. As yet, there is no definitive conclusion, nor will there likely be one for the near-term.

Instructors in the business arena will be developing and using technology-based courses with more frequency. Today, the thrust is in Web-delivered distance learning that incorporates the latest software tools available in the workplace. Constant changes in the technology available for use in the workplace demands that instructors to keep current with technology or risk falling behind in their teaching.

SUMMARY

The business education community is under pressure to incorporate technology-based training into the curriculum for today's students. These students are more diverse and often unbound by geographical location. The opportunity to reach out to a larger and more diverse student population presents the need to effectively assess the quality of these new educational media. Case-based reasoning, electronic portfolios, reflective journals and threaded discussions are some of the technology-based learning methods that can be used to promote the deep learning necessary to not only develop critical-thinking skills required in the workplace, but also to measure them. At this juncture, assessing the long-term effectiveness of technology-based business courses will require additional time and resources.

REFERENCES

Ausubel, D. P. (1967). *Learning theory and classroom practice*. Ontario: The Ontario Institute for Studies in Education.

Basile, A., & Aquila, J. M. (2002). An experimental analysis of computer-mediated instruction and student attitudes in a principles of financial accounting course. *Journal of Education for Business*(Jan/Feb 2002), 137 - 143.

Bauer, J. F., & Anderson, R. S. (2000). Evaluating Students' Written Performance in the Online Classroom. In R. E. Weiss & D. S. Knowlton & B. W. Speck (Eds.), *Principles of effective teaching in the online classroom* (Vol. 84, pp. 65 - 71). San Francisco: Jossey-Bass.

Beard, L., & Harper, C. (2002). Student perceptions of online versus on campus instruction. *Education, 122*(no. 4), 658 - 663.

Bloom, B. S., Engelhart, M. D., Furst, E. J., Hill, W. H., & Krathwohl, D. R. (1956). *Taxonomy of educational objectives: The classification of educational goals. Handbook 1, cognitive domain*. New York: David McKay Co.

Duncan, J., & Wallace, M. K. (2002). Assessing online technology: Edutainment or desktop-rubbishing. *The Delta Pi Epsilon Journal, XLIV*(no. 1), 25 - 38.

Estabrook, N., & Arashino, P. (2002). *Standards for quality online courses*. Retrieved April 2, 2002, from the Michigan Virtual University Web site: http://standards.mivu.org/evaluator

Jorgensen, H. (2002). A precision tool for evaluating student perceptions. *Distance Education Report, 6*(23), 8.

Kolodner, J. L. (1997). Educational implications of analogy. *American Psychologist, 52*(1), 57 - 68.

Lorenzetti, J. P. (2002). Practical course assessment standards from MVU. *Distance Education Report, 6*(21), 2 - 3.

Mariola, E., & Manley, J. (2002). Teaching finance concepts in a distance learning environment - A personal note. *Journal of Education for Business*(January/February), 177 - 180.

Michlitsch, J. E., & Sidle, M. W. (2002). Assessing student learning outcomes: A comparative study of techniques used in business school disciplines. *Journal of Education for Business*(January/February), 125 - 130.

Perreault, H., Waldman, L., Zhao, J., & Alexander, M. (2002). Overcoming barriers to successful delivery of distance-learning courses. *Journal of Education for Business*(Jul/Aug 2002), 313 - 318.

Ross, G. C., & Tuovinen, J. E. (2001). Deep versus surface learning with multimedia in nursing education: Development and evaluation of WoundCare. *Computers in Nursing, 19*(5), 213 - 223.

Simonson, M. (2000). Making decisions: The use of electronic technology in online classrooms. In R. E. Weiss & D. S. Knowlton & B. W. Speck (Eds.), *Principles of effective teaching in the online classroom* (Winter 2000 ed., pp. 29 - 34). San Francisco: Jossey-Bass.

Tuovinen, J. E. (2000). Multimedia distance education interactions. *Educational Media International, 37*, 16 - 24.

Distance Learning Success for the Business School: MERLOT's Facilitation Strategy

Joseph Otto
California State University, Los Angeles
Los Angeles, California

Gerard L. Hanley
California State University, Los Angeles
Los Angeles, California

Cathy Swift
Georgia Southern University
Statesboro, Georgia

Society is "in the midst of an information revolution unmatched since the invention of the printing press" (Victor, 1999, p. 74). Institutions of higher learning are struggling to develop programs to take advantage of this technological transformation. These institutions are increasingly relying on technology innovations that enhance student learning (Dacko, 2001). Educational institutions have made significant progress in enabling student success in distance learning through the delivery of academic programs in the form of course management systems, electronic access to library resources, and the wealth of student services using help desks and campus portals.

Online learning has been growing rapidly and is expected to continue to increase by 33% per year (Pethoukoukis, 2002). Enabling faculty success in researching and designing curriculum for teaching in distance learning programs is an area where institutions still face significant challenges. Institutions must commit to providing resources for faculty training, course design, and course development if these initiatives are to be successful (van Dusen, 2001).

This paper will review a number of the challenges facing educational institutions and describe how MERLOT (Multimedia Educational Resource for Learning and Online Teaching) is an international consortium designed to facilitate successful teaching and learning with technology. Additionally, a description of the business editorial board of MERLOT will be provided, as well as the business peer review process.

TEACHING: PREPARING FOR STUDENT LEARNING

There are two major activities that faculty perform in the preparation of teaching:

1) Collecting and creating academic content (i.e., the research for teaching), and

2) Designing curriculum with content and pedagogy.

The effectiveness and efficiency of faculty who perform these activities will contribute significantly to the quality, scalability, and sustainability of an institution's distance education program.

Research for teaching requires faculty to search and find content provided by commercial publishers, libraries, and individuals (e.g., via the World Wide Web). Faculty also develop their own content to complement the resources produced by others, including syllabi, lectures, units of practice, and learning objects. The critical success factors for faculty doing research for teaching include the ability to identify the relevant content within their academic discipline; the ability to customize the content to satisfy local, programmatic requirements; and the ability to participate in a community of practice for teachers.

If faculty cannot successfully determine the relevance of materials for teaching in their discipline, the process for searching, finding, evaluating, and selecting content will be overwhelming, unreliable, and of poor quality. If faculty cannot effectively and efficiently customize that content, the collection of content may not meet the needs of the students within their specific academic program. Finally, if the faculty cannot participate in a community of practice for teaching, the professional development opportunities for innovation, improved effectiveness, recognition, and feedback will be insufficient to develop and sustain updated knowledge for teaching in the discipline.

Designing curriculum requires faculty to organize the content with pedagogies that add a programmatic and cultural context to the collected content. This context includes defining the learning objectives, the prerequisite skills and knowledge, the learning activities, and the methods of assessment for learning materials. As discussed above, the critical success factors for faculty developing curriculum are identifying the relevant content and pedagogy for the students' capabilities and learning objectives, customizing the learning activities and assessments in ways appropriate for the students and the academic program goals, and participating in the community of practice for teachers.

Ineffective and inefficient curriculum design processes do not produce the desired student learning outcomes and can lead to irrelevant and boring curriculum that doesn't engage the students' readiness to learn. As with research for teaching, if the faculty cannot participate in a community of practice for teaching, the professional development opportunities for innovation, improved effectiveness, recognition, and feedback will be insufficient to develop and sustain excellence in teaching skills and curriculum design.

PREPARING FOR TEACHING IN DISTANCE LEARNING PROGRAMS

Faculty face significant problems when they research and design curriculum for teaching in distance learning programs. Transitioning to online delivery is complicated, time consuming, and professionally challenging (Gibson & Herrera 1999). These challenges are in addition to the many issues of technology infrastructure, access to computing technologies by students and teachers, and administrative systems for managing students learning at a distance. Commercial publishers and libraries do not provide deep, broad, or organized collections of multimedia academic content; however, electronic access to text-based resources is advancing rapidly. A large proportion of the multimedia content has been developed by a cottage industry of individual faculty, academic technology staff, campus technology centers, and professional organizations. Locally developed and managed digital collections of multimedia content are developing, yet are at early stages of reliability, sustainability, and quality. Consequently, faculty can have significant difficulty researching and designing curriculum for teaching in distance learning programs. The successful distance education instructor has to become conversant with new technology and develop a new instructional style, moving from creating instruction to managing resources (Strain 1987).

While these challenges are significant, distance learning programs have also created opportunities for educational communities to respond collaboratively to a number of these challenges. The time and expense for developing and distributing digital content can be reduced if there is more effective sharing of digital content.

Assuring the quality of the content and its use with sound pedagogy is another critical aspect of distance learning that can be addressed through collaboration by establishing evaluation standards and sharing reviews by peers. Professional development programs that enable the academic community to use digital resources successfully can be delivered through the collective discovery and sharing of exemplary practices. Development and management of technology services supporting the sharing of digital resources and professional development programs are pivotal in establishing and sustaining the communities of practice in distance learning.

MERLOT was designed and has evolved to enable educational institutions to overcome the challenges of researching and designing curriculum for teaching in distance learning programs. By collaboratively designing, building, evaluating, and managing a shared digital collection of multimedia academic content, MERLOT enables faculty to perform effective and efficient research for teaching. By building in the capabilities for faculty to customize and contextualize the academic content, MERLOT enables faculty to successfully design curriculum. Finally, by building the MERLOT digital library on the foundation of the community of users, MERLOT enables faculty to participate in communities of practice for teaching with technology. The following sections will review the development of the MERLOT consortium, its digital collection and services, and its strategies for facilitating the success of business education around the world.

Historical Context Shapes MERLOT Today

In 1996, the California State University Center for Distributed Learning (CSU-CDL, at www.cdl.edu) was established to serve the academic technology needs of its 23 campuses. With over 30,000 faculty and over 350,000 students in the CSU system, the CSU-CDL had to design a service that would be easy to use, would leverage the widespread yet uncoordinated development of academic technologies, and would be low cost to operate. Under the leadership of Chuck Schneebeck, CSU-CDL's Director, MERLOT (www.merlot.org) was developed, and free access was provided in 1997. MERLOT was modeled after the NSF funded project, "Authoring Tools and An Educational Object Economy (EOE)" which was led by Dr. James Spohrer and hosted by Apple Computer, and other industry, university, and government collaborators. One of the key design requirements for MERLOT was to have a technology service that enables users to contribute directly to a community's collection of online resources without "human mediation." The goal of MERLOT was to enable the "cottage industry" of campuses and individual faculty's development of academic technology to become scalable and sustainable (Hanley, Schneebeck, & Zweier, 1998; Schneebeck and Hanley, 2001).

In 1998, a State Higher Education Executives Organization/American Productivity and Quality Center (SHEEO/APQC) benchmarking study on faculty development and instructional technology selected the CSU-CDL as one of six best practices centers in North America. Visitations to the CSU-CDL by higher education institutions participating in the benchmarking study resulted in institutional interest in collaborating with the CSU on the MERLOT project. The University System of Georgia, Oklahoma State Regents for Higher Education, University of North Carolina System, and the California State University System created an informal consortium representing almost one hundred campuses. SHEEO was the coordinator for the cooperative of the four state systems.

In 1999, the four systems recognized the significant benefits of a cooperative initiative to expand the MERLOT collections, conduct peer reviews of the digital learning materials, and add student-learning assignments. Each system contributed funds to develop the MERLOT software and in-kind support to advance the peer review process. The CSU maintained its leadership of and responsibilities for the operation and improvement of processes and tools.

In January 2000, the four systems sponsored faculty from the disciplines of biology, physics, business, and teacher education to develop evaluation standards and peer review processes for online teaching-learning material. In April 2000, other systems and institutions of higher education were invited to join the MERLOT cooperative and by July 2000, twenty-three systems and institutions of higher education had become institutional partners of MERLOT.

Facilitating Collaboration Across Borders

Today, the MERLOT consortium comprises over 20 higher education systems, consortia, individual institutions of higher education; over 20 professional academic organizations; and over 15,000 individuals, to form a community of educators who strive to improve the teaching and learning experience with high quality online resources (as of September 2003). The consortium is a diverse and complex mix of institutions, and there are multiple levels of participation. MERLOT's institutional partners include smaller liberal arts colleges and large state university systems, as well as community colleges focused on undergraduate teaching, and research institutions focused on scholarship, research, and graduate education. For institutions of higher education, MERLOT has 4 levels of participation:

- Sustaining Partners pay $50,000 per year and provide over $250,000 of in-kind support.

- System Partners pay $25,000 per year and provide approximately $50,000 of in-kind support.

- Campus Partners pay $6,500 per year and provide approximately $20,000 of in-kind support.

- Institutional Alliances provide in-kind support for advancing the MERLOT project within their institution.

Collectively, MERLOT provides services that require approximately $3 million annually, but no institution has to provide the full funding. The "return on investment" is one of the factors that motivates institutions to join the consortium. The different levels of participation are associated with different levels of MERLOT services; the more an institution commits to MERLOT, the more MERLOT commits its services to the institution. These different levels enable institutions to participate within the constraints acceptable for their institutional culture, resources, and readiness. MERLOT has 19 System and Campus Partners in the U.S. California State University and eduSource.Canada are Sustaining Partners; education.au, which provides academic technology services (EdNa Online) to education institutions throughout Australia, and the National University of Rwanda are alliance partners. Whether the borders are the campus property lines or the international dateline, higher education institutions can participate in MERLOT's consortium. MERLOT's responsibility is to facilitate a productive community and to engage the consortium members in shared governance and program implementation through open communications, cooperative planning, and program delivery.

Though the consortium members are very diverse, they share the commitment to MERLOT's vision to be a premier online community where people from around the world share online learning materials and pedagogy. They also share MERLOT's strategic priority to improve the effectiveness of teaching and learning among diverse members by expanding the quantity and quality of peer-reviewed online learning materials that can be easily incorporated into faculty-designed courses. It is the combination of shared values, the collaborative delivery of quality services, and the public recognition of the partners' contributions to MERLOT that sustains the MERLOT consortium.

SERVING COMMON NEEDS ACROSS BORDERS: EASY ACCESS TO QUALITY DIGITAL CONTENT, PEDAGOGY, AND PEER-TO-PEER INTERACTIONS

Without the delivery of high quality services, the MERLOT consortium would quickly dissolve. MERLOT's services address the difficulties that institutions of higher education and their faculty experience when fulfilling the promises and challenges of technology-enhanced education. Higher education makes regular and substantial investments in the development of instructional technology amidst concerns that someone else may be "reinventing the wheel." Duplication of effort wastes time, staff resources, and funds. Faculty have difficulty reliably producing high-quality online materials, efficiently choosing online materials, receiving appropriate professional recognition for their work, and providing evidence of improvements in teaching and learning. MERLOT's community digital library and services are designed to meet these common needs.

The MERLOT Collection

MERLOT and its institutional and individual members have created a digital library of about 10,000 online teaching/learning materials and a directory of over 15,000 members who can provide peer-to-peer consultation (as of September, 2003). The MERLOT Web site (www.merlot.org) is a cooperatively developed, free, Web-based resource where faculty, staff, administrators, and students can easily find digital learning materials with evaluations and guidance for their use.

In 2003, the Web site had over 1.5 million hits per month with over 15,000 unique users per month. Learning materials from a wide variety of academic disciplines are indexed on the MERLOT site. Most of the learning materials found on www.MERLOT.org are modular (e.g., simulations, tutorials, animations, drill and practice exercises, lecture presentations, case studies, collections, and reference materials), and all designed to be integrated into a larger course. Most of the materials run inside a Web browser, facilitating the use within an online course, or as assignments to students outside the classroom.

MERLOT is designed for easy and effective navigation. Whether users browse the collection or search for targeted learning materials, they will be able to read a preview of the material to help them decide if it is worth their time to investigate the materials more thoroughly. MERLOT does not store the thousands of actual learning materials on its servers but simply provides the links and descriptions of the materials (metadata). Once the materials are found in MERLOT, users simply click on the URL for the materials, which takes them to the material's actual location, where they can check for any licensing regulations or costs involved with use and can incorporate the resources into their curriculum (e.g., enter a link to the material in their course Web site, or e-mail the URL to the students). To find or use materials in the MERLOT collection, users do not need to be members of MERLOT, nor does the user's institution need to be in the MERLOT consortium. This feature of "on-demand" access is a founding principle of MERLOT; it enables faculty to solve their research and curriculum design problems immediately.

MERLOT has recently provided a federated search service that enables users to search MERLOT and other digital libraries simultaneously and provide an integrated hit list. This federated search service provides one-stop-access to collections developed by different communities around the world; MERLOT and Australia's EdNA Online are using the federated search services to leverage each other's collections in the service of their own constituents.

The Collection Built by the Community

A distinctive feature of MERLOT is that individual members perform the cataloging of materials voluntarily. Once a person registers as a member of MERLOT (at no charge), he/she is able to create catalog records of materials deemed worthy of sharing. Every contributed material, comment, review, or assignment is visibly connected to the individual in the MERLOT ePortfolio, which creates some social pressures for members to apply reasonable judgment. It also provides a mechanism for MERLOT to identify and discipline members for abusing their privileges. A premise underlying MERLOT's decision to open the cataloging to the community is that if a faculty member, staff, librarian, or administrator is qualified enough to be hired by a higher education institution, that person is qualified to identify materials that might be valuable to peers. In addition, if a user is concerned about the qualifications of the person submitting the materials, the user clicks on the name of the submitter and learns more about them.

Cataloging by the community enables MERLOT to grow the collection in breadth and depth, so that it is directly meeting the needs of its members. As the community becomes more diverse in its interests, the collection can grow to satisfy the interests. Members of different cultures and nationalities can contribute materials without having to satisfy gate-keeping requirements that could be culturally insensitive.

The process for building the collection is also scalable; if every one of MERLOT's members contributed one material this year, the collection would grow by 15,000, without MERLOT having to hire staff to catalog the materials. The workload cost to catalog one material is low, compared to the benefit of 15,000 new materials that would be available to every member.

Pedagogical Contexts for Learning Content

There are a number of critical features to MERLOT that makes it more than a collection of URLs. The individual members of MERLOT write a description of the materials within the context of teaching and learning. Members can add comments about the quality and usefulness of the materials. MERLOT also provides the capability for members to describe specific techniques for using the materials in teaching; the learning assignments include information about the topics covered, the level of student (e.g. lower division, upper division, graduate), names of courses for which they are appropriate, prerequisite skills and knowledge the students should have before doing the assignment, learning objectives, type of learning activity (e.g. team-based vs. individual; supervised vs. unsupervised), assessment methods, time required to do the assignment, and the text of the assignment. All of the metadata on pedagogy enable faculty to effectively and easily choose and use the best online learning materials for their students that are compatible with their own teaching methods and the learning goals of their own academic programs.

Personalizing the MERLOT Collection

MERLOT recognized that people can easily get overwhelmed by the volume of available materials and easily forget the value and relevance of materials they find. Consequently, MERLOT created the capability for its members to create and annotate personal collections. Once members find material that satisfies their needs, with a click of a button, they can add it to their personal collection and describe what it is and why they found the material valuable. Members can create multiple personal collections that can form the foundations of course portfolios, where the faculty can describe how the selected materials can be used to achieve specific learning objectives.

A critical aspect of the personal collections is that the member defines the pedagogical and/or personal context for selecting and using the materials. The ability of users to contribute their context for the materials enables the user of any country, culture, or language to share their knowledge and purposes for using the online materials.

Access to the MERLOT Community

Although the collection of online materials facilitates the research and design of curriculum, it is MERLOT's directory of members that facilitates participation in the community of practice. The member directory contains contact information, academic areas of expertise, and an ePortfolio of the members' contributions of materials, comments, and assignments to MERLOT. As presented earlier, the personal collections are also part of the member's ePortfolio. The directory enables individuals to find and communicate with colleagues who might advise them on the effective use of digital resources. If faculty find a resource that they want to use in their class, they could contact the author of the materials, the person who contributed the description, and/or the person who wrote a member comment or assignment. The close connections between the academic content and the people who have used the content reduce the isolation of faculty and provide opportunities for dialogue, feedback, collaboration, and mentoring.

THE BUSINESS COMMUNITY MANAGEMENT OF COLLECTION QUALITY

With the MERLOT collection being built by its members, there is a question of how the quality of the collection is managed. MERLOT conducts peer review of online materials in the collection, a process that helps insure that learning materials within the MERLOT collection are contextually accurate, pedagogically sound, and technically easy to use. MERLOT has modeled its peer reviews on the discipline-based peer review of scholarship and research (Hanley & Thomas, 1998; Hanley, 2003). MERLOT's peer review process also provides a mechanism for professional recognition for faculty developing and using instructional technology.

The review and management of the collection is the responsibility of MERLOT's editorial boards. Currently, business is one of the 13 disciplines within MERLOT. Part of the commitment a MERLOT institutional partner makes is to support faculty participation on some of the editorial boards. The criteria used to appoint members of the business editorial board by the partnering systems and institutions are 1) expertise in the discipline, 2) excellence in teaching, 3) experience in using technology in teaching and learning, and 4) connections with their discipline's professional organizations.

Within the business discipline, there are a number of subdisciplines that include accounting, business law, e-commerce, economics, finance, general, information systems, international business, management, and marketing. Each of these subdisciplines is further categorized in more detail. For instance, management includes strategy, human resources, organizational behavior and development, production and operations management, entrepreneurship, ethics, and international management. The business collection currently contains over 1400 learning materials, and the business community itself is composed of over 2000 members.

As discussed above, the business peer review process is modeled on the peer review of scholarship and research. The editor has the overall responsibility of managing the collection and ensuring that the peer review process runs smoothly. Additionally, associate editors from sponsoring organizations are responsible for the peer review of modules within their subdisciplines.

In addition to the sponsored members of the editorial board, the business discipline has also encouraged those in the greater business community of MERLOT to participate in the peer review process. Currently, two "volunteer" board members serve as assistant editors, with responsibility for the review process in their subdisciplines. Additionally, the business editorial board has cultivated an ever-growing group of voluntary peer reviewers. These individuals must meet the same requirements met by sponsored members of the editorial board. Many of these peer reviewers have been recruited from professional discipline organizations, such as the American Marketing Association, American Accounting Association, and the Academy of Management.

MERLOT provides a variety of tools and processes to ensure the integrity and manage the efficiency of the peer review process, including the training of peer reviewers and process controls on the evaluation of the materials. MERLOT also provides conference calls, LISTSERVS, threaded discussions and password-protected Web sites for posting documents, enabling the business editorial board to communicate and coordinate its work in a secure environment.

Business Peer Review Process

The peer review process begins with the business editorial board triaging parts of the collection in their discipline to determine which materials are worthy of the intensive review process. Many of the materials are classified as "will not review." These may include materials that are only resource materials, or they may include materials that are not of the highest quality. Rather than delete materials that don't qualify for peer review, the business editorial board prefers that the materials remain accessible for all.

Once identified as worthy of review, the material is reviewed by at least two trained peer reviewers who have expertise in the area. Faculty reviewers write individual evaluations, and then send these reviews to the editor or associate editor, who then integrates them into a single peer review. During the peer review process, the editorial board members are in communication with the author of the material. Additionally, the author must agree to have the peer review posted to MERLOT.

The outcome of the peer review process is a report containing a description of the learning goals, the targeted student population(s), prerequisite knowledge and skills, the type of learning material included (simulation, animation, tutorial, quiz, lecture/presentation, collection, reference material), a summary of the procedures for using the software, the technical requirements needed, and an evaluation of the quality, potential effectiveness for teaching and learning, and usability. Additionally, the comments and recommendations for the author are included. The authors are also permitted to respond to any comments made by the reviewers, and these can be incorporated into the report.

Evaluation Standards

The business editorial board members are provided three (3) evaluation standards for use when assessing the online learning materials. These standards are operationalized in ways appropriate for the business discipline. After each of the evaluation standards is evaluated, an overall rating is assigned to the module, and also an overall rating of each of the evaluation standards appears. The three evaluation standards are as follows:

1. **Quality of content.** The learning materials must present valid (correct) concepts, models, and illustrations. To evaluate the validity of the content, the reviewers rely on their particular expertise. Quality of content also means that the learning materials present educationally significant concepts, models, and skills for the discipline. To evaluate the educational significance of the content, peer reviewers decide if the content is part of the core curriculum within the discipline, difficult to

teach and learn, and/or is a prerequisite for understanding more advanced material in the discipline. The module is rated on each of the following criteria, and then an overall quality of content rating is determined:

a. Module is clear and concise.

b. Module provides a complete demonstration of the concept.

c. Module demonstrates a core concept.

d. Module is current.

e. Module is relevant to today's situation.

f. Module is self-contained (can be used without requiring an assignment or context).

g. Module provides accurate information.

h. Module is flexible (can be used in several situations).

i. Module includes an adequate amount of material.

j. Module summarizes the concept well.

k. Module integrates the concept well.

l. Overall, the quality of the content is very high.

2. **Potential effectiveness for teaching and learning.** Determining the effectiveness of the material requires the actual use of the digital learning materials by both students and faculty and a systematic assessment of the outcomes. Evaluation of the potential effectiveness of the material requires the peer reviewers to judge the materials based upon their expertise as instructors. The reviews determine if the materials are likely to improve teaching and learning, given the ways the faculty and students could use them. The reviewers are provided an established set of principles to follow to determine if the material is appropriate according to the standards of MERLOT. The module is rated on each of the following criteria and then an overall potential effectiveness of teaching and learning rating is assigned:

a. Module identifies learning objectives.

b. Module identifies prerequisite knowledge.

c. Module reinforces concepts progressively.

d. Module builds on prior concepts.

e. Module demonstrates relationships between concepts.

f. Module is easy to write assignments for.

g. Module is very efficient (one could learn a lot in a short period of time).

h. Overall, this module is very effective as a teaching tool.

3. **Ease of using the material.** Evaluating how easy it is for instructors and students to use the digital learning materials for the first time is the primary feature of this standard. MERLOT provides a summary of the appropriate usability standards to follow as a guideline. The standards are based on Nielson's (1993) heuristics for good instructional design. The module is rated on each of the following criteria and then an overall Ease of Using the Material rating is assigned:

a. Module is easy to use.

b. Module has clear instructions.

c. Module is engaging.

d. Module is visually appealing.

e. Module is interactive.

f. Module is of high design quality.

g. Overall, the usability of this module is very high.

Complementing Peer Reviews with Member Comments

While peer reviewers require training and are appointed by MERLOT, anyone who is an individual member of MERLOT can contribute member comments. The user-centered review process already has precedent in a number of highly used Web sites, such as Amazon.com, and allows individuals to provide their observations and evaluations on the learning materials within MERLOT. Members are asked first to describe how they reviewed the materials (e.g., 5 minutes browsing, or used it in teaching a course), and are then asked to evaluate the quality of the content, effectiveness for teaching and learning, and ease of use.

In summary, the MERLOT collection of modules, peer reviews, comments, assignments, personal collections, and ePortfolios enable faculty to effectively and efficiently choose materials for teaching. Instructors can customize the materials within the design of their own curriculum, and participate in professional development activities within the Business Community.

Institutional and Individual Readiness

The success of any program is determined in large part on its ability meet the immediate needs of the institution and individual. MERLOT provides services that can meet the immediate needs for research and curriculum design in distance learning programs. MERLOT continues to serve the needs and capabilities of institutions and individuals as they mature. For those who need to simply explore and find digital content, MERLOT provides a very low threshold of effort to succeed. For those who need instruction on how to use digital content in teaching and learning, MERLOT provides a professional development program. The annual MERLOT International Conference also provides many opportunities for professional development. The MERLOT Faculty Development Workshop provides its institutional partners with an intensive training program for their staff to learn how to implement MERLOT at their campuses. For those who want to demonstrate leadership in academic technology, MERLOT provides opportunities, resources, and participation in the strategic directions of MERLOT. MERLOT conducts a variety of planning and training meetings for its project directors' council, editors' council, and advisory board, as it continuously shapes its future.

Technology, Teaching, and Tenure

One of the pervasive issues for both faculty and administration is the recognition and reward for effective teaching with technology within the hiring, retention, tenure, and promotion process. The disconnection between stated priorities for using technology and the policies and practices for personnel evaluation is a major barrier to effective and sustained use of technology in teaching and learning. For those institutions that are ready to align priorities with policies and practices, MERLOT provides a means to their success.

Guidelines for evaluating technology in instruction are being published by professional societies and institutions, such as the following:

- Conference on College Composition and Communication
  http://www.hu.mtu.edu/~cyselfe/P&TStuff/P&TWeb/Introduction.htm

- Modern Language Association
  http://www.mla.org/reports/ccet/ccet_frame.htm

- American Association for History and Computing
  http://www.theaahc.org/tenure_guidelines.htm

- Duquesne University
  http://www.tltgroup.org/resources/rduqten.html

- University of Michigan
  http://www.personal.umich.edu/~cberger/FacultyRecandReward.doc

There are a number of common principles emerging from these evaluation guidelines. Peer evaluation and testimony by experts in the field are required to verify the quality and importance of the materials to the discipline. The digital scholarship should be made "visible" to the professional community. Candidates should provide electronic portfolios for review, instead of evidence files of the "crime of doing good work." The evaluation of the materials should be performed in the medium in which the scholarship was created.

MERLOT provides campus administration, review committees, and candidates with resources and tools to implement these evaluation guidelines. MERLOT's peer reviews are performed by an independent panel of experts who have been trained to reliably apply a standards-based evaluation process. Administrators, committees, and candidates can use the peer reviews as external reviews, validating the quality and significance of the candidate's digital scholarship. MERLOT provides an international venue to make the digital scholarship visible and enables the professional community to evaluate, use, augment, and reference in their personal collections. Finally, MERLOT provides documentation for the quality and quantity of digital scholarship contributions that business faculty make through the ePortfolios and with letters of recognition. Authors of peer-reviewed modules are sent letters of recognition for their contributions. Additionally, peer reviewers received recognition for their contributions in the peer review of scholarly material.

CONCLUSION

In conclusion, well-designed Web-based learning materials can significantly improve teaching and learning (Carpi 2003). Internet technology complements and supplements the conventional classroom methodology and can enhance the educational process (Karuppan 1999; 2001). However, faculty members are sometimes worried about the amount of time it takes to prepare coursework (Carr 2000). The online sharing of high quality materials will help promote and enhance learning. As suggested by Brown (2002), professors are better off searching for "chunks" of effective material and then deciding which of them will strengthen their courses.

MERLOT's own success is determined by its ability to facilitate different educational institutions' success, as measured by local variables, through shared and customized services. It is through the expanding, collaborative participation in an international business community that individuals and institutions will be able to more effectively and efficiently prepare their instructors to design and deliver effective, innovative, and customized distance learning programs. As effective programs grow, they will sustain the educational needs of future business leaders.

REFERENCES

Brown, David G. (2001). Searching for chunks. [Electronic Version]. *Syllabus*, August 26. Retrieved October 7, 2003, from http://www.syllabus.com/article.asp?id=6337,

Carpi, Anthony (2003). The visionlearning project. *Journal of College Science Teaching*, 33 (1), 12-15.

Carr, Sarah (2000). Many professors are optimistic on distance learning, survey finds. *Chronicle of Higher Education*, 46 (44), p. A35.

Dacko, Scott (2001). Narrowing skill development gaps in marketing and MBA programs: The role of innovative technologies for distance education. *Journal of Marketing Education*, 23 (3), pp. 228-229.

Gibson, Jane Whitney & Herrera, Jorge M. (1999). How to go from classroom based to online delivery in eighteen months or less: A case study in online program development. *THE Journal*, 26 (6), pp. 57-60.

Hanley, G.L., Schneebeck, C., & Zweier, L. (1998). Implementing a scaleable and sustainable model for instructional software development. *Syllabus*, 11(9), pp 30-34.

Hanley, G.L, & Thomas, C. (2000) MERLOT: Peer review of instructional technology. *Syllabus*, v14, no. 3, 16-20.

Hanley, G.L. (2001). Designing and delivering of instructional technology: A team-based approach. In C. Barone & P. Hagner (Eds.), *Technology-enhanced learning: A guide to engaging and supporting faculty*. Indianapolis, IN: Jossey-Bass Inc.

Karuppan, Corinne M. (1999). Empirically based guidelines for developing teaching materials on the Web. *Business Communication Quarterly*, 62 (3), pp. 37-45.

Karuppan, Corinne M. (2001). Web based teaching materials: A user's profile. *Internet Research*, 11 (2), pp. 138-148.

Pethoukoukis, J. M. (2002). Elearn and earn. *U.S. News & World Report*, 132 (22), p. 36.

Schneebeck, C. & Hanley, G. L. (2001). The California State University Center for Distributed Learning. In Epper, R. M. and Bates, A. W. (Eds.), *Teaching faculty how to use technology: Best practices from leading institutions*. Westport, CT: Greenwood/Oryx Press.

Strain, J. (1987). The role of the faculty member in distance education. *American Journal of Distance Education*, 1 (2). 10-15.

Victor, D. (1999). Electronic classrooms and vertical publishing: A look beyond the writing requirement. *Business Communication Quarterly*, 62 (1), pp. 74-81.

Distance Education Environment: Course Delivery in Cyberspace

Nanda Ganesan

California State University, Los Angeles

Los Angeles, California

Over the years, the enrollment in online courses has increased considerably. Universities have reported steady growth in online enrollment with fully Web-based online degree programs being offered (Hartman, Dzubian, and Moskal, 1999). The trend shows an increase in Internet delivered or supported university courses (Hartman et al.; Koroghlanizn and Brinkerhoff, 2000). There are an estimated 600 courses now offered on the Internet by different academic institutions (Illinois Online Network, 2003). The era in which research studies focused on the viability and validity of online courses has long past, leading current day research into the study of implementing successful online courses. This chapter follows this trend by discussing the technological and the pedagogical issues concerned with the delivery of courses in cyberspace.

The chapter is divided into two sections. The technical issues relating to course delivery in cyberspace are presented in the first section, while the student- and instructor- related issues are discussed in the second section. The information presented is based on the experience gained from implementing Technology Mediated Learning (TML) in a selected number of courses in an urban university (Ganesan, 2002). The experience thus obtained is compared, contrasted, and augmented with the published experience of others who have implemented similar online courses.

SECTION I: TECHNOLOGIES FOR DELIVERING COURSES IN CYBERSPACE

The technologies and tools that could be used for the creation of Web sites, the development of multimedia modules, the experimental configuration of a Cyberlab, and the hosting of online collaboration are discussed in this section.

Web Design, Implementation, and Hosting

A course Web site represents the point of aggregation of information and learning material pertinent to a course. Designing and implementing a Web site would therefore figure prominently in the decision to deliver courses in cyberspace. In most cases, the design and implementation of a course Web site are characterized by the following tasks (that are further discussed in the sections that follow):

- Choice of platform for hosting the course Web site

- Web content development

- Selection of Web development software

Web hosting. Deciding on the right platform to host the course Web site at the initial stages of Web development is important, because it will have an influence not only on the choice of Web design tools, but also on the design itself. There are a number of options available for hosting a Web site. A few are as follows:

- Host the Web site using an e-learning system such as WebCT or Blackboard.

- Use a free Web hosting service to host the Web site.

- Host the Web site on a fee-based Web hosting service.

- Design and implement a Web server locally to host the Web site.

The best choice for those with minimal technical knowledge of designing and hosting Web sites would be to use an e-learning system such as WebCT or Blackboard, two of the leading Web development and hosting systems implemented on campuses. (Other examples of e-learning systems are listed in Table 1.)

The second option, using a free Web hosting service, is often subject to several limitations, such as the restrictions placed on bandwidth and use of storage space. Due to these limitations, the usefulness of free Web hosting services is somewhat restrictive. This option may, however, be used for hosting simple Web sites containing basic course-related information, such as the course syllabus and other descriptive information about the course. Some commercial examples of free Web hosting services are provided in Table 1.

The third option mentioned was to use a fee-based service to host the course Web site (Web Hosts, 2001). Some examples of service providers in this category are listed in Table 1. One of the major advantages of using a fee-based service is that the course designer is spared the challenging task of managing the Web site. The hosting company is responsible for not only hosting the Web site, but also securing the site from attacks from hackers. The obvious drawback with a fee-based hosting service is the cost associated with the service.

Table 1. Sample Products and Selection Criteria for Web Hosting		
Hosting Platform	**Sample Products**	**Selection Criteria**
E-Learning Systems	WebCT, Blackboard, IntraLearn, Top Class, VisualU, and Web Course in a Box	Best choice for anyone in academia with limited knowledge of Web design and hosting.
Free Web Hosting	Tripod, Angelfire, Geocities, Web4Free, and NetCitizen	Suitable for hosting simple Web sites for courses.
Fee-Based Web Hosting	AdGrafix and Bytewerks	May be chosen if none of the other alternatives are available.
In-House Hosting	Apache Server and IIS Server	Suitable for course designer wanting to experiment with different approaches to offering courses, provided the necessary technical support for hosting the Web site is available.

The fourth option mentioned was to install and manage a dedicated Web server for hosting the course Web site. A dedicated Web server offers the most flexible environment for hosting a course Web site, although it brings the added responsibility of installing and managing the server to the course designer. In most cases, the responsibility would rest with the technical support person assigned to assist the course designer. In the case of the TML project, it was decided to install and manage a Web server locally because of the flexibility it offered in terms of experimenting with different approaches to delivering the courses in cyberspace. The decision criteria that could be used for selecting an appropriate Web hosting platform from the four options mentioned are summarized in Table 1.

Web content development. *Course information.* For the effective delivery of courses in cyberspace, the course Web site should be designed to function as a gateway to learning, in the sense that it should be more than merely a repository of course-related information. The course Web site should contain resources that play a supporting role in the learning process. These resources include tutorials, the actual reference material, or the Web links to relevant reference material, study guides, and multimedia learning material. A study that analyzed 230 course Web sites listed, among others, the following categories of information to be prevalent in course Web sites (Grandkowska & Heines, 2002):

The course Web site created in the TML project also contained many of the categories of information listed above. In particular, it contained the following information:

- General course-related information

- PowerPoint slides

- Streamed audio reviews

- Course notes made available in PDF format

- Reference material presented in PDF format

- Extensive links to tutorials and reference sites

- Homework assignments

The general course-related information included the syllabus, a description of the examination requirements, project details, and other requirements of the course. The online learning material consisting of course slides and audio reviews was hosted on the Web site. The multimedia instructional modules that were developed as part of the learning material were not stored on the Web site. The reason for this was that the modules required considerable bandwidth for downloading them over the campus network.

Online references. One of the major advantages of hosting a course Web site online is that it provided the students with instant access to a vast collection of learning resources on the Internet. For the most part, either the links to the appropriate reference material were provided, or the reference material itself was captured in PDF format and posted on the Web site. Due consideration was given to copyright restrictions when posting the reference material Web site. The students preferred the availability of the actual reference material to the instructor's providing them with the links to the references.

The reference material available on the Internet included encyclopedias and Web tutorials, among other formats. In teaching a course in Information Technology, technical encyclopedias such as whatis.com and Webopedia.com were found to be useful in explaining the meaning of many technical terms. A tutorial Web site such as howstuffworks.com was equally helpful in furthering the understanding of a number of topics covered in the course. In addition, Web sites hosted by hardware and software vendors that provided easy access to the latest product-related information and white papers enabled the students to relate theory to practice. A few examples of the types of reference Web sites included in the course Web site are as follows:

- Subject-specific encyclopedias

- Reference papers published in journals

- Articles published in magazines

- White papers published on the Internet

- Links to vendor's Web sites

- Web tutorials

Selection of Web development software. Two different approaches could have been taken with respect to the design and development of the Web site. One approach would have been to design it using a general purpose Web development software such as Microsoft FrontPage or Macromedia Dreamweaver. The other approach would have been to use Web development software specifically designed for developing instructional Web sites, for example, ToolBook, Director, AuthorWare, or TopClass.

Unless one is involved in the extensive production of online courseware, the general purpose Web development software is adequate for designing course sites. Of the two general purpose Web development software mentioned, Dreamweaver is more sophisticated than FrontPage, but FrontPage was chosen for the TML project because it had the capability of incorporating the design features deemed necessary for the course's Web site. If advanced features were to be incorporated, the Macromedia suite of software known as Studio MX (of which Dreamweaver MX is a component) would have been a better choice. Others who have used Macromedia's suite of software have cited its extensive development features and the tight integration of its different components as reasons that persuaded them to choose it for their Web development project (Junaidu & Al-Ghamdi, 2002).

Audio and Video Technologies for Online Learning

Although a course Web site can be effective in functioning as a gateway to learning resources, it cannot by itself disseminate knowledge in the same way an instructor does in a classroom. Audio and video technologies can be used to overcome this shortcoming to some extent when delivering a course in cyberspace. In some cases, it is possible to simulate a learning environment similar to that experienced in a classroom by the innovative use of multimedia technology. In the TML project, streamed audio modules and several sets of CD-ROMs consisting of multimedia instructional modules were produced to achieve this end.

Producing and hosting audio modules. The technology is readily available, at present, to record and present high quality audio in streamed format. The impact of streamed audio on learning, however, is somewhat limited because of the absence of video. It could nevertheless be used for purposes such as chapter reviews and examination reviews. In the TML project, the reviews were streamed and hosted on the course Web site. The streamed audio modules were found to be effective for review purpose because they contained information that had already been presented and discussed.

Audio can be streamed using streaming software such as Microsoft Media Encoder or Real Producer. A sound editing software such as SoundForge could also be used for streaming audio. The relative merits of each approach are described in Table 2, along with names of sample software in each category. The SoundForge sound editing software was chosen for the TML project because of its good sound editing capabilities and the flexibility it offered in recording and storing audio in different formats.

Table 2. Audio Streaming Options and Sample Products

Streaming Software	Advantages	Disadvantages	Sample Products
Encoder	Inexpensive	Limited or no editing features supported	Microsoft Media Encoder, Real Media Producer, and Apple QuickTime
Sound Editor	Good editing features; original sound can be stored in Wav format	Need to purchase the software, although inexpensive	SoundForge and Cakewalk Express

Producing computer screen-based multimedia modules. Compared to the audio modules, the multimedia modules consisting of both audio and video were better suited for simulating an actual classroom lecture. As in the case of the audio modules, there are different methods of producing multimedia instructional modules. Depending on the resources available, the modules can be produced in varying degrees of sophistication, ranging from simple recordings of screen images in real-time, to the complex streaming of taped videos. In the case of the TML project, the multimedia modules were produced based on screen recordings.

Two different approaches could have been taken for recording the computer screens. The first approach would have been to use dedicated screen recording software such as

Camtasia to record the screen images, along with the accompanying audio narration. The second approach would have been to use a streaming software such as Microsoft Media Encoder to capture and stream the screens in real-time. The relative merits of each approach are listed in Table 3, along with a list of software available in each category. In the case of the TML project, the first option was chosen because of the fact that the quality of the audio and video of the modules produced by Camtasia was found to be better than those produced by a streaming encoder.

Table 3. Audio Streaming Options and Sample Products			
Multimedia Production Software	Advantages	Disadvantages	Sample Products
Screen recording software	Offers some editing and production features.	Need to purchase the software.	Camtasia, HyperCam, and CamStudio
Streaming software	Inexpensive	Modules could only be produced in streaming format; few editing features are supported.	Microsoft Media Encoder, Real Media Producer, and Apple QuickTime

Types of multimedia modules produced. Three different categories of multimedia modules were produced in the TML project using the recording technique described earlier. The categories of multimedia modules produced are as follows:

- Lecture modules based on PowerPoint slides

- Lecture modules simulating the chalk-and-talk type of in-class instruction

- Modules demonstrating various functional aspects of computer software

The first set of modules was based on PowerPoint slides used in regular lectures. These modules contained only the slides and the narration that accompanied the slides. As such, it was not possible to simulate the chalk-and-talk type of lectures given in a classroom in these modules. A second set of modules was produced to overcome this drawback. The Seiko InkLink electronic memo pad was used to turn the computer screen into an electronic blackboard for simulating the chalk-and-talk lectures. In this case, the screen images were recorded in real-time, along with the accompanying explanations of how to simulate the chalk-and-talk type of lectures.

The third set of modules was produced for the purpose of demonstrating the functionality of the software. These modules were essentially software tutorials, using computer screens captured in real-time to show various operational features of the software. The modules were superior to any other form of learning aid that could have been used for teaching software applications. All three modules worked well to augment the learning material posted on the course Web site.

Real-Time Access to Computers in Cyberspace

One of the major challenges facing cyber-delivered courses is in providing real-time access to computers. Real-time access is particularly desirable when teaching courses that require hands-on computing experience as part of the course. To address this issue, an experimental Cyberlab was setup in the TML project. The lab was implemented based on a technology well known in the industry, but little used in the academia. The technology is known as *thin-client computing*.

In thin-client computing, a thin-client server is maintained at a remote location from which client computers on the Internet access and execute applications. In this case, the entire execution takes place at the server. The client only functions as a terminal connected to the server over cyberspace. Microsoft's implementation of thin-client technology, known as Terminal Services, was used for configuring the Cyberlab. The choice was made based on the fact that the IT courses for which Technology Mediated Learning was implemented relied on Microsoft's application software for the laboratory component.

The Cyberlab was used for teaching networking courses where students were able to access the server over the Internet to practice network administration tasks from their home computers. Although the Cyberlab was used for completing assignments in network administration, the application potential of thin-client computing is by no means limited to network-related operations. Many applications that run on a regular server can be run equally effectively from a Terminal Server. Thin-client technology can therefore provide the answer to the delivery of courses in cyberspace that have a laboratory component as part of the course requirement.

Collaboration Technologies

In the previous sections, the activities directly related to the delivery of instruction were discussed. In this section, technologies related to collaboration, an indirect but essential part of online learning will be presented.

For a considerable period of time, e-mail was the most prevalent form of collaboration. E-mail represents a passive form of collaboration. In recent times, a more active form of collaboration, known as Web-based conferencing, has made significant advances in terms of the software and services needed to implement collaboration. The collaboration software and services can be grouped into three major functional categories (Wooley, 2003). They are as follows:

Real-time conferencing. Real-time conferencing comprises data conferencing, instant messaging, chat rooms, whiteboards, and video conferencing. An inexpensive way to conduct real-time conferencing, or synchronous communication, is to use Microsoft NetMeeting. The alternative to setting up an online conferencing facility locally is to use the services offered by a conference service provider. Real-time conferencing has a broad appeal in the commercial world. As such, there are several service providers who offer their services for real-time conferencing (Wooley, 2003). Examples of service providers in this category include CentraNow, Click to Meet, eBlvd and WebEx.

Electronic forums. Collaboration can take place in asynchronous mode as well. Electronic forum is an example of the asynchronous form of collaboration. There are several software packages available for hosting electronic forums and message boards locally on a server. E-learning systems such as WebCT also have built-in support for hosting discussion forums. If it is not possible to host an electronic forum locally, the facilities offered by a forum service provider such as Web Crossing, netVillage, and Bravenet can be used.

Group workspaces for collaboration. Collaborative group workspaces can be of help to students participating in group activities. E-learning systems generally support the hosting of group workspaces. Workspaces could also be set up locally on a server using a messaging server such as the Exchange server. There are also newer servers that focus solely on collaboration. An example in this case is Microsoft's SharePoint portal server. It is also possible to use the services of outside vendors to set up collaborative group workspaces. Some vendors have specialized in offering group workspaces to support online courses. Examples of service providers in this category include Campus Crossing, Classroom Assistant, and eTrainer.

Maintaining an electronic forum was not a priority in the case of the TML project, as it focused primarily on implementing a hybrid system that required regular, but shortened, in-class meetings. On the other hand, if a course is designed to be delivered entirely in cyberspace, it is imperative that the students be offered an electronic forum in some form for online collaboration.

Multifaceted Approach to Delivering Courses in Cyberspace

To build an effective online learning environment, it is important to integrate the technologies discussed in the previous sections. A multifaceted online learning model such as the one shown in Figure 1 can achieve this objective. Only a multifaceted approach can successfully combine the flexibility of online learning with the positive learning aspects of in-class learning.

SECTION II: PEOPLE IN ONLINE LEARNING

The flexible learning environment of online education is the result of people using technology to overcome time and space restrictions imposed upon them by the traditional classroom-based learning environment. In this respect, the technology discussed in

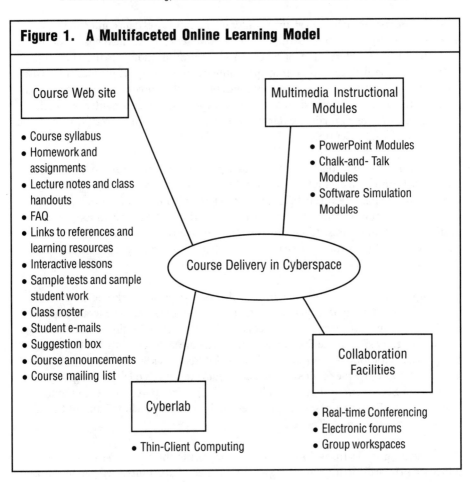

Figure 1. A Multifaceted Online Learning Model

Course Web site
- Course syllabus
- Homework and assignments
- Lecture notes and class handouts
- FAQ
- Links to references and learning resources
- Interactive lessons
- Sample tests and sample student work
- Class roster
- Student e-mails
- Suggestion box
- Course announcements
- Course mailing list

Multimedia Instructional Modules
- PowerPoint Modules
- Chalk-and- Talk Modules
- Software Simulation Modules

Course Delivery in Cyberspace

Collaboration Facilities
- Real-time Conferencing
- Electronic forums
- Group workspaces

Cyberlab
- Thin-Client Computing

the previous section forms one component of online learning. The other component is people—those individuals who are involved in delivering and using online learning. The people involved can be grouped into different categories: instructors, students, administrators, and technical support staff. The issues related to instructors and students are discussed in this second section of the chapter.

Instructor Perspectives

Opportunities and challenges. There are many reasons for instructors to offer online courses. An interest in online teaching and learning and an interest in technology and the Internet were some of the reasons cited by many who have become involved in online courses (Fredericksen, Pickett, Shea, Pelz & Swan, 2000). Others have identified the opportunity to develop new ideas; the opportunity to improve one's teaching; the opportunity to diversify program offerings; the ability to offer greater flexibility to the students in their learning experience; the personal motivation to use technology; the intellectual challenge; and the overall job satisfaction as some of the factors motivating them to offer online courses (Schifter, 2000).

Instructors offering online courses are likely to face a multitude of challenges. Among them are an increase in workload, the lack of recognition of their efforts for tenure and promotion, and the concerns relating to student ratings (Grankowska & Heines, 2002). Many studies have indicated that there would be an increase in the workload of the instructor offering online courses (Hartman et al., 1999; NEA, 2000; Visser, 2000). There is also a minority view that there is no significant increase in the workload when implementing an online course (DiBase, 2000). In the case of the TML project, there was a substantial increase in the workload of the instructor.

Instructors are also concerned that a decrease in face-to-face contact with the students may lead to lower student ratings. Some studies tend to indicate lower student ratings in online courses, whereas others have shown that there is no difference in the ratings between online and regular courses (Durton & Dutton, 2002; Johnson, 2001). There are also studies indicating that the student evaluations for online courses and the overall grade received by students in online courses are higher compared to traditional courses (Fredericksen et al., 2000). In the case of the TML project, the student ratings remained unchanged compared to the ratings received prior to the introduction of Technology Mediated Learning.

Student Perspectives
There are insightful studies that have been carried out to understand various student-related factors that influence student performance of students in online courses. These studies can be grouped into two different categories. First, the performances of the students have been analyzed with respect to the demographic characteristics of the students. Second, the behavioral and learning characteristics of the students that relate to their receptiveness to online learning have been studied. The findings of these studies are briefly discussed in the following sections.

Effect of student demography on online learning. In analyzing the demography of students in relation to their performance in online courses, the studies have basically focused on race and gender. There is limited study to indicate that black students tend to have the highest success rates in online courses, whereas Asian and Hispanic students tend to show the opposite result (Hartman et al., 1999). There are a number of studies that indicate that female students, in general, tend to perform better than their male counterparts in online courses (Fredericksen et al., 2000, issue 2; Hartman et al., 1999; Johnson, 2001). Age is another contributing factor to successful online learning. Older students tend to view online courses favorably compared to their younger counterparts (Fredericksen et al.,2000 (issue 2); Inoue, 1999). Some have suggested that online learning could be an effective alternative method of education for mature and self-disciplined students (Illinois Online Network, 2003). This observation was confirmed in the TML project, where graduate students were found to be more receptive to the challenges imposed upon them by online courses, compared to their undergraduate counterparts.

Characteristics of a successful online student. Other than the demographic characteristics of students, there are also certain behavioral and learning characteristics that contribute to successful online learning. Among these characteristics are self-motivation, ability to work independently, ability to manage time efficiently, possession of organization skills, resourcefulness, and the ability to take responsibility for learning (University of North Texas, 2003). These observations were generally in agreement with the characteristics of the students found to be successful in the courses offered in the TML project.

Grooming students to be successful in online courses. While the students with certain traits are considered to be positively disposed to online learning, others can be equally motivated and trained to become successful online learners. The best approach to motivating them is to groom them into developing an attitude conducive to online learning. In this respect, the factors that should be brought to their attention are that they should be open minded about sharing life, work, and educational experiences; be self-motivated and self-disciplined; be willing to speak up if problems arise; be willing and able to commit to 4 to 15 hours per week per course; be able to meet the minimum requirements for the program; be able to accept critical thinking and decision making as part of the learning process; have access to a computer and a modem; be able to think ideas through before responding; and feel that high quality learning can take place without going to a traditional classroom (Illinois Online Network, 2003).

CONCLUSION

Based on the experience gained in the TML project and the published experience of others engaged in similar projects, it is evident that online learning will play an increasingly important role in higher education and in the delivery of professional courses. At the undergraduate level, the best approach would be to use a mixed model that combines online learning with the traditional form of in-class learning. At the graduate level, the courses can be fully delivered in cyberspace. Many professional courses and training seminars stand to benefit from online learning because of the fact that they are offered to mature students.

The effectiveness of online learning can be significantly increased by taking a multifaceted approach to the delivery of courses in cyberspace. A course Web site alone cannot deliver the desired results in learning. Innovative use of multimedia and other e-learning tools, techniques, and services must be incorporated as part of the course plan to build a successful online learning environment. Only a multifaceted approach to online learning can be effective in combining the benefits of the vast e-learning resources of the Internet with the positive learning aspects of in-class learning.

To maximize the impact of online learning on students, the instructors also need to learn to adjust and adapt to a changing environment. Their role will now change from teachers to facilitators of learning. It is important for the instructors to make the students aware of the fact that online learning requires a somewhat different outlook, attitude, and approach to learning, compared to traditional in-class learning. The instructors will thus have to bear the responsibility of guiding and training the students into becoming successful online learners.

Finally, given the emerging computer literacy of students entering colleges and the rapidly advancing speed and affordability of computer and communication technologies, it is apt to conclude that cyber-delivered courses will play an increasingly important role in the delivery of instruction in higher learning institutions.

REFERENCES

DiBase, D. (2000) Is distance learning more work or less work? *The American Journal of Distance Education, 14*(3).

Durton, J., Dutton, M. & P. (2002, July). How do online students differ from lecture students? *Journal of Asynchronous Learning Networks, 6* (1).

Fredericksen, E., Pickett, A., Shea, P., Pelz, W. & Swan, K. (2000, September). Factors influencing faculty satisfaction with asynchronous teaching and learning in the SUNY Learning Network. *Journal of Asynchronous Learning Networks, 4* (2).

Fredericksen, E., Pickett, A., Shea, P., Pelz, W. & Swan, K. (2000, September). Factors influencing faculty satisfaction with asynchronous teaching and learning in the SUNY Learning Network. *Journal of Asynchronous Learning Networks, 4* (3).

Ganesan, N. (2002/2003). A multifaceted approach to technology mediated learning. *Journal of Educational Technology Systems, 31* (2).

Grankowska, S., & Heines, J. (2002, December). Course Web sites: State-of-the-art. *USDLA Journal, 12* (12).

Hartman, J., Dziuban, C., & , Moskal, P. (1999). Faculty satisfaction in ALNs: A dependent or independent variable? *Proceedings of the 1999 Summer ALN Conference, University of Chicago.*

Inoue Y. (1999-2000). The university student's preference for learning by computer-assisted instruction. *Journal of Educational Technology Systems, 28* (3).

Illinois Online Network (2003). *Learning styles and the online environment.* Retrieved August 22, 2003, from http://illinois.online.uillinois.edu/IONresources/instructionaldesign/learningStyles.asp

Illinois Online Network (2003). *Weakness of online learning.* Retrieved August 22, 2003, from http://www.ion.illinois.edu/IONresources/onlineLearning/weaknesses.asp.

Illinois Online Network (2003). *What makes a successful online student?* Retrieved August 22, 2003, from http://www.ion.illinois.edu/IONresources/onlineLearning/StudentProfile.asp

Johnson, Susan M. (2001, January). Teaching introductory international relations in an entirely Web-based environment: Comparing student performance across and within groups. *Ed at a Distance, 15* (10).

Junaidu, S. & Al-Ghamdi, J. (2002, December). Tips for developing media-rich online courses. *USDLA Journal, 12* (12).

Koroghlanian, C.M., & Brinkerhoff, J. (2000-2001). An investigation into students' preexisting computer skills and attitudes toward Internet delivered instruction. *Journal of Educational Technology Systems, 29*, (2).

National Education Association (2000, June). *A survey of traditional and distance learning higher education members.* Retrieved September 5, 2003, from http://www.nea.org/he/abouthe/dlstudy.pdf

Schifter, C.(2000, January), Factors influencing faculty participation in distance education: A factor analysis, *Ed at a Distance, 13* (1).

University of North Texas (2003). *Distributed learning@ U, how do I know if distributed learning is for me?* Retrieved September 5, 2003, from University of North Texas Web site: http://Web2.unt.edu/cdl/CDL_ECAMPUS/default.cfm?pfile=isitrightforme.htm

Visser, J. A. (2000). Faculty work in developing and teaching Web-based courses: A case study of time and effort. *The American Journal of Distance Education, 14*(3).

Web Hosts. (2001). Retrieved September 6, 2003, from http://www.onlinebusiness.com/OnlineBusiness/WebHosts.shtml.

Wooley, D. R. (2003). Conferencing on the Web. Retrieved September 6, 2003 from http://www.thinkofit.com/Webconf/.

Essential Tips for the Planning and Development of Online Courses

Ok D. Park
University of Arkansas
Fayetteville, Arkansas

Frederick Nafukho
University of Arkansas
Fayetteville, Arkansas

Technological advances, especially in the area of computer technology, have led to the development and implementation of new and innovative instructional strategies. Mundrake (2003, p. 130) noted, "Information technology is an important part of business education curriculum at all levels." In the case of business teachers, it is noted, "As a result of the development of the microcomputer and new office technologies, business educators are not strangers to technology. In fact, in most educational settings business education teachers are known for being the *experts* in the area of computers and technology" (Wallace, 1996, p. 106). The teaching and learning process has been dramatically changed by an emergence of a variety of technological and instructional developments in recent times (Smith, 2002). Advances in technology have led to a paradigm shift in the instructional process. "Online learning is attracting increased attention from individuals, school districts, higher education providers, and for-profit companies" (Donley, 2003, p.117). Because of technology, the teacher has become a facilitator in a learner-centered environment. Using the Internet's resources, students actively research needed information by participating as expert knowledge providers. The teacher is viewed as a coach and supporter who actively encourages students to use their personal knowledge and skills to create unique solutions to problems (Newby, Stepich, Lehman & Russel, 2000). The use of online instruction has made educational opportunities accessible particularly to students, who in the past, lacked opportunities due to factors such as work, geography, time, family responsibilities, and lack of money (Nafukho, Thompson & Brooks, 2003). Computer-related course instruction has made a significant impact on the provision of instruction and student learning in higher education (Piotrowski & Vodanovich, 2000).

This chapter looks more closely at the planning and development of online instruction courses. The key issues addressed in the chapter include preparation for online learning and instruction, main components of online instruction, interactive online instructional design, incorporation of interactivity and multimedia into online instruction, important resources for online instruction, course design considerations, use of electronic mail for instruction purposes, and bulletin boards. Advantages and disadvantages of the various online delivery methods are discussed.

PREPARING FOR ONLINE LEARNING AND INSTRUCTION
Online learning environments can be of three types: Web use as a supplement to face-to-face instruction, Web use in a mixed mode with face-to-face instruction, and use for Web-based instruction exclusive of face-to-face instruction (Berge, Collins & Dougherty, 2000).

Mishra (2002, p.493) observed, "The online environments of the third type are referred to in the literature as Web-based instruction, virtual learning, online learning, and e-learning." In this chapter, we use online learning to refer to any of the other three types of learning. The Web can be technically defined as, "A client/server information service based on Hyper Text Transfer Protocol" (Bostock, 1997, p.226). Melara (1999) emphasized the notion that before providing online learning, instructors must prepare the learner regarding the expected study habits such as time management. The other important preparations that Melara recommends include, clearly defining the role of the learners; ensuring knowledge of the expected communication protocol; ascertaining background knowledge of the virtual learners; clarifying virtual instructor/student interaction strategies; providing feedback; estimating learners' degree of technical knowledge; and communicating the availability of student support services. Based on the experience of these instructors, Melara's views deserve strong support. Failure to pay attention to the factors mentioned here may interfere with the efficient and effective delivery of online courses. As in traditional instruction, a conducive learning environment must be provided prior to launching online instruction. Mishra (2002) and Harris (1999) point out that using the Internet to deliver instruction requires more than creating good content. Instructors must make an effort to provide a complete learning environment.

On the importance of learning environment and availability of resources for successful on-line instruction, Khan (1997) observes that online learning environment requires many resources, technical support, a clear instructional/learning framework, and support for both novices and experts. Business educators, like all other educators, should be concerned with how to use technology to enhance and enrich the students' learning environments (Barker, 2000; Bianco & Curr-Chellman, 2002). While using online instruction, business educators should endeavor to develop rich classroom environments that encourage active learning and higher level thinking skills, especially reflection, problem solving, flexible thinking, and creativity (Hopson, Simms & Knezek, 2001).

MAIN COMPONENTS OF ONLINE INSTRUCTION

In order to design and deliver online courses, instructors must have a clear knowledge of the main components of online learning. Khan (1997, p. 7) identifies the following important components: "content development, multimedia component, Internet tools, computers and storage devices, service providers, authoring programs, servers, browsers and other applications." The content and development component of online courses require the instructor to be aware of the important learning and instructional theories (Mishra, 2002). In addition, the instructors require a sound knowledge of instructional design and curriculum development theories. This component is a must for all professional teachers. Thus, professional teachers should be equipped with a specific body of knowledge related to effective teaching strategies.

The multimedia component of online instruction refers to the aspect of stimulus variation in the instruction process. For online learning to accommodate learners' learning styles, such as auditory, visual, and kinesthetic, online course designers need to use text and graphics, audio streaming, video streaming, and graphical user interface (GUI). Online learning can also be made interesting and real by using the variety of search engines that currently exist. In addition, instructors should make use of asynchronous communication tools such as e-mail, listervs, newsgroups, and online chats. Synchronous communication tools such as audio, Internet phone, and conferencing tools can also be incorporated in online instruction. Experience with teaching online courses has shown that learners face a number of problems, such as not being able to download the class material, and having slow computers. To overcome such problems, instructors should make use of several computers and storage devices such as computer platforms for running Unix, DOS, Windows, and Macintosh operating systems, as well as servers, hardrives, and CD-ROMs. Course material should be saved on CD-ROMs and be made available to students who may be having problems with accessing online material. Using online instruction software such as WebCT and Blackboard, the instructors do not require learning HTML.

WebCT and Blackboard are the two main online instruction packages commonly used in the field of education. WebCT is a course development software package that utilizes the Internet to deliver online courses. The software creates a user-friendly environment and is quite convenient for online instruction. WebCT has become an important component of online course delivery and is now used by over 2000 universities worldwide. It has several advantages such as communication, assessment, tracking, and presentation tools. These tools allow for the development of online courses suited to several learning/teaching styles. Like the WebCT, Blackboard has become the leading provider of Internet infrastructure software for e-Education. "The software offers a complete suite of enterprise software products and services that power a total *e-Education Infrastructure* for schools, colleges, universities, and other education providers" (Blackboard Inc., 2003, p.1). Since its initial development in 1997, the software has grown to "serve many of the largest, innovative, and best known institutions in the world, from universities to associations to corporations. Blackboard is Web-based server software that provides industry- leading course management, an open architecture for customization and interoperability, and a scalable design that allows for integration with student information systems and authentication protocols (Yaskin & Gilfus, 2002). The College of Education and Health Professions at the University of Arkansas, where the authors of this chapter are based, uses Blackboard software package for all online instruction courses. The advantages of this software are that it is quite versatile and learner-friendly.

Successful design and delivery of online courses requires a variety of features. Khan (1997) further divides these features into two: (1) key features and (2) additional features. As noted, a well-designed Web course should have the following key features:

> Interactive, multimedia facilities, open system, online search, device distance-time independent, globally accessible, electronic publishing, uniformity world wide, online resources, distributed, cross cultural interaction, multiple expertise, industry supported, learner controlled, convenience, be self contained, ease of use, online support, authentic, course security, environmentally friendly, non-discriminatory, cost effective, ease of coursework development and maintenance, collaborative learning, formal and informal environments, online evaluation, and virtual cultures (p. 8).

Online instructors should work with the Web master to ensure that these features are incorporated in the online courses that they plan to teach.

INTERACTIVE ONLINE INSTRUCTIONAL DESIGN

For instructional Web sites to engage students in active learning environments, they should have interactive multimedia capabilities. "Multimedia refers to applications that add sound, animation, and support for both analog and digital video" (Wallace, 1996, p. 110). Wallace observes further that multimedia for business education can entail using multimedia to assist instruction for business education and prepare students to develop multimedia materials using authoring software packages. The design of the sites with multimedia capabilities should adhere to principles of instructional design. The principles require that the Web sites must have the main components, key features, and additional features. The Web sites should ensure that they cater to the learners' personality and learning styles, cultural differences, learners' disabilities, and aim at promoting supportive learning environments. Gillani and Relan (1997, p.236) provide the following useful multimedia design guidelines for online instructional design:

- Keep frames simple and be consistent in design of text, graphics, and sound. Simplicity and consistency eliminates cognitive overload.

- Do not distract the attention of the learner by providing unnecessary elements in a multimedia presentation.

- Use multimedia components to reinforce rather than distract from learning.

- Combine colors attractively to appeal to students. (For example, the color orange attracts attention, whereas the color blue creates a non-threatening environment.)

- Multimedia should convey information rather than an art piece.

- Always keep the size of animation as small as possible.

- Use dual coding as an effective means of instruction.

On the importance of an online instructional framework, Mishra (2002) and (Villalba & Romiszowski, 2001) note that three schools of thought have been widely used and explored to provide guidance for instructional practice. These include: behaviorism, cognitive psychology and constructivism. Of the three, constructivism has been identified as the most suitable one for online learning (Mishra, 2002; Hung 2001). The constructivist school of thought argues that teaching is more efficient when students engage in activities within a supportive learning environment and when they get proper guidance mediated by learning tools.

HOW TO INCORPORATE INTERACTIVITY AND MULTIMEDIA INTO INSTRUCTIONAL WEB SITES

The intention here is not to advise instructors to produce an accomplished Web master, but to mention the tools that can enable instructors to incorporate interactivity and multimedia features in their Web courses. Internet explorer is the most widely used tool for browsing the Internet. (See the browser survey results Web site shown in the index.) The other tool used for browsing the Internet is the Netscape Navigator. Both Internet Explorer and Netscape Navigator support a number of plug-ins such as Java, Java Scripting, and Shock Wave. Brief explanations of Java Scripting and Shock Wave are provided because of their importance in the design and delivery of online courses.

JavaScript

JavaScript is a scripting language that is full-feature object-based. It works best when it is embedded into HTML codes. The main advantage of using JavaScript is that it makes the content not static. JavaScript can also be used to create programs that interact with the user without relying on Common Gateway Interface (CGI) programs, which define how the browser, server, and script communicate. The other advantages of JavaScript as identified by Gillani and Relan (1997, p. 236) include the following features:

- It is an interpretive language and not compiled.

- Its codes can be embedded in HTML files and be interpreted on the fly.

- The language is object oriented.

- It can create reusable data objects.

- It can create its own objects or interact with objects that are included in the browser.

- It can be used to create mathematical units that monitor and interact with student's input.

- It can be used to verify students' answers, their names, their scores, and text inputs such as their passwords.

- It creates superior Web sites.

Shockwave

This is another important tool that can be used to create interactive multimedia Web sites for educational purposes. Just like JavaScript, Shockwave is designed to embed into interactive multimedia titles created with Director or Authorware, and then into HTML Tag and Plug-in (Gillani & Relan, 1997). Incorporating interactive multimedia features in online classes enables learners to develop group skills such as collaboration and cooperation. Learners are also provided with numerous opportunities to discuss material and to learn teaching and sharing with other group members. In addition, learners receive feedback from discussion group members and eventually develop interpersonal skills. They also observe that authoring for learning offers several advantages over authoring for more fixed media such as CD-ROM. For example, interactive multimedia enables the user to constantly update information, requires less equipment for production, requires less high-level graphics and provides a constantly updated source of design models for the structuring of large bodies of information.

While the interactive and multimedia features are important for online instruction, these features cannot replace the instructor. The instructors must always be available to the students. Willis and Dickinson (1997, p. 82) concluded that the challenges faced by the distant teacher are imposing. They suggested that the teachers do the following to be successful:

1. Look at the course in a new way. In many cases, the more comfortable the instructor is in teaching in a traditional setting, the more difficult it is to face the reality that significant re-thinking and adaptation will be required for effective distant course delivery.

2. Shift from the role of content provider to content facilitator.

3. Gain comfort and proficiency in using technology as the primary teacher-student link.

4. Learn to teach effectively without the visual control provided by direct eye contact.

5. Develop an understanding and appreciation for the distant students' lifestyle.

IMPORTANT RESOURCES FOR ONLINE INSTRUCTION

Bostock (1997) argues that educational uses for personal computers are well-known and suggests the following resources to be important for business instructors planning to use online instruction:

1. Data resources. Data resources include Web based resources found on the global hypermedium that are interactive in nature and Local CD-ROMs that can be used in combination to promote active learning. A combination of the two should help in solving problems faced by learners who have older versions of computer models that are usually slow in accessing Web material. Such learners might find the CD-ROMs very useful.

2. Tools. As pointed out in the earlier sections of this chapter, there are several components that enable learners to share information on the Web. For example, using the interactive multimedia tools, learners are able to use computers as word processors, spreadsheets, databases, and graphics to create effective and interesting learning environments. These tools enable students to share information with each other by publishing their own work on the Web.

3. Business simulations. Business simulations enable online users to program the computer to create games, simulations, models, microworlds, and programming languages by sharing one feature. All these can enhance and promote online instructional learning environments.

4. Tutors. Online instructors should make use of a variety of tutoring programs that have been developed. Web pages and course material can be used to create branching course tutorials, computer aided assessment, branching computer aided instruction (CAI) with remediation, adaptive computer aided learning (CAL) and Intelligent Tutoring Systems.

5. Communication. While learners and instructors using online instruction cannot engage in face-to-face communication, several other communication channels exist. For example, online instructors should make use of e-mail as a means of effective communication that is fast and less expensive. Communication by electronic mail needs to be integrated with the Web for efficient instruction purposes (p. 227-228).

Course Design Considerations

Business educators need to remember learner motivation while designing online courses. Examples of motivational strategies that should always be considered include creating learner interest, stimulus variation, increased learner curiosity, relevance, challenge level, positive learning outcomes, and positive learner impression.

Interest in the course content affects the attitude of the learners towards the course and the technology being used. Therefore, business instructors using online learning must endeavor to create interest in the instruction as early as possible. Opportunities

215

Chapter 15

should be provided in the beginning of the course to allow students to interact with others, with the technology being used, and with the instructional materials.

Instructors using online instruction must make appropriate changes in the organization and presentation of course material as a way of capturing learners' interest and raising their level of curiosity. They should create learning activities that require learners to browse several Web sites. This is a powerful way of engaging the learners mentally by exposing them to several different ways of thinking. Another good way to engage online students in active learning is to create intranet-based group discussions among students based in different sites or locations. In the authors' class at the University of Arkansas in Fayetteville, for example, active group discussions take place between students based at the Fayetteville, Hope, Fort Smith, Harrison, and Blytheville campuses. As mentioned earlier, instructors should endeavor to develop a diversity of online learning environments that appeal to students with different learning styles.

While creating variations, there is need to remain focused on the goals of the course. The diversity in learning activities should not distract learners from achieving course objectives. Effort should be made to build a strong relationship between what is being learned and the course objectives. Learning should proceed from known to unknown knowledge. For the course to remain relevant, the instructor should build in activities that relate to the learners' work experience, interests, background, career goals and learning styles. The Web-based instructor should also be highly motivated and use the powerful medium of the Internet for self-directed learning.

The challenge for online instructors is to create active learning environments that challenge their students. Learners should be provided with opportunities to ask questions and to receive answers. In addition, the students should be provided with detailed study guides and advance planners, showing when the quizzes and tests will be taken, when assignments are due, and when the course examination is scheduled. The expected goals and performance requirements should be clearly stated. For students enrolled in online courses to be fully challenged, they should continuously interact with their instructor and other students in the class. Therefore, while designing the course, more interaction avenues should be provided. To insure that students remain focused throughout the course, the instructor should provide instruction in short segments. For example, course content should be posted in topics instead of in its entirety, which can overwhelm some of the students. Frequent summaries and reviews of the course content should also be provided, a strategy that has proven effective in the authors' classes. When quizzes and tests are taken, corrective feedback should be posted on the Web site. Students should be regularly encouraged to follow the course schedule. Students who fall far behind the schedule often end up dropping the course. To ensure 100% course completion, students should be encouraged to sign a contract with the instructor stating their intentions and willingness to complete the online course. This serves as an important reminder, and it challenges the students to remain focused.

To achieve positive outcomes with online instruction, students should be provided with the opportunity to share work done in class with others who are in different locations. In addition, collaborative methods of teaching and learning should be employed. Class assignments and projects should require students to work together.

To create a positive impression of online classes, instructors can provide opportunities for the students to experiment with the courseware before actual classes. This helps in removing fears and stress associated with taking online classes for the first time. Organizing the instructional text will also help in creating a positive impression of the course. Use of appropriate color, good graphic and text design principles such as use of white space, complimentary colors, and attractive background makes the course material presentable and attractive to learners. To create a positive impression of the online courses, Web designers should use pictures, maps, graphics, diagrams, charts, arrows, figures and appropriate sound. This should help make the course material easier to understand and hold the learners' attention. When designing the content, instructors should use active voice in the instruction right from the beginning. Also, they should use sentences that are moderate in length and a variety of vocabulary. To take care of students who are visually impaired, font sizes 14 and above and clear, large figures should be posted on the Web sites. After an assignment is completed, just like in the face-to-face classes, students in online classes should be provided with positive feedback for their accomplishments as a way of sustaining their motivation in the course.

Use of E-mail for Instructional Purposes

Electronic mail can be used effectively for instruction purposes. Bauer and Jerz (2000) provide ten tips for writing effective electronic e-mail that we consider important. These tips are as follows:

- Each time you send e-mail to your students, write a meaningful, recognizable subject line. For example, Subject: "Important—read immediately," or "Quiz 1 due on Friday."

- Both instructors and students in a Web class should keep their messages focused and readable. For example; if multiple questions are put in an e-mail, students are likely to hit "return" after the first question that sparks their interest, and completely ignore the second or third questions. Therefore, learn to be very specific.

- For effective instruction, attachments should be used sparingly. This is because the attachments, unless they are essential, take time to download; they could transmit viruses; they could take up space on your recipient's computer, and they don't always transmit correctly. Instead of sending a whole word processor file, you might copy and paste the relevant text into the e-mail.

- At the end of every e-mail message, the sender needs to include a clear identification, such as a name known to all class members.

- Senders should be kind in messages, and avoid "flaming," or angry messaging. Students need to be careful and remember that if they flame their instructor, for example, the message might surface someday when they want a letter of recommendation. The same rules of civility apply to instructors.

- Before sending the message, always proofread.

- Remember that there is no privacy with e-mail. Other people—not just those in your class—may access your message. E-mail users often forget and include personal information or commentary that may do harm to other class members. In some organizations, the e-mail administrator has the ability to read any and all e-mail messages.

- Encourage learners to distinguish between formal and informal situations.

- Keep up-to-date with the class; check the inbox regularly.

- Always reply promptly.

An instructor in an online class should encourage his or her students to remember that if they want to be taken seriously by professionals and other class members, they need to follow the ten tips of e-mail etiquette.

Bulletin Boards

There are two types of bulletin board systems (BBS) that can be used for instruction purposes in online classes. These are information bulletin systems and interactive systems. Information bulletin boards are important since they direct the users to other sites. Online learning instructors should make use of information bulletin boards to encourage students to search for additional information. Interactive bulletin boards on the other hand, encourage learners to react to messages posted by the instructor or other students in the class. French (1997) observes that an example of such a board is, "Howdy and welcome to Aggieland –Jim Segers" (p. 67). In online courses, the main functions of bulletin boards are that they...

1. Are used to save students time.

2. Help facilitate the study of single copy information posted on the board.

3. Can help stimulate interest in the subject being discussed.

4. Encourage active student participation.

5. Enable learners to review information.

6. Assist learners to communicate ideas visually.

7. Make learning dynamic and interesting.

8. Are used to inform learners.

9. Can be effectively used to promote certain ideas and concepts.

10. Provide a medium for individual or group reports.

Advantages of Online Delivery

In general, online methods of instruction have been found to have several advantages. Empirical studies support the advantages of Internet for instruction. According to computer technology research, these methods are able to cater to the learners' learning styles by incorporating all the five senses. As noted "Comprehension is raised to 80 when one sees, hears, and interacts with instructional material. This comprehension rate is very high, compared to 20% to 30% for just sight and sound respectively." (Multimedia source guide cited in Wallace, 1996, p.110). Tull (2001, p.1) observed that while few online courses are self-paced, "Students have better control over their time, since they can arrange weekly class hours around their own schedules—even if the only time to join the discussion is after midnight or on Sunday morning." She noted further that because online discussions are asynchronous in nature, students are not pressured for immediate, off-the-cuff answers. Thus, learners have time to think about questions before responding.

Online courses encourage cooperative learning. Since most of the class work is posted, students have plenty of opportunity to learn from anyone in the class and can compare their work to those of others in the class. One method is to post the course material online for the entire semester. Students have found this method very useful. While in the traditional method of instruction, instructors have to find ways of dealing with absentees; it is not a problem with online instruction. The fact that all discussions, answers to student questions, and lessons are available online solves the problem of missing classes. Therefore, students have the opportunity to print all the information and read it at their own pace. It is also easier to study the course material or to review sections that may have presented a student with difficulty.

Distance learning opportunities through online instruction have brought the classroom from the educational setting into the home. This has provided many students the opportunity to learn and earn degrees without the inconvenience of having to travel to campus for classes (Beard & Harper, 2002). Online instruction has been found to offer students the greatest chance to discover their strengths and weaknesses and the best opportunities to discover their paths to achieving success. Chamberlin (2001) observed that online communication assists in diminishing student inhibitions related to communication by removing psychological and social barriers to student-teacher and student-student interactions. While many advantages exist for online instruction, the primary advantages are that it allows flexibility for the learners, instructors, and employers; provides accessibility to many online resources that enhance learning; allows instructors to communicate to one or all of the students; provides easy communication using a variety of communication methods such as discussion groups, bulletin boards, and e-mail; allows meetings, brainstorming sessions, and monitoring of students' involvement in learning activities; allows instructors to monitor learner progress and offer timely feedback; provides access to students who in the past lacked opportunities due to factors such as work, geography, time, family responsibilities, and lack of money; and may in the long run be cheaper when compared to traditional instruction.

Disadvantages of Online Delivery Methods

While online instruction has many advantages, Tull (2001) observed that online courses do not work for everyone. For example, online instruction can present a communication problem, since it has no body language, facial expression, nor tone of voice to guide the interactions with the students and their instructor. Often, the instructor is at the mercy of the student with regard to feedback, if students who decide to respond to questions, take quizzes and tests on their own time. Some instructors and students find online instruction isolating and frustrating. The lack of actual contact that exists in a traditional class setting is a major limitation with the asynchronous method of instruction for some individuals. Students who lack self-discipline in terms of organization and time management face a major disadvantage.

Beard and Harper (2002) noted that many students learn best through direct interaction provided by their instructors and other students, something that is lacking in online learning environments. The other disadvantages of online learning, as reported by Piotrowski & Vadanovich (2000), include a lack of socialization that is a common feature of traditional campus classes, problems experienced by students who lack technological skills, problems related to privacy issues, and learners' focus on the technology instead of the content being taught. In summary, online instruction faces the following disadvantages: lack of direct student interaction, limited group participation, less team learning, lack of nonverbal communication, lack of immediate feedback, no eye contact, lack of ability to know the individual responding, and a focus on technology instead of content.

SUMMARY

This chapter shows the development of online courses using several formats including multimedia, text-based Web pages, e-mail writing for academic purposes, and bulletin boards. The chapter explains how to prepare for online learning and instruction, main components of online instruction, and interactive online instructional design. It demonstrates how to incorporate interactivity and multimedia into instructional Web sites and find important resources for online instruction. It covers course design considerations, use of electronic mail for instruction purposes, and bulletin boards. The chapter examines the advantages and disadvantages of the various online delivery methods and provides a detailed list of resources for business instructors who are contemplating the development of online courses.

REFERENCES AND SUGGESTED READINGS

Barker J. (2000, November). Sophisticated technology offers higher education options. *The Journal of Technology Horizons in Education, 28* (4), 58.

Bauer, J. & Jerz, D.G. (2000). Writing effective e-mail's: Top 10 tips. Retrieved April 29, 2004, from http://jerz.setonhill.edu/writing/e-text/e-mail.htm.

Beard, L. & Harper, C. (2002). Student perceptions of online versus on campus instruction. *Education,* 122(4), 658-664.

Berge, Z., Collins, M. & Dougherty, K. (2000). Design guidelines for Web-based courses. In B. Abbey (ed). *Instructional and cognitive impacts of Web-based instruction.* Hershey, IDEA Group. 32-40.

Bianco, M. B., & Carr-Chellman, A. A. (2002). Exploring qualitative methodologies in online learning environments. *The Quarterly Review of Distance Education,* 3(3), 252-260.

Blackboard Inc. (2003). Transforming the Internet into a powerful environment for the education experience. Retrieved July 29, 2003, from http://company.blackboard.com/.

Bostock, S. J. (1997). Designing Web-based instruction for active learning. In B. H. Khan (Ed.) *Web-Based Instruction.* (pp.225-230). Englewood Cliffs, NJ: Educational Technology Publications.

Bostock, S. J. (1996, June). A Critical review of Laurillard's classification of educational media. *Instructional Science,* 24, 71-88.

Chamberlin, W. S. (2001). Face to face vs. cyber-space: Finding the middle ground, *Syllabus,* 15, (11).

Cornell, R. & Martin, B. (1997). The role of motivation in Web-based instruction. In B. H. Khan (Ed.) Web-*Based Instruction* (pp.93-100). Englewood Cliffs, NJ: Educational Technology Publications.

Donlevy, J. (2003). Teachers, technology and training. *International Journal of Instructional Media.* 30 (2), 117-121.

French, D. (1999). Skills for developing, utilizing and evaluating Internet-based learning. In French, D., Hale, C., & Farr, G. (Eds.)(1999). *Internet based learning: An introduction and framework for higher education and business* (pp.63-86). Sterling, VA: Stylus Publishing, Inc.

French, D., Hale, C., & Farr, G. (Eds.)(1999). *Internet based learning: An introduction and framework for higher education and business* (pp. 87-96). Sterling, VA: Stylus Publishing, Inc.

Gillani, B. B. & Relan, A. (1997). Incorporating interactivity and multimedia into Web-based instruction. In B. H. Khan (Ed.) *Web-Based Instruction* (pp.231-237). Englewood Cliffs, NJ: Educational Technology Publications.

Harris, D. (1999). Creating a complete learning environment. In French, D., Hale, C., & Farr, G. (Eds.)(1999). *Internet based learning: An introduction and framework for higher education and business* (pp. 139-164). Sterling, VA: Stylus Publishing, Inc.

Hopson, M. H., Simms, R. L., Knezek, G. A. (2002, Winter). Using a technologically enriched environment to improve higher-order thinking skills. *Journal of Research on Technology ineducation,* 34(2), 109-119.

Hung, D. (2001). Design principles for Web-based learning: Implications for Vygotskian thought. *Educational Technology,* 41(3) 33-41.

Khan, B. H. (Ed.) (1997). *Web-Based Instruction*. Englewood Cliffs, NJ: Educational Technology Publications.

Lynch, M. M. (2002). *The Online Educator: A guide to creating the virtual classroom*. New York: Routledge, Falmer.

McLellan, H. (1997). Creating virtual learning communities via the Web. In B. H. Khan (Ed.) (1997). *Web-Based Instruction* (pp.185-190). Englewood Cliffs, NJ: Educational Technology Publications.

Melara, G. (1999). Softwaretools for building and nurturing virtual learning communities.http://muspin.gsfc.nasa.gov/conferences/99conference/99proceedings/melara-vides.ppt. Retrieved May 23, 2003.

Mishra, S. (2002). A design framework for online learning environments. *British Journal of Educational Technology*, 33, (4), 493-496.

Mundrake, G. A. (2003). Information technology. In M. H. Rader (Ed) *National Business Education Association Yearbook*, 41, (pp. 130-146.)

Nafukho, F. M., Thompson, D. & Brooks, C. (2003). Factors predicting success in a distance learning undergraduate HRD degree program. In S. A. Lynham & T. M. Egan (Eds.), *Proceedings of the Academy of Human Resource Development Annual Research Conference. (pp. 89-95). Bowling Green, OH: AHRD*.

Newby, T. J, Stepich, A. S., Lehman, J. D., & Russell, J. D. (2000). *Instructional Technology for Teaching and Learning*, 2nd Ed. Columbus: ASPEN.

Piotrowski, C. & Vodanovich, S. J. (2000). Are the reported barriers to Internet-based instruction warranted? A synthesis to of recent research. *Education*, 121, 48-53.

Smith, R. (2002). Successfully incorporating Internet content and advanced presentation technology into collegiate courses: Lessons, methodology, and demonstration. *Unpublished Manuscript*, Massachusetts Maritime Academy.

Tull, B. A. M. (2001). *About online Learning*. Retrieved July 29, 2003, from http://online.ohlone.cc.ca.us/english/btull.

Villalba, C., & Romiszowski, A. J. (2001). Current and ideal practice in designing, developing and delivering Web-based training in H. B. Khan (ed), *Web-based Training*, Englewood Cliff, NJ, ETP 325-342.

Wallace, I. G. (1996). Technology as an instructional strategy. In H. R. Perreault (Ed.), *Classroom strategies: The methodology of business education*. Reston, VA: National Business Education Association.

Willis, B., & Dickinson, J. (1997). Designing Web-based instruction for active learning. In B. H. Khan (Ed.) Web-*Based Instruction*. (pp.81-84). Englewood Cliffs, NJ: Educational Technology Publications.

White, K. W., & Weight, B. H. (2000). *The online teaching guide: A handbook of attitudes, strategies, and Techniques for the virtual classroom*. Needham Heights, MA: Allyn & Bacon.

Yaskin, D. & Gilfus, S. (2002). *Balckboard 5: Introducing the 5 learning system*. Retrieved July 31, 2003, from http://www.Blackboard.com.

Educational Delivery: Intellectual Property Rights/Privacy Issues

Marsha Bayless
Stephen F. Austin State University
Nacogdoches, Texas

Betty S. Johnson
Stephen F. Austin State University
Nacogdoches, Texas

J. Keaton Grubbs
Stephen F. Austin State University
Nacogdoches, Texas

The E-world of educational delivery covers a vast array of ever expanding resources and means of communicating and storing information. Intellectual property is "a commercially valuable product of the human intellect, in a concrete or abstract form, such as a copyrightable work, a protectable trademark, a patentable invention, or a trade secret" (Garner, 2000, p. 649). This chapter will focus primarily on significant laws pertaining to copyright in the belief that this is the most common area addressed by educators and students in daily educational delivery. In addition, ownership and privacy rights will be examined. The central points of the discussion will be aimed at delivery through multimedia, online, and distance learning.

WHEN ARE ELECTRONICALLY GENERATED WORKS SUBJECT TO COPYRIGHT?

The general rule is to initially assume that everything is subject to copyright. A copyright in original works occurs automatically at the moment that the work is put into a tangible form (Copyright Act of 1976, Chap. 1, § 102(a)). That is, copyright protection attaches when the work ceases to be just an idea and is put on paper, a disc, a tape, film, canvas, the Internet, and so forth. It is no longer a requirement that the work be published, display the Ó or *copyright* or *copr.*, or be registered with the U.S. Copyright Office for the work to be protected by copyright (Copyright Act of 1976, Chap. 4, § 408(a)). Registration is required, however, before an infringement lawsuit may be filed and in order to receive the full range of remedies (Copyright Act of 1976, Chap. 4, § § 411-12).

The U. S. Copyright Act of 1976 (the "Act") governs copyrights (Copyright Act of 1976 *et seq.*). It is a federal law that preempts state law governing copyright (Copyright Act of

1976, Chap. 3, § 301). To be subject to copyright, a work need only be originally authored and embodied ("fixed") in a material object (Copyright Act of 1976, Chap. 1, § 101). Section 102 of the Act provides copyright protection for "original works of authorship fixed in any tangible medium of expression, now known or later developed.... Works of authorship include the following categories: (1) literary works; (2) musical works, including any accompanying words; (3) dramatic works, including any accompanying music; (4) pantomimes and choreographic works; (5) pictorial, graphic, and sculptural works; (6) motion pictures and other audiovisual works; (7) sound recordings; and (8) architectural works" (Copyright Act of 1976, Chap. 1, § 102(a)). Additionally, computer programs were defined and included in the literary work category in 1980 (Computer Software Copyright Act of 1980). The historical and statutory notes to §102 indicate that the list is illustrative and not exhaustive, and that there may be overlap within the categories (Copyright Act of 1976, § 102 Hist. Notes).

From the generality and breadth of the Act, it is apparent that virtually all E-world resource material is subject to copyright. Internet Web sites, online courses, multimedia presentations, and recorded distance education presentations, are subject to copyright. This includes all of the creative material within these works. E-mail even qualifies. Any original work that would qualify in one of the Copyright Act categories outside of E-world educational delivery will also qualify in the multimedia, Web-based, Web-enhanced, distance education delivery environment.

There are limits and exceptions, however. Ideas, government works, works in the public domain, and facts do not have copyright coverage. Specifically not included as original works of authorship are "any idea, procedure, process, system, method of operation, concept, principle, or discovery, regardless of the form in which it is described, explained, illustrated, or embodied in such work" (Copyright Act of 1976, Chap. 1, § 102(b)). Although an educator cannot copy without permission another educator's online course and materials, an educator can look at the course and materials and use the ideas reflected there to create his or her own course. Originality, not novelty, is the standard.

Government works and works already in the public domain are also excluded from protection by statute (Copyright Act of 1976, Chap. 1, § 105 and Chap. 3, § § 302-305). Works may be in the public domain by expiration of copyright (Cornell Institute, 1999) or by an author placing the works in the public domain. A common misconception is that works in public view, without a copyright symbol, ©, or located in a personal Web site, or any educationally-oriented Web site are automatically in the public domain. The rule to follow is to assume copyright, unless the site or the material is explicitly denoted as in the public domain, or unless there is specific language authorizing copying or some other use.

Facts are not copyrightable, because even in the initial discovery, they are not original works of the author. They are in the public domain available to everyone. A compilation of facts may be copyrightable, as an original work, if there is independent collection and assembly of the facts and a minimum degree of creativity by the author in the selection, placement, and arrangement of the facts in the work (Feist v. Rural, 1991). This copyright protection only goes to the compilation work itself, and others may use the same facts in a competing work, so long as the same selection, placement, and arrangement are not used. These rules apply no matter how much "sweat of the brow" was expended by the initial fact discoverer/compiler (Feist v. Rural, 1991).

WHAT ARE THE LEGAL REQUIREMENTS FOR USING COPYRIGHTED WORKS IN MULTIMEDIA?

Copyright protection consists of enumerated exclusive rights granted to the copyright owner together with various remedies employed to enforce infringement of those rights. "Fair use" is a judicial and now legislated limitation on the owner's copyright protection. Under proscribed circumstances, it allows educators to use copyrighted works for education and scholarly research purposes without having to obtain permission from the author.

Copyright Owner's Exclusive Rights

A copyright owner has *exclusive* intangible rights to (1) reproduce the work, (2) prepare derivative works (modifications or adaptations) based on the original, (3) distribute the work, (4) perform the work publicly, (5) display the work publicly, and (6) publicly perform a sound recording work by means of digital audio transmission (Copyright Act of 1976, Chap. 1, § 106).

"Copying" is the generic term commonly used to denote the violation or infringement of any one or more of these rights by a non-owner user of the work. In traditional educational delivery, one of the most common violations is reproduction by photocopying articles or chapters or pictures or music. Educators may also have occasion to record material from the television or radio or from a video or audiocassette. An educator may play the entire or a portion of an original video or audiocassette.

Copying constitutes infringement when it is shown (1) that the user had access to the work, and (2) there is a substantial similarity between protected aspects of the original work (not mere facts or ideas) and the alleged competing work (Sony v. Universal, 1984). Copying may include the entire work or a substantial portion, and schools are "public" places in the context of copyright (Copyright Act of 1976, § 106 Hist. Notes). In E-world delivery, copying from a source to a disc is the same thing. Download or copy-and-paste reproduction from the Internet, sharing software and copied materials, and performance and display uses in Web sites, online courses, and multimedia presentations, would be common examples of E-world infringements.

Avoidance of Infringement Claims

There are two ways for educators to avoid infringement claims for the use or "copying" of copyright works. The first is to have permission from the copyright owner, called a license, for the intended use of the work, such as reproduction or performance or display. The second is to come within or assert one or more of the limitations to the exclusive rights of copyright owners contained in the Copyright Act.

Only the copyright owner may grant a license. Licensure permission should always be obtained in writing, by mailed or faxed email letter or more formal document. The owner may or may not require payment of a fee or royalty for the requested use. The request for permission and the corresponding grant of the license should always describe the exact nature and extent and duration of the permitted use. E-world licenses are commonly encountered with software, whether purchased at a store or downloaded from the Internet. When the educator clicks "agree" or "accept" at the beginning of the program, he or she is agreeing to the copyright owner's terms of permitted use for the product. These license agreements have become more extensive and detailed in recent years. Educators should expect the courts to take the view that the Internet makes it easier for users to locate and communicate with copyright owners for permission.

Copyright Limitations and Fair Use

To achieve a balance of copyright ownership protection and the needs for access and use of educators and others, Congress followed the exclusive rights granted in the Act with statutory limitations of those rights. A copyrighted work use or activity that comes within one of these statutes does not require the permission of the copyright owner and cannot be the basis for an infringement claim. Sections 107 through 122 of the Copyright Act contain these limitations (Copyright Act of 1976, Chap. 1, § § 107-122). By far, the judicial fair use doctrine, codified in § 107, is the broadest and most far-reaching limit on exclusive rights. Fair use is not defined in the Act. It is an "equitable rule of reason," and each occasion of its application must be made on a case-by-case basis. The statement of fair use in the statute offers guidance, but it is not intended to "freeze the doctrine in the statute, especially during a period of rapid technological change" (Copyright Act of 1976, § 107 Hist. Notes). Section 107 of the Act states the fair use limitation.

Fair Use Analysis

An educator confronted with the issues of whether and in what manner to use a copyrighted work in any E-world delivery can apply a fair use analysis provided in Section 107. The first part of the analysis involves determining whether the broad purpose of the intended use is for criticism, comment, news reporting, teaching (including multiple copies for classroom use), scholarship, or research. Teaching, scholarship, and research would be the most typical categories for educators.

Having determined that the use may qualify as fair use in one of these categories, the educator uses the "four-factor test" (purpose, nature, portion, and effect) to gauge whether the particular manner of use should qualify. The first factor concerns the narrower *purpose or character of the use*, and educational, noncommercial, nonprofit use would weigh more favorably toward fair use than commercial, for-profit use. The *nature of the work* in factor two refers to the originality and degree of creativity in the work, such that informative works, more factual and nonfiction, would be more of a candidate for fair use than more creative, imaginative, fictional works. Published works would be more favored than nonpublished works.

The third factor to be used in determining fair use is the *amount or portion* to be used, small or large, excerpt or entire article or chapter; and using the least amount needed will weigh more favorably. Note, however, that a small part of a work may count against fair use, if that piece is so significant or substantial to the work that it is the complete essence of the entire work. The fourth factor, *effect on potential market or value*, includes considerations of the potential loss of sales of the original or the avoidance of paying for available permission or payment of royalties. This last factor necessarily involves the first three factors as well as the identifiability of the copyright owner, market for and availability of the original, and availability of and market for licensed permission (Bartow, 1998; Harper, "Fair Use", 2002; Groton, "Fair Use", 2003).

If, after analysis, an educator questions whether a prospective use will pass as fair use, diligent efforts to obtain permission should be made. Another reason to use the Section 107 analysis is that there is an innocent infringer/good faith defense in the Act (Copyright Act of 1976, Chap. 5, § 504(c)(2)). When statutory damages are sought, Section 504(c)(2) provides that a court must reduce damages when a nonprofit educational institution or its employee or agent, acting in the scope of employment, reasonably believed that the use of the copyrighted work was a fair use under Section 107.

Fair Use Guidelines

There have been a number of efforts to develop fair use guidelines for educational copying, distribution, display and performance of others' works. Such guidelines are not law, and the various guidelines have all been intended to portray minimum [not maximum] standards of fair use as a "safe harbor" (Crews, 2001; Bartow, 1998; Harper, "Fair Use", 2002; Groton, "Fair Use", 2003). Certain of these guidelines have gained acceptance and are utilized in the policies of educational institutions. A typical institutional policy statement includes the following: guidelines are not law and reflect the minimum and not maximum standards of what may constitute fair use; guideline limits may not be sufficient for the needed use; additional copying might still be fair use under a Section 107 analysis; and the further one exceeds the guidelines, the greater the risk that the use will not be a fair use and will constitute infringement. These admonitions actually come from the preambles to the guidelines (Harper, "Fair Use", 2002; Groton, "Fair Use", 2003).

For the more traditional delivery of education the early guidelines addressed copying general print media (books and periodicals), printed music and sound recordings, interlibrary loan materials, and television broadcasts. These early traditional delivery guidelines are titled,

- Guidelines for Classroom Copying in Not-For-Profit Educational Institutions with Respect to Books and Periodicals ("Classroom Guidelines" 1976)

- Guidelines for Educational Uses of Music ("Music Guidelines" 1976)

- Guidelines on Photocopying Under Interlibrary Loan Agreements ("CONTU Guidelines" 1979)

- Guidelines for Off-Air Recordings of Broadcast Programming for Educational Purposes ("Off-Air Guidelines" 1982)

The emphases in the Classroom Guidelines are reflected in some fashion in all of the traditional and electronic environment educational delivery guidelines. There are excellent resources for detailed summaries and models for applications of the respective guidelines (U. S. Copyright Office, 1995; Harper, "Fair Use", 2002; Heartland, 1999; Davidson; CNI-Coalition; Groton, "Fair Use", 2003).

According to the Classroom Guidelines, teachers may make a single copy of a chapter of a book, an article from a periodical or newspaper, a short story, a short essay, or short poem, or a chart, graph, diagram, drawing, cartoon or picture from a book, periodical, or newspaper for scholarly research, or for use in teaching or preparation to teach a class. Multiple copies of not more than one per student may be made by or for the teacher of the course for classroom use or discussion, if the copying meets the tests of brevity, spontaneity, and cumulative effect, as defined in the guidelines, and if each copy includes a notice of copyright (U. S. Copyright Office, 1995).

Fair Use Guidelines for Multimedia and Web-based Delivery
In 1994, representatives of interested user and owner organizations collected to negotiate guidelines for the new electronic environment, called the Conference on Fair Use (CONFU). Working groups were set up for multimedia, digital images, distance learning, interlibrary loans, electronic reserves, and computer software. None of the user/owner groups were able to reach a consensus agreement on guidelines. By 1996, all but the interlibrary loan group had developed some form of written proposal for guidelines (U. S. Patent and Trademark Office, 1998; Harper, "CONFU", 1997; and Harper, "Fair Use", 2002). The proposals were as follows:

- Fair Use Guidelines for Educational Multimedia (1996)

- Draft of Proposal for Educational Fair Use Guidelines for Digital Images (1996)

- Revised Draft for Educational Fair Use Guidelines for Distance Learning (1996)

- Draft of Fair Use Guidelines for Electronic Reserve Systems (1996)

- Statement on Use of Copyrighted Computer Programs (Software) in Libraries—Scenarios (1996)

A group of interested authors, publishers, and educators, known as the Consortium of College and University Media Centers (CCUMC), had already begun the process of devising multimedia guidelines prior to CONFU. The CCUMC consortium of parties was subsumed within the CONFU multimedia group, and because of the considerable majority support, guidelines were submitted to the Subcommittee on Courts and Intellectual Property, Committee on the Judiciary, U. S. House of Representatives, and were recognized in the adoption of a 1996 nonlegislative report of the subcommittee (Penn State, 2002).

Although not a legal document and not legally binding, the Fair Use Guidelines for Educational Multimedia are widely endorsed and used in the same sense as the Classroom, Music, Interlibrary Loan, and Off-Air Recording Guidelines. The other electronic environment guidelines have been used or referenced by different educational institutions and other user organizations, as adopted for their own policies as general reference, and as a basis for developing their own guidelines. Similar to the earlier traditional delivery guidelines, excellent resources are available for reviewing all educational electronic environment guidelines in their entirety, for summaries, and for models of application (Harper, "CONFU," 1997; Harper, "Fair Use," 2002; Stanford University; Groton, "Fair Use," 2003; Groton, "Implementation," 2002; Music Library Association, 2003; Music Publisher's Association, 2003; Davidson, n.d.).

Fair Use Guidelines for Educational Multimedia

The Multimedia Guidelines (U. S. Trademark Office, "Final Report" Appendix J, 1998; Penn State, 2002) "apply to the use, without permission, of portions of lawfully acquired copyrighted works in educational multimedia projects which are created by educators or students as part of a systematic learning activity by nonprofit educational institutions"(Penn State, 2002, para. 1.3). The document states that the Guidelines "…do not supercede other preexisting educational fair use guidelines that deal with the Copyright Act of 1976." (Penn State, 2002, footnote 1) Thus, other guidelines would be consulted for questions outside of the multimedia context or where the Multimedia Guidelines do not address a specific instance for a multimedia project.

"Educational multimedia projects created under the Multimedia Guidelines incorporate students' or educators' original material, such as course notes or commentary, together with various copyrighted media formats including but not limited to, motion media, music, text material, graphics, illustrations, photographs, and digital software which are combined into an integrated presentation" (Penn State, 2002, para. 1.3). Following the Introduction paragraphs of Preamble, Background and Applicability, the Guidelines address the use of copyright works when developing multimedia projects (Penn State, 2002, Part 2, paras. 2.1 & 2.2). Students are allowed to incorporate portions of lawfully acquired copyrighted works into their own multimedia projects for a specific course. Educators are allowed to incorporate portions of lawfully acquired copyrighted works in "their own multimedia programs for their own teaching tools in support of curriculum-based instructional activities at educational institutions." Lawfully acquired is defined as, "… copyrighted works…obtained by the institution or individual through lawful means such as purchase, gift, or license agreement but not pirated copies" (Penn State, 2002, para. 1.3). These allowances are subject to the portions limits and attribution and citation requirements specified in the Guidelines.

Permitted uses of the educational multimedia projects are subject to portion, time, copying, and distribution limitations in the Guidelines. According to the Guidelines, (Penn State, 2002, para. 3.1-3.4), students may

- perform and display their own projects for educational uses in the course for which they were created, and

- use them in their own portfolios as examples of their academic work for later personal uses such as job and graduate school interviews.

Educators may

- perform and display their own educational multimedia projects for face-to-face instruction; for directed self-study by students; for remote instruction to students enrolled in curriculum-based courses and located at remote sites, provided over the educational institution's secure electronic network in real-time; or for after class review or directed self-study, provided there are technological limitations on access to the network and educational multimedia project (such as password or PIN), and provided further that the technology prevents the making of copies of copyrighted material [Web CT with copy-blocking technology, for example],

- perform or display their own projects for presentations to peers at workshops and conferences, and

- retain educational multimedia projects in their personal portfolios for later personal uses such as tenure reviews or job interviews.

In the event the institution's network or technology is not adequate to meet the security provisions, students and educators may only use their projects over an otherwise secure network (the institution's intranet network, for example) for 15 days after the first real-time remote use or 15 days after the assignment for self-study. After that, one of the two permitted use copies must be placed on reserve for on-site use by students enrolled in the course, and students are to be advised that they may not make their own copies of the multimedia project.

Preparation and use of educational multimedia projects are subject to specific time, portion, copying, and distribution limitations contained in Part 4 of the Guidelines (Penn State, 2002). For students, the time limitations include the duration of the course for which they were created and, thereafter, for personal portfolio uses. For educators, multimedia projects may be used for teaching courses for up to two years after the first instructional use with a class. Any use beyond the two years requires obtaining permission for each copyrighted portion contained in a project.

Portion limitations of the amount of a copyrighted work that may be incorporated apply regardless of the original source medium of the work. Furthermore, portions are measured both "in the aggregate" and cumulatively. The phrase, "in the aggregate," refers to the total amount of copyrighted material that may be incorporated into a single multimedia project from a single copyrighted work without permission. The limits are cumulatively applied "to each educator's or student's multimedia project(s) for the same academic semester, cycle or term." Students are to be admonished about copyright and following the guidelines. The specific portion limitations (Penn State, 2002, para. 4.1-4.3) are as follows:

- Motion Media – up to 10% or 3 minutes, whichever is less, in the aggregate

- Prose Text Material – up to 10% or 1000 words, whichever is less, in the aggregate

- Poetry – entire poem of less than 250 words, but no more than three poems by one poet or five poems by different poets from any anthology. For poems of more than 250 words, 250 words may be used, but no more than three excerpts by a poet or five different poets from an anthology.

- Music, Lyrics and Music Video – up to 10% or 30 seconds, whichever is less, or in the aggregate of extracts from a single work, and there may be no change in the basic melody or fundamental character of the work

- Illustrations and Photographs – entire illustration or photograph, but no more than 5 images by a particular artist or photographer; if taken from a published collective work, up to 10% or 15 images, whichever is less

- Numerical Data Sets – up to 10% or 2500 fields or cell entries, whichever is less; field entry is a specific item of information like a name in a database; cell entry is the intersection where a row and a column meet in a spreadsheet

For copying and distribution, only three copies of a multimedia project are permitted in the Guidelines, an original use copy, plus one other use copy, and one copy for preservation. Only one use copy may be placed on reserve in the event the institution's network or technology is insufficient to provide security as stated above, and the preservation copy may only be used or reproduced to replace a use copy that is lost, stolen, or damaged. Joint creators are each entitled to retain a copy of a project, but only for peer presentations and personal portfolios in the case of educators and use in the specific course and in a personal portfolio as to students (Penn State, 2002, para. 4.3). Thus, in the case of a student team project, each member of the team could retain a copy for his or her personal portfolio.

Fair Use Guidelines – Individual Permissions
Part 5 of the Multimedia Guidelines include instructions to educators and students to obtain individual permissions for copyrighted works in their multimedia projects before any commercial use and for duplication or distribution of the projects beyond the Guideline limitations (Penn State, 2002). Part 6 includes a warning about downloading digital material from the Internet, since the Internet has both copyrighted and public domain works, and in addition, some copyrighted works may have been posted without permission. Also, students and educators are reminded to appropriately credit the original sources, display the copyright symbol, ©, and include copyright ownership information for all copyrighted works incorporated into a project. Crediting the source requires full bibliographic information, such as author, title, publisher, and place and date of publication (Penn State, 2002).

Copyright ownership information includes the symbol, year of publication and name of the copyright holder. Use of an image should include the copyright symbol and creator's name on the image, but these may appear separately but simultaneously on the screen with the image or separately but appropriately linked to the image, if that is more compatible with the instructional objectives.

Fair Use Guidelines – Credit for Copyrighted Works
Also included in Part 6 of the Multimedia Guidelines is a requirement that the project have a notice on the opening screen advising that the project contains copyrighted works and is produced pursuant to fair use under the U. S. Copyright Act, such that further use is restricted. If educators or students believe that there may be a possibility of further use beyond those allowed in the Guidelines, they should seek permission during development rather than waiting until the project is completed. Alterations of incorporated copyrighted works are permitted only if they support specific educational purposes and are duly noted in the project. The Guidelines do not provide for reproduction or decompilation of computer programs and portions thereof, and educators and students are advised to determine if incorporated copyrighted works specifically require or are subject to a license, since license or contractual obligations will control over the guidelines (Penn State, 2002).

WHO OWNS THE COPYRIGHT IN AN INSTRUCTOR-DEVELOPED ONLINE COURSE?
The Copyright Act is clear that the author or authors of the work initially own the copyright in a work that comes within the Act. The author is the person who actually creates the work, that is, "the person who translates an idea into a fixed, tangible expression entitled to copyright protection" (Community v. Reid, 1989). Authors of a joint work are co-owners of the copyright (Copyright Act of 1976, Chap. 2, § 201(a)).

There is a distinction between ownership of the intangible rights of copyright and the material object created by the author. Transfer of any object subject to copyright, or the copy in which the work is first fixed, does not of itself convey ownership of the copyright, or any of the intangible exclusive rights. Conversely, transfer of copyright does not affect ownership in the material object (Copyright Act of 1976, Chap. 2, § 202). An author's ownership is subject to the "first sale doctrine" in §109 of the Act (Copyright Act of 1976, Chap. 1, § 109).

A party lawfully in possession of an original or authorized print of an artist's painting, such as by commissioning or purchasing the work, may transfer ownership of his or her painting or print without seeking permission. The painting or print owner, however, does not own the right to make other prints of the work for sale or other use. Likewise, the person who has bought instructional software owns the disc and can transfer the disc by sale or gift, but the creator of the program still owns the copyright, and a new owner of the disc is subject to the same rights and license in favor of the creator/copyright holder. These rules would apply to an online course as well.

An online course copyright holder can transfer the copyright much like any item of property. The actual transfer of a copyright may be made by "any means of conveyance [e.g., sale, gift, lease, or mortgage] or by operation of law, and may be bequeathed by will or pass as personal property by the applicable laws of intestate succession" (Copyright Act of 1976, Chap. 2, § 201(d)) [Emphasis added.]. It can be conveyed in whole or in part, such as a one-half interest. And, because a copyright consists of a "bundle" of exclusive rights, the individual rights themselves may be conveyed separately and in parts, such as selling the rights to perform or display a work while retaining the rights of reproduction and distribution (Copyright Act of 1976, Chap. 2, § 201(d)(1) and (d)(2)). Any transfer of copyright ownership is required to be in writing and signed by the owner of the right(s) conveyed or by an authorized agent of the owner (Copyright Act of 1976, Chap. 2, § 204).

Exceptions to Ownership in the Creator/Author

There are three qualifications to copyright ownership in the original creator or author of a work. The first two are encompassed within the *work made for hire* doctrine. The third is an *implied license* arising out of the conduct of the parties under the *shop-right* doctrine, or *equitable estoppel.*

Work made for hire. Under the work made for hire rules, an employer or other person (in the case of commissioned work) is deemed to be the original author for purposes of initial ownership of copyright. This has been codified in the Copyright Act (Copyright Act of 1976, Chap1, § 101 and Chap. 2, § 201(b)). The definition of a "work made for hire" includes (1) a work prepared by an employee in the scope of his or her employment and (2) specially ordered or commissioned work (Copyright Act of 1976, Chap. 1, § 101). The Copyright Act attributes authorship and ownership of works made for hire to the employer or other person for whom the work is prepared, unless the parties have expressly agreed otherwise in writing (Copyright Act of 1976, Chap. 2, § 201(b)).

Whether the creator is an "employee" depends upon such factors as the hiring party's right to control the manner and means by which the product is accomplished; the skill required; the source of instrumentalities and tools; the location of the work; the duration of the relationship of the parties; the right of hiring party to assign additional projects; the hired party's discretion over when and how long to work, method of payment; the hired party's role in hiring and paying assistants; whether the work is part of the regular business of the hiring party; whether the hiring party is in business; the employee benefits; and the tax treatment of the hired party. General agency law is used to determine "scope of employment" (Community v. Reid, 1989). Under the Restatement (Second) of Agency §228, (1958) conduct of an employee is "within the scope of employment," if (a) the activity is the kind he or she is employed to perform, (b) it occurs substantially within the authorized time and space of the employment, and (c) it is actuated, at least in part, by a purpose to serve the employer (Quinn v. Detroit, 1997). The notes to § 229 of the Restatement (1958) also indicate that activities "incidental" to employment may also fall within the scope of employment. (Miller v. CP Chemicals, 1992)

In the situation involving specially ordered or commissioned work, the work will be considered a "work made for hire," when the parties expressly agree that it is work for hire in a signed, written instrument, and the work falls within one or more of the following nine specific categories: contribution to a collective work, part of a motion picture or other audiovisual work, a translation, a supplementary work, a compilation, an instructional text, a test, as answer material for a test, or as an atlas (Copyright Act of 1976, Chap. 1, § 101). Thus, an independent contractor or an employee acting outside the scope of employment who is commissioned to create a work subject to copyright is the owner of the copyright to the work, unless the work falls within one of the enumerated categories, and there is a signed, written agreement that the work is made for hire. If the work falls within a category, and there is a written work for hire agreement, then the commissioning party is deemed the author and owns the copyright, unless there is some other written agreement to the contrary.

Implied license. The last exception to unqualified original-creator ownership of a work arises out of an implied right and license to use the creator's work. An implied nonexclusive, cost-free, nontransferable right to use an employee's copyrighted work may exist in the event that the creation of the work is using employer time or other resources, but the activities are not in the scope of employment or incidental to it. This is the equitable shop-right doctrine, and the employer may use the work but may not interfere with the employee's enjoyment of his or her exclusive rights. Another implied right and license may arise by equitable estoppel through allowed or encouraged use of a work by a third party, which may or may not be an employer, without fee or stated expectation of compensation (LaFuze & Wooten, 2001).

For example, if a business instructor whose primary job is to create online courses does so during working hours at the institution's location with institution personnel and/or equipment, the instructor is completing a "work made for hire." The educational institution will own the course. Contrarily, if the business teacher is interested in independently designing an online course after working hours and is using personal equipment, and the course is not an employment requirement, the teacher would own the course. Under the general rules, if the course is created independent of regular job assignments, but is developed using institution time and resources, the copyright would ordinarily be owned by the teacher as creator, but the institution could assert an implied shop-right license to use the course.

Academic policies. In the educational setting, these issues are commonly dealt with by recognition of academic traditions in policies that delineate different ownership applications. By policy, many institutions provide for copyright ownership in the instructor to nonspecifically commissioned or sponsored works, while typically reserving a shop-right license. Policies also provide for institution ownership of commissioned or sponsored works or will generally establish joint ownership rules with divisions of royalties to be negotiated on a case-by-case basis (University of California, 1992; Harvard University, 1998). Some have detailed formulas for sharing remuneration (Columbia University, 2000). Other institutions provide that all employee work product in or incidental to the scope of employment is owned by the institution, often with provision for sharing any royalties after allowing for costs and expenses (Harper, "Regent's Rules," 2002). In this latter case, any online course that is developed with the use of institutional resources would be owned by the institution.

WHAT ARE THE INSTRUCTOR'S RESPONSIBILITIES IN MONITORING ONLINE STUDENTS?

Prior to passage of the TEACH Act in 2002, instructors in E-world were most likely to face a copyright infringement claim for a student's violation on the basis of direct infringement in the case of a joint work or on the indirect basis of vicarious or contributory infringement. Indirect infringement involves pursuing someone other than the person engaged in the actual copying. Vicarious infringement occurs when a person has a financial interest in the infringing (copying) activity and has a right to control or supervise the activities of an infringing person (Sony v. Universal, 1984). An employer-employee or other agency relationship would be involved. Broadly construed, a financial interest could be anything that is of beneficial value to the person (or instructor or institution). An employer whose employee pirates copyrighted software off of the Internet (or just borrows a friend's purchased copy), places it on the employee's computer or the company network, and uses it in his or her job, is thus subject to vicarious liability, even without knowledge of the conduct. Contributory infringement is established when someone, with *knowledge* of the infringing activity, causes or materially contributes to the infringement (Sony v. Universal, 1984). A supervisor or fellow employee who encourages or facilitates the pirating employee or who uses the known infringing software would be an example of contributory infringement. Showing a student how to burn a collection of music onto a CD for the after-game dance would be contributory. It is also potentially vicarious for the institution. Consider also as contributory and potentially vicarious the teacher who knows or discovers that a student has posted his or her class multimedia project to a personal Web site, and further, that the project contains numerous current hit songs virtually in their entirety that the teacher let slide when the project was presented in class. Proof of indirect infringement requires such elements as benefit and control or knowledge and contribution. The TEACH Act is more explicit and demanding in the case of performances and displays in E-world.

Technology, Education, and Copyright Harmonization (TEACH) Act of 2002

In October 2002, President Bush signed into law the Technology, Education and Copyright Harmonization (TEACH) Act. The new law is specifically aimed at distance education and amends the limitations of exclusive rights in §110 of the U.S. Copyright Act (TEACH Act, 2002). It applies only to *accredited* nonprofit educational institutions. The new §110(2) expands performance and display uses of works subject to copyright to include virtually all works. However, commercially available digital education works and unlawfully made or acquired works are specifically excluded (provided, that the institution knew or reasonably should have known). Receiving locations are expanded to include any location that distance education reaches students (Copyright Act of 1976, Chap. 1, § 110(2) and § 112(f)(1); Crews, 2003; Harper, "TEACH Act," 2002).

The TEACH Act requires *the institution* to assure its proper accreditation, devise a copyright policy, prepare and disseminate the appropriate copyright information to all appropriate persons, insure the proper notice to students, and insure that transmission only go to and be received by enrolled students. The institution's *technology officials* have to limit access to transmissions to members of the intended class and implement a system for terminating access after the appropriate time and for preventing any unauthorized further dissemination of the work in accessible form. *Instructors* are required to supervise such things as making sure that the works to be included in a distance education delivery are specifically allowed, that is, that they are not commercially available educational works or are not unlawfully made or acquired. The performance or display materials must be included at the instructor's direction, must be integral to the class session and part of mediated instructional activities (analogous to live classroom), and must directly relate to the teaching content of the transmission (Crews, 2003; North Carolina State). These mandates now place the institution, technology personnel, and instructors at the forefront of policing student E-world works for infringement. Institutions may, however, limit their exposure pursuant to the Digital Millennium Copyright Act.

Digital Millennium Copyright Act (DMCA) of 1998

The DMCA amends Chapter 5 of Title 17, U.S. Copyright Act, by creating a new §512.(DMCA, 1998; DMCA Copyright Office Summary, 1998; Association of Research Libraries, 2003). The new section provides for a limitation of liability for nonprofit educational institutions and libraries as online service providers (OSPs). Four categories of service provider activities covered are transitory communications (data conduit, Web pages, chat room discussions); system caching (retaining copies for limited time of material made by someone other than the provider then transmitted to subscriber at his or her direction); storage of information on systems or networks at directions of users (hosted Web sites); and information location tools (hyperlinks, online directories, search engines). Detailed rules govern the qualifications for protection under the Act, but of special significance to educators in higher education is § 512(e). That section further limits the liability for the institution and provides additional protection from the activities or knowledge of its faculty or graduate student employees performing teaching or research (Copyright Act of 1976, Chap.5, § 512(e)).

WHAT STUDENT PRIVACY ISSUES ARE CONSIDERATIONS IN ONLINE EDUCATION?

Consider the potential scenario of a student downloading copyrighted musical works or gaming software from the Internet on a school computer during slow periods in a lab course or while in the library, making copies, and selling them to classmates. Might the institution or an instructor be vicariously or contributorily liable? The U.S. Supreme Court has recognized teacher and student rights of free speech and expression under the First Amendment (Kemerer &Walsh, 2000, 211-221; *Tinker v. Des Moines*, 1969); privacy and against unreasonable searches and seizures under the Fourth Amendment and Fourteenth Amendment (Kemerer & Walsh, 2000, 322-333; New Jersey v. T.L.O., 1985); and due process under the Fourteenth Amendment (Kemerer & Walsh, 2000, 270-272; Goss v. Lopez, 1975). These valuable rights are inexorably linked to the right of privacy. How do institutions and individual instructors keep a watchful eye or even investigate infringing activities?

Right to Preserve Order

The protection against unreasonable searches and seizures applies to the student, but the Supreme Court also recognizes schools' needs to preserve order. So, the full protections of the Constitution do not apply. The principles for a student search were established in *New Jersey v. T.L.O., 1985*. In that case, the Court held that search of a student required a school official to show (1) that there was *reasonable cause to believe* that the student had violated or was violating a student rule or a law, and (2) that the search was reasonable in scope in light of the age and sex of the student and the nature of the offense. [Italics added.] "Reasonable cause to believe" is a much lesser standard than the probable cause standard for issuing a search warrant under the Fourth Amendment, and a warrant is not required if the standard is met.

With reasonable cause, a search that is reasonably limited in scope, meaning the items or places searched and the mechanics of conducting the search, will be the focus for determining whether a student's privacy and Fourth and Fourteenth Amendment rights have been improperly exceeded. Notably in this regard, the Children's Internet Protection Act of 2000 (CIPA) requires monitoring student computer use. Thus, with reasonable cause, searching a school computer or jointly-held school-furnished equipment, such as a locker, desk, disc file, or loaned disc, for infringing activities, would ordinarily be appropriate in light of typical school policies and student codes warning of the practice. The closer one gets to the student's person or areas where the student keeps personal as well as educational things, the greater the expectation of privacy, and the closer the courts will scrutinize the scope of the intrusion. Searching a personal laptop, backpack, purse, coat, or pants pockets for evidence of infringement would require stronger reasons for the belief of violation. Refusal of consent to the search by the student should ordinarily be followed by parent or police engagement. (Kemerer & Walsh, 2000, 322-333)

Privacy and Federal Legislation

Federal legislation has also addressed privacy issues. Of significance to Web-based and other distance education delivery is the Family Education Rights and Privacy Act of 1974 (FERPA). It applies to any educational institution receiving federal funds. FERPA specifically gives parents and students the right to restrict publication of personally identifiable information pertaining to the student. Arguably multimedia projects and performances and displays of student works, whether or not containing copyrightable work, would fall into the purview of the Act. A "record" is any information recorded in any way, including but not limited to, handwriting, print, computer media, video or audiotape, film, microfilm, and microfiche. An "education record" is a record that directly relates to a student and is maintained by the institution or a party acting for the institution. An education record does not include records of instructional personnel kept in the sole possession of the maker and not accessible to or revealed to any other person.

"Personally identifiable information" includes, but is not limited to the student's name; the name of the student's parent or other family member; the address of the student or student's family; a personal identifier, such as the student's social security number or student number; a list of personal characteristics that would make the student's identity easily traceable; or any other information that would make the student's identity easily traceable.

New FERPA regulations include student email addresses and photos in "directory information" subject to FERPA. Directory information may be disclosed only if the institution has given public notice to parents of minors or to an eligible student (over 18 or in postsecondary education) of personally identifiable information that may be included and the right and procedure for refusal. FERPA rules require detailed consideration when posting group photos to Web sites, giving identification or accreditations to students over distance channels, establishing chat rooms or bulletin boards, or displaying student works or performances.

Consider also the conditions in the DMCA that must be met to qualify for the OSP protections (Copyright Act of 1976, Chap. 5, § 512(a), (b), (c), (d)) and the duties of the institutions and instructors in the TEACH Act (Copyright Act of 1976, Chap. 1, § 110(2)). Both sets of federal legislation raise privacy issues related to restricting and monitoring access to distance education materials and transmissions. Section 512(m) of the DMCA specifically provides that nothing in the Section 512 requires an educational institution service provider to monitor its services or access material in violation of law, such as the Electronic Communications Privacy Act, in order to be eligible for any of the limitations of liability. No similar provision is stated in the TEACH Act. Instructors will have to monitor student distance education works under the TEACH Act to insure compliance with content policies and transmission requirements. This raises the question whether and to what extent instructors must intercept and review student Web sites, email, chat room, and news group transmissions to look for copyright violations and more specifically pirating conduct that may be involved with E-world educational activities. Previewing projects will conceivably become a must. Previewing and especially intercepting activities raise First Amendment free speech issues in addition to privacy.

HOW DO ACCEPTABLE USE POLICIES BENEFIT ONLINE EDUCATION?

Due process requires fairness in the procedure of enforcing legal rules. Knowledge and consent are important ingredients. This is an important basis for educational institution acceptable use policies (AUP's), Web development policies (Web DP's), comprehensive copyright policies (CCP's), and student online course agreements. Such policies also include considerations of the Electronic Communications Privacy Act (ECPA) of 1986, which prevents the unauthorized accessing or interception of electronic transmissions without express consent of one of the parties directly involved in the communication.

Acceptable use policies establish the conditions for using the Internet and other technology at school. At the least they should inform users as to monitoring, require execution of waiver and consent forms, ensure supervision by trained personnel, limit computer access as to times and places, set clear guidelines for use, and instruct and warn about internet safety, (Kemerer & Walsh, 2000, 75-76). Web DP's apply to students and staff, as well as community organizations that may be allowed access and use of the school site. Such policies outline publishing standards for content and format, and they address communication issues. They should address at least six key areas: "roles and responsibilities, content/educational value, privacy/safety, adherence to copyright laws, technical standards, and use of commercial sites and services" (Levine, 2001).

These same general considerations apply to a CCP, and in addition, the CCP should contain the requisite DMCA and TEACH Act information and notices, information about ownership of copyright and works made for hire, and a statement about permitted and prohibited uses of particular works. (Harper, "Copyright Management", 2001; Groton, "Implementation," 2002; Washington State University, 2002) All policies should admonish about policy violations and disciplinary sanctions.

The authors recommend that E-world instructors incorporate pertinent policy provisions as a hardcopy handout and in the course curriculum portion of the online course, with each student signing or otherwise acknowledging that he or she has received, read, and understood the policies.

APPLICATIONS OF ACCEPTABLE USE POLICY

1. To illustrate differences in nonverbal communication among countries, Cheri incorporated video clips from a popular movie in her online class. *A few short clips with appropriate credit, related to the topic being taught, carried over a network with protected access and copy-blocking technology, would be acceptable fair use under §107, Multimedia*

Guidelines, and the TEACH Act. If the network is not secure, then after 15 days a copy of the online material with the copyrighted works should be placed on reserve for students in the class with instruction not to make their own copies. After two years of using the clips, the teacher should get permission for continued use or get new clips.

2. To motivate his students to keyboard faster, Rick encouraged his students to download at least 45 minutes of their favorite music and play it on the system while they practiced their keyboarding. Is this a legal use of downloaded music? *This attempted use of downloaded music does not focus on instruction related to the music but for another purpose. Additionally, the length of the music to be used is excessive. This use does not weigh favorably for fair use under either the § 107 analysis or the music guidelines. Also, the teacher and the institution risk a contributory infringement claim, especially if school computers are permitted to be used for downloading.*

3. Jordan has developed a very popular online course in Web page design and has been asked to sell the course to other schools who wish to use it. Jordan used information from many other sources to create the course. What legal issues might Jordan face? This is fair use, isn't it? *A fair use analysis, considering § 107, guidelines, and the TEACH Act, would apply for use by Jordan for teaching. If Jordan copied other copyrighted material for the course, then that material should be used in a course for sale only with permission from the copyright holder. Copyright protection should not be an issue if Jordan looked at other information that sparked ideas that Jordan then developed as original work.*

CONCLUSION
E-world educators must become more aware of copyright laws and guidelines, particularly the details of exclusive rights of copyright holders and fair use limitations and analysis. Knowledge of Multimedia Guidelines and others are also useful and important. These should not substitute in every case, however, for a reasoned fair use analysis and common sense. E-world educators are being required by the new TEACH Act and the policies of their respective institutions to more closely instruct about and supervise uses of copyright-related works. This will require being informed about the exact responsibilities imposed; together with understanding the parameters of student privacy rights; and knowledge of the district, college or university policies regarding uses of institutional technology and course materials.

As the law and courts race to catch up with technology, many answers about E-world educational delivery remain unclear. It is all new in the law and in the courts—TEACH Act (2002), CIPA (2000), DMCA (1998), Multimedia Fair Use Guidelines (1996), and the other electronic environment guideline proposals of 1996.

Online educators must continue to be aware of the impact of the rapidly evolving law in the distance classroom, because today's E-world educators are pioneering the parameters of educational delivery in the modern technological era.

REFERENCES

Association of Research Libraries, Washington, D.C. *DMCA*. (2003, October 29). Retrieved December 22, 2003, from http://www.ala.org

Bartow, A. (1998). Educational fair use in copyright: Reclaiming the right to photocopy freely. *University of Pittsburg Law Review*, 60, 149-230.

Children's Internet Protection Act of 2000 (CIPA), 47 U.S.C. § 254(h)(5)(B)(i) (West 2001 and Supp. 2002), *and see* Children's Internet Protection Act Rule, 47 CFR 54.520(c)(1)(i) (2000).

CNI-Coalition for Networked Information (n.d.) *Information policies: CONTU*. Retrieved December 22, 2003 from www.cni.org/ docs/info.policies/CONTUv2.html

Columbia University, New York. (2003, June 3). *Statement of policy on proprietary rights in the intellectual products of faculty activity*. Retrieved December 22, 2003, from http://www.columbia.edu/ cu/provost/docs/copyright.html

Community for Creative Non-Violence v. Reid, 490 U.S. 730, 737 (1989).

Computer Software Copyright Act of 1980, Pub. Law. No. 96-517, 94 Stat. 3015, 3028 (1980).

Copyright Act of 1976, 17 U.S.C. § 101, *et seq*, U. S. Copyright Office Circulars and Brochures, *Circular 92 Copyright Law of the United States*. Retrieved December 22, 2003, from http://www.copyright.gov/title17/.

Copyright Act of 1976, 17 U.S.C.A. § 102, Historical and Statutory Notes. West 1996 and Supp. 2002.

Copyright Act of 1976, 17 U.S.C.A. § 106, Historical and Statutory Notes. West 1996.

Copyright Act of 1976, 17 U.S.C.A. § 107 Historical and Revision Notes House Report No. 94-1476. West 1996.

Cornell Institute for Digital Collections. *When works pass into the public domain in the United States: Copyright term for archivists*. (2003, January 15). Retrieved December 22, 2003 from http://www.copyright. cornell.edu/training/ Hirtle_Public_Domain.htm Reprinted from Hirtle, P. B. (1999, January/February) Recent changes to the copyright law: Copyright term extension, *Archival Outlook*.

Crews, K. D. (2003). *The technology, education and copyright harmonization (TEACH) act*. American Library Association. Retrieved December 22, 2003, from http://www.ala.org/washoff/teach.html

Crews, K. D. (2001). The law of fair use and the illusion of fair-use guidelines. *Ohio State Law Journal*, 62, 599, 605-612.

Davidson, H. (n.d.) *Copyright resources*. Retrieved December 22, 2003 from http://www.halldavidson.net/downloads.html.

Digital Millennium Copyright Act of 1998 (DMCA), Pub. Law No. 105-304, 112 Stat. 2860 (Oct. 28, 1998).

Digital Millennium Copyright Act of 1998, U. S. Copyright Office Summary (December 1998), Retrieved December 22, 2003 from http://www.copyright.gov/laws.

Electronic Communications Privacy Act of 1986 (ECPA), 18 U.S.C. § § 2510, *et seq*. West 2000 and Supp. 2002.

Family Education Rights and Privacy Act of 1974 (FERPA), 20 U.S.C. § 1232g West 2000 and Supp. 2002.

Feist Publications, Inc. v. Rural Telephone Service Company, Inc., 499 U.S. 340, 345-348 (1991).

Garner, B.A., ed. (2000). *Black's law dictionary* (Abridged 7th ed.). St. Paul: West Group.

Goss v. Lopez, 419 U.S. 565 (1975).

Groton Public Schools, Mystic, CT. (2002, February 26). *Copyright implementation manual.* Retrieved December 22, 2003, from http://www.groton.k12,ct.us/mts/cimhp01.htm.

Groton Public Schools, Mystic, CT, (2003, June 16). Part 4. Fair use and the guidelines. *Copyright implementation manual.* Media Technology Services. Retrieved December 22, 2003, from http://www.groton.k12.ct.us/mts/mtspol.htm.

Harper, G. K. (1997, June 11). *CONFU.* Office of the General Counsel of the University of Texas System. Retrieved December 22, 2003 from http://www.utsystem.edu/ogc/IntellectualProperty/confu2.htm

Harper, G. K. (2001, August 10). *Copyright management.* Office of General Counsel, University of Texas System. Retrieved December 22, 2003, from http://www.utsystem.edu/ogc/IntellectualProperty/copymgt.htm

Harper, G. K. (2002, May 24). *Regents' rules and regulations on intellectual property.* Office of the General Counsel of the University of Texas System. Retrieved December 22, 2003, from http://www.utsystems.edu/OGC/IntellectualProperty/2xii.htm

Harper, G. K. (2002, November 13). *The TEACH act.* Office of the General Counsel of the University of Texas System. Retrieved December 22, 2003, from http://www.utsystem.edu/ogc/IntellectualProperty/teachact.htm

Harper, G. K. (2002, November 14). *Fair use of copyrighted materials.* Office of the General Counsel of the University of Texas System. Retrieved December 22, 2003, from http://www.utsystem.edu/ogc/Intellectual Property/copypol2.htm

Harvard University. *Statement of policy in regard to inventions, patents and copyrights.* (1998, August 10). Retrieved December 22, 2003, from http://www.techtransfer.harvard.edu/ PatentPolicy.html.

Heartland Area Education Agency 11, *Copyright condensed.* (1999). Published with permission by Groton Public Schools Media Technology Services. Retrieved December 22, 2003, from http://www.groton.k12.ct.us/mts/copyright_condensed.pdf.

Kemerer, F. & Walsh, J. (2000). *The educator's guide to Texas school law.* Austin, TX: University of Texas Press.

LaFuze, W. L. &. Wooten, D. K., & Vinson & Elkins, L.L.P. (2001). Chapter 3: Selected topics regarding litigation on the internet. *Helping clients with e-commerce and the internet* 49-52. Presented for the State Bar of Texas CLE, March 29-30, 2001.

Levine, E. (2001). A Web policy primer. *American School Board Journal,* 188(7). Electronic version available at http://www.asbj.com/2001/07/0701coverstory3.html.

Miller v. CP Chemicals, Inc., 808 F.Supp. 1238, 1243-44 (D.S.C. 1992).

Music Library Association Guidelines. Retrieved Fall 2003, from http://www.lib.jmu.edu/org/ mla/Guidelines.

Music Publishers Association of the United States Guidelines. Retrieved Fall 2003, from http://www.mpa.org/crc.html.

New Jersey v. T.L.O., 469 U.S. 325 (1985).

North Carolina State University Libraries and Office of Legal Affairs.(n.d.). *The TEACH toolkit*. Retrieved Fall 2003 from http://www.lib.ncsu.edu/scc/legislative/teachkit.

Penn State University Libraries. (2002). *Fair use guidelines for educational multimedia*. Retrieved December 22, 2003, from http://www.libraries.psu.edu/mtss/fairuse/guidelines.html.

Quinn v. City of Detroit, 988 F.Supp. 1044, 1049-52 (E.D. Mich. 1997).

Restatement (Second) of Agency § 228 (1958).

Restatement (Second) of Agency § 229 comment b (1958).

Sony Corp. v. Universal City Studios, Inc., 464 U.S. 417 (1984).

Stanford University Libraries. *Copyright & fair use*. Retrieved Fall 2003, from http://fairuse.stanford.edu.

Technology, Education and Copyright Harmonization Act of 2002 (TEACH Act), Public Law 107-273, 116 Stat. 1910 (Nov. 2, 2002).

Tinker v. Des Moines School District, 393 U.S. 503 (1969).

University of California. (1992, August 19). *Policy on copyright ownership*. Retrieved December 22, 2003, from http://www.ucop.edu/ucophome/uwnews/copyr.html.

U. S. Copyright Office Circulars and Brochures. (1995). *Circular 21 Reproductions of copyrighted works by educators and librarians*. Retrieved December 22, 2003, from http://www.copyright.gov.

U. S. Patent and Trademark Office. *Final report to the commissioner on the conclusion of the conference on fair use*. (1998, November 24). Retrieved December 22, 2003, from http://www.uspto.gov/web/offices/dcom/olia/confu/confurep.htm.

U. S. Patent and Trademark Office. The conference on fair use. (November 24, 1998). *Final report to the commissioner on the conclusion of the conference on fair use*, 14-15 and Appendix J, 49-59. Retrieved December 22, 2003, from http://www.uspto.gov/web/offices/dcom/olia/confu/indexx.html.

Washington State University. (2002). *Copyright policy*. Retrieved Fall 2003, from http://www.wsu.edu/Policies.html.